RED, WHITE & BLUE
RIBBON
2004

Winning Recipes *from the past year's*
Top Recipe Contests & Food Festivals

Red, White & Blue Ribbon 2004

ISBN 1-889593-10-9/EAN 823467593102

Printed in USA

Design: Tracey Ranta

Editing: Marlene Blessing Editorial, Melissa Craven, Carol Faino, Susan Larson, Jordan Salcito

Front Cover Photos © (l to r): National Beef Cook-off; Laura Johansen/StockFood; David Loftus/StockFood
Back Cover Photos © (l to r): John Montana/Stockfood; Nestlé; Cazals/StockFood
Chapter Title Photos (in order of appearance): The Almond Board of California; Phillips Seafood; National Beef Cook-off; Finlandia Cheese Great Sandwich Recipe Contest; Veg•All; Maple Leaf Farms; Florida's Naturals Growers; Dole Food Company, Inc.; Maple Leaf Farms; Adirondack Life Magazine; Nestlé; Nestlé; the Cherry Marketing Institute; Nestlé

A number of familiar brand-name food products are used in recipes throughout this book. While the publisher has not included the trademark symbols of ™ and ®, readers can identify such products and their parent companies by noting the capitalization of the products' names and the names of the companies. All of these brand-name products are the registered trademarks of the parent companies.

3D Press, Inc.
Denver, CO 80203

INTRODUCTION

Good food is always cause for celebration, and the pages of *Red White & Blue Ribbon 2004* are filled with over 230 crowd-pleasing reasons to celebrate. *Red White & Blue Ribbon* is an annual compilation of winning recipes from the past year's recipe contests and cook-offs. This book offer a culinary treasure trove of America's best flavors. All ages and geographic regions are represented within its pages. Prepare to embark on an edible adventure across America!

Red White & Blue Ribbon 2004 offers a diverse menu collection, ranging from easy-to-prepare snacks to gourmet entrées. The true authors of this book are the men and women nationwide who share the same passion for cooking that you do.

The winning cooks and chefs embody all levels of culinary expertise. From five-year-old Breanna Lynn, whose Bucket of Dirt & Worms (page 236) won the Clarke County Fair Bake-off in Winchester, Virginia, to aspiring professional chef Carmine Peluso, who won a $70,000 scholarship to Johnson & Wales University in the National High School Recipe Contest with his Stuffed Roasted Quail with Wild Grains, Broccoli Rabe and a Port Wine Reduction (page 150).

Red White & Blue Ribbon 2004 offers you a culinary tour of America. Recipes cross the country. The Maine Lobster Fest, California Avocado Festival, the National Cornbread Cook-off in Tennessee and Illinois' Morton Pumpkin Festival all shine in the following pages – and all the dishes are the best of their kind.

Whether fixing brunch for friends, trying to impress the in-laws with gourmet fare or searching for perfect after-school cookie for the kids, *Red White & Blue Ribbon 2004* has something for everyone, from first-time cooks to committed foodies. Pick up *Red White & Blue Ribbon 2004* and begin the adventure today. As you experiment with these recipes, you may be inspired to create some prize-winners of your own!

*"Coleridge holds
that a man cannot
have a pure mind who
refuses apple dumplings.
I am not certain but
that he is right."*

Charles Lamb (1775-1834)

Table of Contents

"Life expectancy

would grow

by leaps and bounds

if green vegetables

smelled as good

as bacon."

Doug Larson (1902-1981)

APPETIZERS

MEDITERRANEAN CEVICHE

Russell C. Koza of Wakefield, Oregon, won second prize at the annual Charlestown Seafood Contest in Charlestown, Oregon. Charlestown is a unique fishing village is an ideal getaway, with easy access to outdoor recreation, stunning scenery and an array of attractions.

Makes About 4 Cups

8   ounces bay scallops
8   ounces shrimp, peeled and
     deveined, with tails left on
½   cup lime juice
¼   cup water
3   tablespoons olive oil
¼   cup chopped green onion
3   tablespoons chopped cilantro
     or parsley
1   tablespoon capers
Salt and pepper, to taste
1   large tomato
8   ounces lobster, chopped
Cherry tomato halves or tomato
     wedges, for garnish (optional)
Crackers, for serving (optional)

Bring a saucepan of water to a boil. Add scallops and shrimp; cook until scallops are opaque and shrimp are just pink. Drain and rinse under cold water to stop cooking.

Combine lime juice and water in a large ziplock plastic bag. Add shrimp and scallops; seal and refrigerate for at least 8 hours, turning bag occasionally.

In a bowl, combine olive oil, green onion, cilantro, capers, salt and pepper. Drain shrimp and scallops; add to green onion mixture and toss gently to combine. Cover and chill for 2 hours.

Cut tomato into very thin slices, then cut each slice in half. Put tomato slices around edge of a serving platter. Put shrimp and scallop mixture in center of platter. Arrange shrimp with tails up. Put lobster meat on top of scallop mixture. Garnish platter with cherry tomato halves. Serve with plain crackers, such as water crackers, if desired.

Smoked Salmon Cheesecake

Christopher Caruana of East Elmhurst, New York, won the Just Smoked Salmon recipe contest. Olympic Peninsula alder smoked salmon is the same delicacy early American pioneers discovered when they encountered the native tribes of the Pacific Northwest. This recipe contest is a celebration of these foods.

Makes 10 to 12 Servings

2	cups (½-inch) diced French bread, lightly toasted
½	cup toasted walnuts (or pine nuts or pistachios)
1	tablespoon minced fresh dill
1	stick plus 3 tablespoons butter
2	large shallots, minced
3½	(8-ounce) packages cream cheese, softened
½	cup grated Swiss or Gruyère cheese

Dash of Worcestershire (optional)
Tabasco sauce, to taste

½	cup sour cream

Pinch of kosher salt
Coarse ground pepper, to taste

4	eggs
½	cup heavy cream, lightly whipped
½	pound Just Smoked Salmon, thinly sliced

Fresh dill or caviar, for serving
French baguette slices or crackers, for serving

In a food processor or blender, combine French bread, walnuts and dill; process until crumbled. Transfer to a bowl. Melt 1 stick of butter; add to walnut mixture. Mix well and press into bottom and 2-inches up sides of a well-greased 10-inch springform pan. Chill well.

Preheat oven to 350°F. In a skillet over medium heat, melt the 3 tablespoons of butter. Add shallots; cook until tender; set aside to cool.

In a large bowl, beat cream cheese until fluffy. Beat in Swiss cheese, shallots, Worcestershire, Tabasco, sour cream, salt and pepper. Add eggs, 1 at a time, beating briefly after each addition. Fold in lightly whipped cream. Fold in salmon. Pour into crust.

Bake for 45-60 minutes, until set and a toothpick inserted in center comes out clean. Cool, then cover and chill thoroughly.

Before serving, bring to room temperature and garnish with fresh dill and/or caviar. Serve with baguette slices (toasted, if desired) or crackers.

LOBSTER POBLANO ROULADE OVER AZTEC SUCCOTASH WITH JALAPENO TOMATILLO SAUCE

Chef Alan Lake won the "Master Garlic Chef" title for the third consecutive year at the 2003 Delray Beach Garlic Fest, topping a field of professional chefs from south Florida.

Makes 4 Servings

Court bouillon:
1   carrot, roughly chopped
1   onion, roughly chopped
2   stalks celery, chopped
½   bunch parsley
1   tablespoon black peppercorns
3   bay leaves
1   lemon, halved
9   cups water
3   cups white wine

Lobster poblano roulade:
1   (1½-pound) lobster
1   tablespoon brown sugar
8   cloves garlic, roasted*
2   ounces Boursin cheese
2   tablespoons pine nuts, toasted
Salt and pepper, to taste
2   poblano chile peppers, roasted, skinned, seeded and halved lengthwise

For the court bouillon: Bring all bouillon ingredients to a boil, lower heat and simmer for 10 minutes.

For the lobster: Bring court bouillon to a boil. Add lobster and boil for 10-12 minutes. Immediately shock lobster in ice water, then shell and chop into ½-inch dice; discard court bouillon. Make a paste of brown sugar and roasted garlic. Gently mix brown sugar mixture, lobster, Boursin cheese and pine nuts. Season with salt and pepper.

Put poblano halves peeled-side-down on a work surface. Fill bottom half of each pepper with lobster mixture and roll up tightly, like a cigar. Cover with a damp towel and set aside.

Jalapeno tomatillo sauce:

4	tablespoons olive oil, divided
1	large jalapeño, seeded and chopped
4	cloves garlic, crushed
1	stalk celery, chopped
½	small onion, chopped
½	red bell pepper, chopped
1	bunch cilantro, chopped
3	pounds tomatillos, husked*
2	cups chicken stock or broth

Salt and pepper, to taste
Garlic chives, green onions or
  cilantro sprigs, for garnish

Aztec succotash:

½	stick unsalted butter
1	cup fresh corn (about 2 ears)
1	red bell pepper, finely diced
½	red onion, finely diced

Salt and pepper, to taste

¼	cup Noilly Prat sweet vermouth
2	tablespoons chopped cilantro
2	ounces nopales, julienned **
2	hearts of palm, sliced diagonally
1	red apple, diced
2	tablespoons chopped walnuts

For the sauce: Heat olive oil in a saucepan. Add jalapeño, garlic, celery, onion and bell pepper; cook for 3 minutes. Add cilantro and cook until wilted. Add tomatillos and chicken stock. Bring to boil, lower heat and simmer for 30 minutes, stirring frequently (tomatillos should start to break down; pierce remaining whole ones with a knife). Season with salt and pepper. Cool slightly, then purée.

For the succotash: Melt butter in a skillet over medium heat. Add corn, bell pepper and onion; cook for 3 minutes. Season with salt and pepper. Deglaze pan with vermouth, stirring to scrape browned bits free. Reduce liquid slightly to cook off alcohol. Add cilantro, nopales, hearts of palm and apple. Mix well and heat through. Adjust seasonings. Add walnuts just before serving.

To serve: Make a bed of succotash in center of each plate. Put sauce around outside of succotash to edge of plate. Cut poblano roulades into 1½-inch slices with a sharp knife. Lean roulades on outside of succotash and over sauce. Garnish with garlic chives.

*Note: Tomatillos are small, tart Mexican green tomatoes with a papery husk that is easily removed. They can be found in most larger groceries.

**Note: Nopales (cactus leaves) from a jar may be used and can be found at Mexican markets and in the Mexican food section of larger groceries.

OYSTER WRAPS WITH ASIAN DIPPING SAUCE

Jack Campbell of Clackamas, Oregon, won the gold medal in the "appetizer" category at the OysterFest in Shelton, Washington. Campbell travels across the country to compete in cooking contests. This recipe earned him a repeat trip to the 2003 National Oyster Cook-off in Maryland, where he took second prize in 2002.

Makes 6 to 12 Servings

Oyster wraps:
1   teaspoon grated peeled ginger
6   slices bacon, cooked crisp, drained and crumbled
4-6 white mushrooms, minced
1   tablespoon mirin*
1   tablespoon minced lemon grass
2   tablespoons thinly sliced green onion
2   tablespoons brown sugar
1   pint fresh extra-small Pacific oysters, drained and diced
8   ounces crabmeat, picked to remove shells
12   gyoza or pot sticker wrappers
3-4 tablespoons sesame oil
Fresh orange slices, for garnish
Green onions, for garnish

Asian dipping sauce:
½   cup light soy sauce
1   tablespoon regular soy sauce
1   tablespoon finely chopped green onion
1   teaspoon grated peeled ginger
½   teaspoon minced garlic

In a small skillet over medium heat, cook ginger, bacon, mushrooms, mirin, lemon grass, green onion and brown sugar, stirring gently, for 2-3 minutes. Mix in oysters and crab; cook until liquid is absorbed.

Spoon 1 tablespoon of oyster mixture into center of each gyoza wrapper. Fold each wrapper in half, brush edges with a small amount of water and crimp edges with a fork to seal (wraps may be made ahead to this point, covered and refrigerated for up to 24 hours).

Heat sesame oil in a large skillet over medium-high heat. Add wraps and cook until browned on both sides, about 1-2 minutes per side. Serve with Asian dipping sauce. Garnish with orange slices and green onions.

For the sauce: Combine all ingredients and serve in small dipping bowls.

*Note: Mirin is salted, sweet rice cooking wine found in the Asian section of larger groceries.

FIREBALL MEATBALLS

Lois Woods of Millbury, Massachusetts, won the Frank's RedHot Sauce recipe contest, held to celebrate the company's 80th anniversary. Frank's RedHot Sauce is best known as the secret ingredient in the Original Buffalo Wings, created in 1964 at the Anchor Bar & Grill in Buffalo, New York.

Makes 50 Meatballs

1½ pounds ground beef
½   cup Italian-flavor breadcrumbs
1   egg
½   onion, minced
1½ teaspoons plus ½ cup Frank's RedHot Cayenne Pepper Sauce
1   cup ketchup
¾   cup beer or non-alcoholic malt beverage

Preheat oven to 400°F. Combine beef, breadcrumbs, egg, onion and 1½ teaspoons of cayenne pepper sauce. Shape mixture into 1-inch meatballs. Put meatballs in a baking pan. Bake for 10 minutes, until cooked through.

In a large pot, bring ½ cup of cayenne pepper sauce, ketchup and beer to a boil. Lower heat and simmer for 10 minutes, until slightly thickened. Add meatballs; stir to coat with sauce. Simmer for 5 minutes until meatballs are heated through. Serve in a chafing dish.

ASIAN LETTUCE WRAPS WITH PEANUT SAUCE

Margee Berry of White Salmon, Washington, bested hundreds of contestants from across the nation to win first prize in the "salads & main dishes" category at the Peanut Institute's annual Plains Peanut Festival. Peanuts are one of America's favorite foods, comprising 68 percent of the nuts eaten in the United States.

Makes 6 Servings

2   teaspoons peanut oil
1   teaspoon toasted sesame oil
3   boneless, skinless chicken breast halves, cut into 2-inch wide strips
1   teaspoon minced garlic
1   teaspoon grated peeled ginger
¼   cup chicken broth
¼   cup smooth peanut butter
2   tablespoons mango chutney
18   large Bibb lettuce leaves, washed and dried
1   medium red bell pepper, cut into 2-inch matchsticks
1   cup snow peas, trimmed and cut into 2-inch matchsticks
4   green onions, cut lengthwise into 2-inch matchsticks
¾   cup honey-roasted Georgia peanuts, roughly chopped

Heat peanut and sesame oil in a wok or large skillet over medium-high heat. Add chicken; stir-fry for 4 minutes. Add garlic and ginger; stir-fry for 1 minute more, or until chicken is no longer pink. Lower heat and add chicken broth, peanut butter and chutney; cook, stirring, until smooth and heated through, about 3 minutes. Remove from heat.

To assemble: Put equal amounts of bell peppers, snow peas and green onions in center of each lettuce leaf. Spoon some chicken mixture on top, then sprinkle with peanuts. Roll each lettuce leaf up. Serve 3 lettuce wraps per person.

ALMOND & CHICKEN SPRING ROLLS

With entries from across America and recipes from sushi to flan, the Almond Board of California's Almond Inspirations Recipe Contest proved that almonds inspire creativity in chefs around the country. Martin Wolf, chef and owner of Wolf Cuisine in Matthews, North Carolina, won first prize in the "ethnic" category.

Makes 12 Rolls

Almond dipping sauce:

1	teaspoon vegetable oil
¼	cup plus 2 tablespoons diced onion
1	tablespoon minced garlic
1	tablespoon minced peeled ginger
1	teaspoon red pepper flakes
¼	cup slivered almonds
½	cup plus 3 tablespoons coconut milk
⅓	cup soy sauce
1½	teaspoons brown sugar
1	tablespoon curry powder
2	tablespoons lime juice

Spring rolls:

2	ounces thin Chinese rice noodles
1	pound boneless, skinless chicken breast, cooked and shredded
2	tablespoons slivered almonds
2	tablespoons julienned carrot
2	tablespoons julienned red bell pepper
2	tablespoons thinly sliced green onion
1	tablespoon chopped mint
1	tablespoon chopped cilantro
12	round rice paper wrappers

For the sauce: Heat oil in a skillet over medium heat. Add onion, garlic, ginger and red pepper flakes; cook for about 3 minutes, or until onion is soft but not browned.

In a blender, combine onion mixture, almonds, coconut milk, soy sauce, brown sugar, curry powder and lime juice; purée until slightly chunky.

For the spring rolls: In a saucepan in rapidly boiling water, cook noodles for about 5 minutes, or until tender. Drain and rinse in cold water. Cut noodles 3-4 times with a knife or scissors to make shorter pieces.

Transfer noodles to a bowl; toss with remaining spring roll ingredients, except rice paper wrappers. Dip 1 rice paper wrapper in very hot water for a few seconds, until soft and flexible; blot on a towel to remove excess water.

Put about ⅓ cup of noodle mixture on each rice paper wrapper. Fold bottom of wrapper over filling, fold in sides and roll up tightly. Serve rolls at room temperature with dipping sauce.

CARAMEL PEANUT CRUNCH SNACK MIX

Nettie Crafton of Sebring, Florida, won the Good Earth Peanut Company recipe contest with this sweet and crunchy snack. Enjoy it at home, or add raisins for a delicious, caramel-y alternative to trail mix. Peanuts are unusual because they flower above the ground, but fruit below the ground.

Makes 12 Cups

Crunch mixture:
2½ cups lightly sweetened oatmeal cereal squares (such as Quaker Oat Squares)
2½ cups rice and corn cereal squares (such as Life)
1½ cups toasted "O" oat cereal (such as Cheerios)
2 cups pretzel twists
2 cups peanuts

Caramel mixture:
¼ cup light Karo syrup
1 cup packed brown sugar
1 stick butter
½ teaspoon salt
½ teaspoon vanilla extract
½ teaspoon baking soda

For the crunch mixture: In a large roasting pan, combine cereals, pretzels and peanuts; set aside.

For the caramel mixture: Preheat oven to 250°F. In a large Dutch oven over medium heat, combine Karo syrup, brown sugar, butter, salt and vanilla. Bring to a boil and boil for 5 minutes. Stir in baking soda (mixture will foam). While mixture is still foaming, pour over crunch mixture; mix well.

Spread crunch mixture on a rimmed baking sheet. Bake for 45 minutes, stirring every 15 minutes (a wooden spoon works the best). Spread mixture on wax paper to cool. As it cools, break into smaller pieces. Store in an airtight container.

HONEY FIGS WITH GOAT CHEESE & PECANS

Virginia Willis of Atlanta, Georgia, took first prize in the "light honey" category in the National Honey Board's Viva Variety Recipe Contest. This Tuscan-inspired dish combines the delectable flavors of figs, sweet clover honey, creamy goat cheese and crunchy pecans.

Makes 6 Servings

1 cup chopped pecans, toasted, if desired

Coarse salt and pepper, to taste

1 (6-ounce) log goat cheese

12 fresh figs (such as Calimyrna or Black Mission), halved

¾ cup clover honey

Put pecans in a shallow dish. Season with salt and pepper. Roll goat cheese in pecans to evenly coat. Refrigerate until firm, then cut into 6 rounds.

Divide figs among shallow bowls or dessert cups. Top figs with a round of pecan-crusted goat cheese. Drizzle 2 tablespoons of honey over each serving (warm honey slightly to aid drizzling, if desired). Serve immediately.

Roasted Eggplant Marmalade on Rice Noodle Pancakes

Debbie Kulig won second prize in the "appetizer" category at the 12th annual Loomis Eggplant Fest. The festival attracts great chefs and some of the most colorful food and arts and craft booths in California.

Makes 6 to 8 Servings

Eggplant marmalade:

4	medium eggplants (unpeeled) cut into ½-inch cubes
¼	cup minced garlic
¼	cup minced peeled ginger
¼	cup red wine vinegar
2	teaspoons fennel seeds
½	cup firmly packed brown sugar
2	tablespoons sesame oil
2	tablespoons chopped fresh tarragon or 1 teaspoon dried
1	cup chicken or vegetable broth

Noodle pancakes:

7	ounces rice noodles

Vegetable oil, for frying

For the eggplant marmalade: Preheat oven to 400°F. On a baking sheet, combine eggplant, garlic, ginger, vinegar, fennel seeds, brown sugar, sesame oil and tarragon. Bake, stirring occasionally, until liquid evaporates and eggplant begins to stick to pan, about 90 minutes. Add ½ cup of broth and deglaze pan by stirring to scrape browned bits free. Continue baking until eggplant begins to brown, about 20 minutes.

For the noodle pancakes: Cook noodles according to package directions; drain and dry on paper towels. Divide noodles into 6-8 small portions. Heat vegetable oil in a skillet over medium heat. Add noodle portions and flatten with a spatula. Cook noodles until crisp and golden brown on both sides; remove and drain on paper towels. Serve noodle pancakes topped with eggplant marmalade.

"DIP-IN" THE PALOUSE

Pam Steele of Moscow, Idaho, created this winning appetizer for the 2003 National Lentil Festival cook-off in Pullman, Washington. Pullman is located in the Palouse region, which produces most of the lentils grown in the United States, and the highest quality lentils grown in the world.

Makes 8 to 12 Servings

1	cup dry lentils
1	(12-ounce) bottle red taco sauce (mild, medium or hot)
1	(28-ounce) package frozen peas, thawed
1	tablespoon fresh lemon juice
¼	teaspoon salt
½	teaspoon pepper
1	cup sour cream
½	cup mayonnaise
1	(1-ounce) package taco seasoning
1	large bunch green onions, chopped
1	green bell pepper, chopped
1	yellow bell pepper, chopped
1	(2-ounce) can sliced olives
3	tomatoes, chopped
1½	cups grated cheddar cheese

Tortilla chips, for serving
Carrot and celery sticks, for serving

Bring 4 cups of water to a boil in a large saucepan. Add lentils, lower heat, cover and cook for 20-30 minutes, until tender. Drain and cool lentils. Purée lentils and taco sauce together in a blender (leave some lentils whole, if desired); set aside. Spread lentil mixture onto a large, shallow platter.

Purée peas, lemon juice, salt and pepper in a blender. Spread pea mixture over lentils. Combine mayonnaise, sour cream and taco seasoning; spread over pea mixture. Top with onions, green and yellow bell peppers, olives and tomatoes. Sprinkle with cheese.

To serve: Spoon dip onto small plates. Serve with tortilla chips and/or carrot and celery sticks.

CHAMPIONSHIP GUACAMOLE

Tim Bridwell won first prize in the California Avocado Festival's Best Guacamole Recipe Contest, held annually since 1984 in Carpinteria, California. The festival has grown into one of the largest in California, with three days of food, music and great family fun.

Makes About 2 Cups

3   ripe Haas avocados
¼   cup plus 2 tablespoons minced shallot
2   tablespoons minced cilantro
2   jalapeños, seeded and minced
1   tablespoon chopped oil-packed sun-dried tomato
1   teaspoon minced garlic
2   tablespoons crumbled goat cheese
1   Roma tomato, chopped
Lime juice, to taste
Tortilla chips, for serving

Mash avocados to desired consistency. Add remaining ingredients; stir well. Serve with tortilla chips or use as a spread on sandwiches.

Texas Proud Pineapple Salsa

A. Keith Hebert of Humble, Texas, took first prize in the fourth annual Houston Hot Sauce Festival. Each year, thousands of "chiliheads" flock to the Houston for the nation's largest hot sauce festival.

Makes About 3 Cups

1	fresh pineapple, quartered
2	green jalapeños, seeded
3	red jalapeños, seeded
½	large Vidalia onion
1	tablespoon minced garlic
½	bunch cilantro
1	cup chicken stock or broth
½	cup sugar
¼	cup fresh lime juice
2	teaspoons salt
1	teaspoon cumin

Put all ingredients in a food processor and process for 45-60 seconds, to desired consistency.

CHILLIE WILLIE'S CHILI SALSA

2003 International Chili Society salsa champ Judy Omerza of Wilkes-Barre, Pennsylvania, earned the distinction of being the winner who was furthest from home. With two types of onion, three varieties of tomato and three kinds of chiles, Omerza's salsa is not for the feint of heart.

Makes About 4 Cups

1	medium Vidalia onion (or other sweet onion), chopped
1	medium white onion, chopped
2	large anaheim chiles, seeded and chopped
2	jalapeños, seeded and minced*
2	habanero chiles, seeded and minced*

Juice of 1 lime
Juice of 1 lemon

1	large bunch cilantro, chopped
1	pint cherry tomatoes, chopped
1	pint grape tomatoes, chopped
2	vine tomatoes, chopped
1	small turnip, chopped

Salt and cumin, to taste

Combine all ingredients.

CONFETTI GRILLED CORN & OLIVE SALSA

Roxanne Chan of Albany, California, won the California Ripe Olives' Outdoor Olive Recipe Contest with this unusual Mediterranean/Southwestern fusion. As an accompaniment to grilled beef, pork or chicken, this one's a winner.

Makes About 3 Cups

4   ears corn, husked
1   tablespoon vegetable oil
1   small red bell pepper, halved
1   (6½-ounce) jar marinated quartered artichoke hearts, undrained
½   cup sliced black olives
¼   cup minced green onion
¼   cup sliced almonds
2   tablespoons chopped parsley
1   tablespoon chopped chipotle pepper in adobo sauce*
1   teaspoon lemon juice
1   teaspoon honey

Preheat grill to low. Brush corn with oil. Grill corn, turning to brown evenly, until slightly charred, about 8-10 minutes. Remove corn kernels from cobs. Grill bell pepper halves, cut-side-up, until skins are evenly blackened. Seal pepper halves in a paper bag for a few minutes to steam. Remove peppers; peel and dice. Put peppers, corn, and remaining ingredients in a large bowl; mix well. Cover and chill until serving.

*Note: Chipotle chiles are smoked jalapeño peppers canned in a spicy adobo sauce. They can be found in the Mexican food section of most larger groceries.

APPLE RELISH

Nicole Gilbert of East Henderson, North Carolina, won the "low-cal" category in the 57th annual North Carolina Apple Festival in Hendersonville, North Carolina. The festival pays tribute to everything apple – from apple breakfasts and orchard tours to apple arts and crafts.

Makes About 2 Cups

2	large (or 3 small) Granny Smith apples, cubed
1	large dill pickle, chopped
1	medium onion, finely chopped
⅓	cup sugar
¼	cup cider vinegar

In a medium bowl, combine apples, pickle and onion. In a small bowl, combine sugar and vinegar; stir until sugar is dissolved. Add sugar mixture to apple mixture; toss to combine. Cover and chill for 1 hour. Serve with roast pork or other meat dishes.

BLAKE-O'S RED HOT SAUCE

Team Blake-O of Houston, Texas, won the Amateur Salsa Competition "People's Choice Award" at the 2003 Tex-Mex Gourmet Houston Hot Sauce Festival. Every year, ten to twenty thousand brave souls attend the festival.

Makes About 4 Cups

Vegetable oil
1   teaspoon chili powder
2   medium white onions
1   ancho chile
5   whole cloves garlic, peeled
6   ripe medium tomatoes (overly ripe is okay)
12   large ripe cherry tomatoes
12   arbol chiles, stemmed and seeded (it is not necessary to remove all seeds – just get what you can)
5   medium red jalapeños
2   large pickled jalapeños
Salt, to taste
1   bunch cilantro, chopped

Heat a small amount of oil (about ⅛-inch deep) in a small skillet over high heat. Add chili powder. Quarter 1 onion. Lower heat to medium and add quartered onion, ancho chile and garlic. Cook, turning ancho chile, until onion and garlic are lightly browned (do not let chile burn – remove it to a paper towel when it is browning slightly and/or has a puffy appearance). Remove onion and garlic to paper towels and pat dry. Stem, quarter and seed ancho chile.

Boil medium and cherry tomatoes until skins start to fall off, about 30 seconds. Remove tomatoes (reserve tomato cooking water to thin the sauce). Slip skins off medium tomatoes. Remove or leave cherry tomato skins.

Put tomatoes, onion mixture, ancho and arbol chiles and red and pickled jalapeños in a food processor (do not use a blender – it does not work well for this recipe). Process mixture until very thin (this may take a little while). For a thinner sauce, add reserved tomato cooking water a little at a time. Taste and add salt. For a spicier sauce, add more stemmed red jalapeño peppers, 1-2 at a time, and process until puréed.

Chop remaining onion and add to sauce with cilantro, a handful at a time, to taste (do not process).

SOUTH OF THE BORDER PESTO SAUCE

Sycamore Farms' annual Basil Festival in Paso Robles, California, is a chance to explore new ways to use basil. Barb Wilcox of Paso Robles, won first prize in the new "non-traditional best o' pesto" category, which was added in 2003 because of entrant' creativity in past years.

Makes About 2 Cups

2	cups fresh basil, coarsely chopped
½	cup chopped fresh cilantro
4	cloves garlic, minced
6	tomatillos, husked*
1-2	jalapeños, seeded
½	cup grated Parmesan cheese
½	cup crumbled feta cheese
½	cup pine nuts, toasted
½	cup chopped walnuts, toasted
1	tablespoon lemon juice
½	cup olive oil
2	teaspoons Seasoned Salt by Barb**

In a food processor, combine all ingredients in order given; process until puréed to desired consistency. If not using immediately, refrigerate in an airtight container with a thin coating of oil on top to keep the sauce from turning dark. This pesto will keep for a week or more in the refrigerator. It also freezes well.

*Note: Tomatillos are small, tart Mexican green tomatoes with a papery husk that is easily removed. They can be found in most larger groceries.

**Note: Seasoned Salt by Barb is a salt and herb blend. It is available at www.seasoningsbybarb.com. If unavailable, substitute another favorite salt blend.

BREAKFAST & BRUNCH

FRESH PLUM & PECAN WAFFLES

Alexandra Ricciuti, a pastry chef from Boston, Massachusetts, won first prize in the "breakfast" category at the Eat California Fruit Make It Special With California Peaches, Plums and Nectarines Recipe Contest. Made with juicy California plums, this is a wonderful twist on traditional waffles. In the finished waffle, the plums become intense and jammy in flavor.

Makes 6 Servings

¾ cup coarsely chopped pecans, divided
1½ cups all-purpose flour
1½ teaspoons baking powder
¼ teaspoon salt
3 tablespoons brown sugar
1½ cups milk
2 large eggs
1 teaspoon vanilla extract
3 tablespoons unsalted butter, melted
1 cup diced (½-inch) fresh California plums (any variety), plus additional sliced fresh California plums, for serving
Maple syrup, for serving

Preheat oven to 325°F. Preheat waffle iron. Spread pecans on a baking sheet in a single layer and toast in oven just until lightly browned and aromatic. Spread pecans on parchment or wax paper and cool.

In a large bowl, combine flour, baking powder, salt and brown sugar. In a small bowl, beat milk, eggs and vanilla. Whisk half of egg mixture into flour mixture, then whisk in remaining egg mixture (do not overmix). Stir in butter. Fold in diced plums and ½ cup of toasted pecans.

Spoon batter onto a preheated greased or non-stick waffle iron; bake until golden brown. Serve with maple syrup. Garnish with fresh sliced plums and remaining ¼ cup of toasted pecans.

BANANA PANCAKES WITH RICOTTA CREAM & CARAMEL SAUCE

These pancakes won second prize in the spring 2003 Ready, Set, Cook Recipe Contest. In this recipe, fluffy pancakes combine beautifully with bananas and caramel sauce, and are served with a delicious ricotta cream. If serving as a dessert, rum or brandy can be added to the caramel pecan sauce.

Makes 6 Servings

Ricotta cream:
1   cup ricotta cheese
¼   cup powdered sugar
2   tablespoons orange juice
½-1 teaspoon grated orange zest

Caramel pecan sauce:
6   ounces caramels, chopped
¾   cup cream (light or whipping)
⅓   cup chopped pecans
1   tablespoon flaked coconut
1   tablespoon rum or brandy
       (optional)

Banana pancakes:
1¼   cups buttermilk
2   tablespoons butter, melted
2   large eggs, separated
½   teaspoon vanilla extract
1   tablespoon caster sugar
       (superfine sugar)
1   cup all-purpose flour
Pinch of salt
2   teaspoons baking powder
½   teaspoon baking soda
2   medium bananas, sliced

For the ricotta cream: Whisk together all ingredients until well combined. Cover and refrigerate until using.

For the caramel sauce: In a small, non-stick saucepan over low heat, melt together caramels and cream, stirring occasionally, until smooth and combined. Add pecans, coconut and rum or brandy; stir to combine, then remove from heat. Set aside and keep warm.

For the pancakes: In a small bowl, mix buttermilk and butter. Lightly beat yolks; whisk into buttermilk mixture. Add vanilla and caster sugar; stir until sugar is dissolved. Sift together flour, salt, baking powder and baking soda into a large bowl. Add buttermilk mixture; whisk until batter is thick and smooth.

In a clean, dry bowl, beat egg whites until stiff. Carefully fold egg whites into batter until combined (bananas can be added now or during cooking). Pour ½-¾ cup of batter into a small, lightly greased skillet over medium heat; swirl skillet quickly to spread batter evenly over bottom of skillet. Cook until bubbles begin to appear on surface; lay some banana slices on top. Cook pancakes until golden brown on both sides; keep warm.

To serve: Drizzle warm caramel sauce over each pancake and top with a generous dollop of ricotta cream.

CREPES A LA FRENCH FESTIVAL

Steve Hoegerman of Santa Barbara, California, won the "Golden Franc" award at the 2003 Santa Barbara French Festival. Hoegerman's winning recipe was inspired by a classic French recipe.

Makes 4 to 6 Servings

1   cup all-purpose flour
2   eggs
Pinch of salt
⅔   cup milk
⅔   cup water
1   tablespoon butter, melted
1   tablespoon vegetable oil
Butter, sugar and/or jam, for serving

Put flour in a bowl; make a well in flour. Crack eggs into well in flour. Add a pinch of salt; mix thoroughly with a wooden spoon. Gradually add milk and water; whisk until smooth. Stir in melted butter and oil. Cover batter and refrigerate for at least 2 hours.

Lightly butter a hot crêpe pan or skillet. Stir crêpe batter and add enough batter to pan to cover bottom of pan in a thin, even layer (tilt pan from side to side, or spread gently with a spatula).

Cook crêpes for 1-2 minutes, until golden. Turn and cook for about 1 minute more. Serve warm, with butter and sugar, or your favorite jam, and folded into thirds.

POTATO PANCAKE WITH SMOKED SALMON & CAVIAR

Lillian Julow of Gainesville, Florida, won the Shuckman's Fish Company & Smokery recipe contest with this fabulous take on a classic dish. Shuckman's was founded in 1919 by Issa Shuckman and is now in its fourth generation of family ownership.

Makes 6 to 8 Servings

3	medium Yukon gold potatoes, peeled and coarsely grated
1	stick butter, melted
Salt and pepper, to taste	
2	teaspoons extra-virgin olive oil
½	cup sour cream
3	shallots, minced
5	sprigs fresh dill, chopped, or 2 teaspoons dried dill
Juice of ½ lemon	
6	ounces Shuckman's Smoked Nova Salmon, thinly sliced
3	ounces Shuckman's Kentucky Spoonfish Caviar
4-5	fresh chives, finely chopped

Preheat oven to 425°F. Toss grated potatoes in melted butter. Season with salt and pepper. Heat olive oil in a large skillet over medium-high heat. Add potato mixture; spread into a large, thick pancake. Cook for 1 minute. Lower heat to medium and cook until bottom of pancake is browned.

Turn pancake by sliding it onto a large plate, covering it with another plate and turning over. Slide pancake back into skillet and cook until other side is browned. Slide pancake onto a baking sheet and bake for 3-5 minutes.

In a bowl, combine sour cream, shallots, dill and lemon juice. Season lightly with salt and pepper; mix well.

To serve: Remove potato pancake from oven and place on a large platter. Spread sour cream mixture over top of pancake. Cover with slices of smoked salmon. Garnish with caviar and chives. Slice and serve immediately.

Potato & Maple Sausage Pancakes

Deborah Puette of Lilburn, Georgia, won second prize in the Old Farmer's Almanac's *2003 recipe contest. Since 1792, The* Old Farmer's Almanac *has published useful information for people in all walks of life: tide tables for those who live near the ocean; planting charts for those who live on the farm; and recipes for those who live in the kitchen!*

Makes 6 to 8 Servings

2½ cups mashed potatoes
1 large Granny Smith apple, peeled, cored and grated
½ pound maple-flavored sausage, browned and crumbled
2 green onions, chopped
2 eggs
⅓ cup flour
½ teaspoon salt
½ teaspoon ground white pepper
Vegetable oil, for frying
Sour cream, for serving (optional)

In a large bowl, combine all ingredients, except oil and sour cream. Heat 1-2 tablespoons of oil in a large skillet over medium-low heat. Drop enough batter into skillet to make 4-inch pancakes.

Brown cakes on both sides, about 3 minutes per side. Remove pancakes from pan and drain on paper towels. Repeat with remaining batter, adding oil to skillet between batches as needed. Serve pancakes immediately, topped with a dollop of sour cream, if desired.

Smoked Salmon Frittata Gremolata

Roxanne Chan of Albany, California, was the grand prize winner in the Shuckman's Fish Company &
Smokery recipe contest. This easy and versatile recipe is perfect served warm for breakfast, lunch or
dinner, or cut into small squares and served cold or at room temperature as an appetizer.

Makes 6 Servings

Frittata:
8   eggs
8   ounces Shuckman's Smoked
     Salmon Spread*
1   cup sour cream
1   cup Shuckman's Smoked Alder
     Salmon, flaked
½   cup diced red bell pepper
2   green onions, sliced
½   teaspoon pepper

*Gremolata:***
⅓   cup chopped parsley
2   cloves garlic, minced
1   teaspoon grated lemon zest

For the frittata: Preheat oven to 350°F. Whisk together eggs, smoked salmon spread and sour cream until well blended. Stir in smoked salmon, bell pepper, green onion and pepper until well mixed.

Pour egg mixture into a greased 9x13-inch baking dish. Bake for 30 minutes, or until set. Cut into squares and sprinkle with gremolata to serve.

For the gremolata: Combine ingredients in a small bowl.

*Note: Shuckman's Smoked Salmon Spread is a mixture of smoked salmon and cream cheese. If unavailable, use store-bought smoked salmon cream cheese.

**Note: A gremolata is an Italian garnish made of parsley, garlic and lemon zest.

SOUTHWEST-STYLE EGGS BENEDICT WITH JALAPEÑO HOLLANDAISE

Executive Chef Erick Neuharth of Hidden Valley Lake Country Club in Middletown, California, won first prize in the "entrée" category in Mission Tortilla's Think Outside The Tortilla Recipe Contest.

Makes 4 Servings

Potatoes:
3   pounds baby red potatoes
3   tablespoons vegetable oil
Salt and pepper, to taste
1   medium yellow onion, diced
2   Anaheim chiles, preferably red, seeded and diced
Nopales (cactus leaves), sliced*

Jalapeño hollandaise sauce:
2   sticks butter
4   egg yolks
2   tablespoons lemon juice
Dash of Tabasco sauce
Dash of Worcestershire sauce
1   small jalapeño

For the potatoes: Put potatoes and 3 quarts of salted cold water in a large pot. Cover and bring to a boil. Lower heat and simmer until potatoes are tender; drain potatoes and place in an ice-water bath to stop cooking. When potatoes are cool, drain and cut into ½-inch thick slices (potatoes can be prepared to this point the night before).

Heat oil in a skillet over medium heat. Add potatoes. Season with salt and pepper. Turn potatoes once they have browned. Add onion, chiles and nopales; cook for 5 minutes. Turn and cook for 5 minutes more, or until potatoes are golden brown. Remove from heat.

For the sauce: In a saucepan, bring butter to a vigorous boil. In a stainless steel bowl, beat egg yolks and lemon juice with a mixer (or in a blender). With mixer running, beat in melted butter in a slow, steady stream. (The sauce should be thick and custard-like – if it is too thick, thin it with a little water.) Stir in Tabasco and Worcestershire.

Oil jalapeño and grill or broil until skin begins to blister. Once skin has blistered all the way around, put pepper in a paper bag to steam. After a few minutes, remove skin and seeds. Mince jalapeño and stir into sauce.

*Note: Nopales (cactus leaves) from a jar may be used and can be found in Mexican markets and the Mexican food section of larger groceries.

Eggs Benedict:
Oil, for frying
4   (6-inch) Mission corn tortillas
2   tablespoons vegetable oil
12 ounces bulk chorizo sausage
2   teaspoons vinegar
8   eggs
8   cilantro leaves, for garnish

For the eggs Benedict: Heat oil for frying to 375°F. Cut tortillas into 8 rounds with a round cookie cutter. Fry tortillas until crisp and golden brown. Place on paper towels to drain.

Heat 2 tablespoons of oil in a skillet over medium heat. Form chorizo into 8 small patties. Cook chorizo for 3-5 minutes per side, until cooked through.

Bring 1½ quarts of water and vinegar to a simmer. Add eggs and poach to desired doneness, about 3-4 minutes.

To serve: Put 2 fried tortilla rounds in center of each plate. Put 1 chorizo patty on each tortilla. With a slotted spoon, put 1 egg on each chorizo patty. Top eggs with hollandaise sauce and surround with potatoes. Garnish with a cilantro leaf and serve.

AMERICAN EGG BAKE

The Iowa Egg Council recipe contest was created as a way to increase egg consumption across the United States. Derrick Walton of Des Moines, Iowa, won first prize in the "breakfast" category in the 2003 event. Iowa is the nation's leading egg producer with over 42 million hens laying over 10 billion eggs per year.

Makes 3 to 4 Servings

2	tablespoons olive oil
1	potato, cubed
½	cup chopped green onion
4	mushrooms, sliced
¼	cup finely chopped red bell pepper
1	clove garlic, minced
1	cup chopped cauliflower
1	cup chopped broccoli
6	large eggs
½	cup grated Asiago cheese
¼	cup white wine
½	teaspoon dried basil
¼	teaspoon salt
¼	teaspoon pepper
½	cup grated Parmesan cheese

Heat oil in a skillet over medium heat. Add potatoes and cook until tender. Add green onion, mushrooms, bell pepper and garlic; cook until green onion is soft. Add broccoli and cauliflower. Lower heat to medium-low and cook for about 5 minutes more.

Beat eggs, Asiago cheese, wine, basil, salt and pepper; pour over ingredients in skillet. Cook for 5 minutes (be careful, if heat is too high, eggs will overcook).

As eggs set, lift edges of egg mixture with a spatula and let uncooked portion flow underneath. Continue cooking, lifting edges of eggs and letting uncooked portion flow underneath until mixture is almost set (the top will still be moist). Remove pan from heat. Cover and let stand until top is set. Sprinkle with Parmesan cheese and serve.

EGGLICIOUS SANDWICH

Jenny Chung of Ames, Iowa, bested 200 entrants to take the $750 third prize in the "student" division at the 2003 Iowa Egg Council recipe contest. In the past, practically every town in Iowa included a hatchery where people could buy baby chicks.

Makes 6 to 8 Servings

1	(1-pound) loaf French bread, unsliced
4	tablespoons butter, softened and divided
2	tablespoons mayonnaise
2	tablespoons honey mustard
4	thin slices deli ham
4	thin slices deli turkey
4	strips cooked bacon
1	large tomato, sliced
1	small onion, thinly sliced
8	eggs, lightly beaten
4	slices cheddar cheese
4	slices pepper Jack cheese

Halve bread lengthwise. Carefully hollow out top and bottom, leaving a ½-inch shell; discard removed bread. Spread mayonnaise and 3 tablespoons of butter over bottom half of bread. Spread honey mustard over top of bread. Layer bottom of bread with ham, turkey and bacon. Top with tomato and onion.

Preheat oven to 375°F. In a skillet over medium heat, melt remaining 1 tablespoon of butter. Add eggs and cook, stirring occasionally, until eggs are almost set. Spoon eggs into bottom of bread shell over tomato and onion. Top with cheddar and pepper Jack cheese. Cover with bread top. Wrap in greased foil. Bake for 15-20 minutes, or until heated through and cheeses are melted. Slice and serve.

ARTICHOKE BREAKFAST BURRITO

Julia Perez Magana of Castroville, California, wowed the judges at the Castroville Artichoke Festival's Fresh Artichoke Recipe Contest. This weekend-long event includes music, wine tastings, arts and crafts, a farmer's market and an old-fashioned parade.

Makes 4 to 8 Servings

½ pound bulk Italian sausage, crumbled
2 tablespoons olive oil
½ cup chopped onion
1 clove garlic, minced
1 jalapeño, seeded and minced
1 large tomato, diced
2 cups trimmed, cooked and diced artichoke hearts
Salt and pepper, to taste
3 large eggs
8 medium flour tortillas
2 cups grated Monterey Jack and/or cheddar cheese

In a skillet over medium heat, cook sausage until done; drain grease. Add olive oil to sausage. Add onion, garlic and jalapeño; cook until onion is soft. Add tomatoes and artichokes; cook, stirring occasionally, for 3-4 minutes. Season with salt and pepper. Add eggs and cook, stirring, until eggs are done.

Heat tortillas (on a griddle, if possible). Fill middle of each tortilla with artichoke mixture. Sprinkle with cheese. Fold in ends, then roll up tortilla.

ZUCCHINI & CHICKEN QUICHE

Rebecca Cicio of Windsor, Florida, won the grand prize at the 18th annual Windsor Zucchini Fest, America's first zucchini festival. Windsor is semi-famous for their marching band, which appeared in the movie Doc Hollywood, *starring Michael J. Fox.*

Makes 6 to 8 Servings

- 1 tablespoon olive oil
- 1 medium zucchini, quartered and sliced
- 1 medium onion, chopped
- 2 chicken bouillon cubes, divided and crumbled
- 1 chicken breast, cut into ½-inch cubes
- 4 eggs, beaten
- 1 cup light cream
- ¾ cup milk
- 1 tablespoon all-purpose flour
- ½ teaspoon salt
- 1½ cups grated sharp cheddar cheese
- 1 deep dish pie crust

Preheat oven to 325°F. Heat oil in a skillet over medium heat. Add zucchini, onion and 1 crumbled bouillon cube. Cook until zucchini is almost tender; set aside. In a saucepan, bring 4 cups of water and remaining crumbled bouillon cube to a boil. Add chicken, lower heat, cover and simmer until chicken is cooked through. Stir chicken into zucchini mixture.

In a bowl, beat eggs. Add cream, milk, flour and salt; mix well. Add zucchini mixture and cheese to egg mixture; mix well. Pour into pie crust and bake for 50-60 minutes, or until a toothpick inserted in center comes out clean.

CRISPY POTATO QUICHE

Amy Kerby of Omaha, Nebraska, won third prize in the Old Farmer's Almanac's *2003 Potato Recipe Contest. Her delicious quiche uses hashbrowns for the crust in a new twist on an old favorite. Leave the hashbrowns in the oven a bit longer for an extra-crispy crust!*

Makes 6 to 8 Servings

1   (24-ounce) package frozen shredded hash browns, thawed
5⅓ tablespoons butter, melted
1   cup grated hot pepper cheese
1   cup grated Swiss cheese
1   cup diced cooked ham
½   cup half & half
2   eggs
¼   teaspoon seasoned salt

Preheat oven to 425°F. Press hash browns between paper towels to remove moisture. Press hash browns into a greased 10-inch pie pan, forming a solid crust. Brush with melted butter, especially the top edges. Bake for 25 minutes, or until golden. Remove and cool slightly.

Lower oven temperature to 350°F. Spread hot pepper and Swiss cheese and ham evenly over potato crust. Beat half & half, eggs and salt; pour over cheese and ham. Bake for 30-40 minutes, until a toothpick inserted in center comes out clean.

Sun-Dried Tomato Quiche

In the 2003 Iowa Egg Council recipe contest, Zach Pierce of Cedar Rapids, Iowa, won first prize in the "student" category. Egg contains the highest quality food protein known. It is so nearly perfect, in fact, that egg protein is often the standard by which all other proteins are judged.

Makes 6 to 8 Servings

Crust:

1	large baking potato, thinly sliced
2	tablespoons butter, melted

Filling:

⅔	cup oil-packed sun-dried tomatoes, chopped
1	green onion, chopped
1	tablespoon minced garlic
⅓	cup cubed smoked ham
2	cups grated provolone cheese
4	large eggs
1½	cups whipping cream
2	teaspoons Italian seasoning
⅛	teaspoon salt
⅛	teaspoon pepper

For the crust: Preheat oven to 350°F. Butter a pie pan. Arrange potato slices on bottom of pan. Brush potatoes with melted butter. Bake for 10 minutes (or longer for a crispier crust).

For the filling: Layer sun-dried tomatoes, green onion, garlic, ham and cheese on top of potato crust.

Whisk together eggs, cream, Italian seasoning, salt and pepper. Pour egg mixture over ingredients in pie pan. Bake for 40-50 minutes, or until a toothpick inserted in center comes out clean. Let stand for a few minutes, then slice and serve.

CRAB & VEGGIE QUICHE

Veg-All invited cooks from across America to use its canned vegetables to add a new twist to a home-cooked favorite. The result? More than 1,400 different ideas on how to add convenience and nutrition to family favorites, such as this quiche from Jack Simson of Buffalo, New York.

Makes 6 Servings

1   (9-inch) refrigerated pie crust
1   cup grated Swiss cheese
2   (4½-ounce) cans crabmeat, drained
2   slices bacon, cooked crisp and crumbled
1   (15-ounce) can Veg-All Original Mixed Vegetables, drained
2   green onions, sliced
3   large eggs
1½ cups half & half
½   teaspoon salt
⅛   teaspoon cayenne pepper
Pinch of minced parsley, plus parsley sprigs, for garnish
Pinch of garlic powder
Dash of nutmeg
Lemon wedges, for garnish

Preheat oven to 375°F. Prepare pie crust according to package directions. Put crust in a quiche or pie pan. Sprinkle crust with cheese, crabmeat, bacon, Veg-All and green onion.

Beat eggs, half & half, salt, cayenne, minced parsley, garlic powder and nutmeg; pour over ingredients in crust. Bake for 45-60 minutes, or until a toothpick inserted in center comes out clean. Let stand for 5 minutes before slicing. Garnish with parsley sprigs and lemon wedges.

SWEET ONION PIE

Tammy Gordon of Walla Walla, Washington, won the prize for "best entrée" at the 2003 Walla Walla Sweet Onion Festival recipe contest with this quiche. The Walla Walla onion is a big, sweet variety that can weigh up to two pounds. It owes its sweetness not to sugar, but to a high water and low sulfur content.

Makes 6 to 8 Servings

2	tablespoons unsalted butter
3	cups (½-inch) rings Walla Walla sweet onion
1	(9-inch) pie crust
4	large eggs
1½	cups heavy cream
¼	teaspoon Italian seasoning
1½	cups grated Swiss cheese

Preheat oven to 325°F. Melt butter in a skillet over low heat. Add onion and cook, stirring occasionally, until golden brown and caramelized, about 30-45 minutes. Spread onions in bottom of pie crust. Beat eggs, cream and Italian seasoning; pour over onions in crust. Sprinkle with Swiss cheese. Bake for 30-35 minutes, until set. Let stand for 10 minutes, then slice and serve.

CHERRY PEANUT GRANOLA

Amy Oliver of Bangor, Maine won second prize in the "snacks & appetizers" category at the 2003 Plains Peanut Festival recipe contest. Granola was created by Sylvester Graham (1794-1851), the father of the graham cracker!

Makes About 8 Cups

3	tablespoons butter, melted
¼	cup peanut oil
½	cup honey
½	cup packed brown sugar
1	teaspoon vanilla extract
½	teaspoon cinnamon
3	cups old-fashioned rolled oats
1	cup flaked coconut
¼	cup wheat germ
½	cup sesame seeds
1	cup peanuts
½	teaspoon salt
1	cup dried cherries
1	cup chopped pitted dates

Preheat oven to 300°F. In a large bowl, combine butter, oil, honey, brown sugar, vanilla and cinnamon. Add oats, coconut, wheat germ, sesame seeds and peanuts; toss well to coat. Spread mixture onto a non-stick or parchment paper-lined rimmed baking sheet.

Bake granola for 30 minutes, checking and stirring every 10 minutes, until mixture is golden brown. Stir well and return to oven for 15 minutes more, if needed. Remove from oven and sprinkle with salt. Transfer granola to a bowl. Stir in dried cherries and dates. Cool, then store in an airtight container.

To serve: For a European-style breakfast, serve granola with yogurt and cut-up fresh fruit. For trail mix, just add some chocolate (such as M&M's, chocolate chips and/or chocolate-covered peanuts), pretzels, peanut butter chips and/or cereal.

AWESOME HEALTHY CHEESECAKE SMOOTHIE

Logan Stewart of Simsonville, South Carolina, won Friendship Dairies' monthly recipe contest with this creamy, yet light smoothie. It is a perfect option for breakfast, or as a cool treat on a hot day.

Makes 2 Servings

1   cup 1% milk
1½   cups crushed ice
1   (4½-ounce) box sugar-free Jell-O pudding mix (flavor of your choice)
¼   cup low-fat Friendship sour cream
¼   cup low-fat cream cheese
6   packets Splenda sweetener (or 2 tablespoons of sugar)
1½   cups blueberries or strawberries (optional), plus extra for garnish
Whipped topping, for serving
2   sheets regular or cinnamon graham crackers, crushed

In a blender, combine milk, crushed ice, pudding mix, sour cream, cream cheese, Splenda and berries; blend at high speed until ice is dissolved and mixture is smooth. Pour into serving glasses. Garnish with a spoonful of whipped topping, crushed graham crackers and berries.

CHOCOLATE VELVET

*Rachel Winzer of Stockton, California, was a finalist in the Got Leche? Cook-off. Winzer said of her recipe,
"I was reading through my cookbooks one day and found a story on the Aztecs, who prepared and drank a
beverage like this 'Chocolate Velvet' for energy during hard days of work in the mountains."*

Makes 4 to 6 Servings

2   tablespoons sugar
1   teaspoon ground cinnamon
1   teaspoon nutmeg
3   teaspoons arrowroot or
    cornstarch
6   cups whole milk, divided
4   ounces semisweet chocolate,
    finely chopped
4   ounces white chocolate, finely
    chopped
1   egg, slightly beaten
1   teaspoon vanilla extract
Shaved chocolate, for garnish
    (optional)

Combine sugar, cinnamon, nutmeg and arrowroot or
cornstarch in a saucepan over medium heat. Add ⅓ cup
of milk; cook for 2 minutes. Stir in remaining milk. Add
semisweet and white chocolate; bring to a gentle simmer.

Put egg in a small bowl. Mix 1 cup of chocolate mixture
into egg, then fold egg mixture into saucepan; whisk
until thickened. Remove from heat and stir in vanilla.

Pour hot chocolate into a large bowl. Beat only the top
of the hot chocolate with a mixer until foamy. Pour hot
chocolate into wide cups. Garnish with shaved chocolate.

SOUPS, CHILIS & CHOWDERS

QUICK TURKEY RAGOUT WITH PIMENTO CORNBREAD DUMPLINGS

For this rib-sticking stew, Norita Solt of Bettendorf, Iowa, won third prize in the 2003 National Cornbread Festival's National Cornbread Cook-off in South Pittsburg, Tennessee.

Makes 4 Servings

Turkey ragout:
2   tablespoons butter
1   cup chopped onion
½   cup chopped celery
1   (10- to 14-ounce) uncooked turkey breast tender, cut into bite-size pieces*
1   cup sliced mushrooms
½   teaspoon rosemary
1   teaspoon dried sage
½   teaspoon thyme
1½ cups water
1   tablespoon chicken soup base (or chicken bouillon granules)
1   (10½-ounce) can condensed cream of chicken soup
1½ cups milk

Pimento cornbread dumplings:
1   (6-ounce) package Martha White Buttermilk Cornbread Mix
1   (2-ounce) jar chopped pimentos, undrained
1   teaspoon onion powder
⅓   cup milk
1   tablespoon minced parsley

For the ragout: Melt butter in a 3-quart cast-iron chicken fryer over medium-high heat. Add onion, celery and turkey; cook, stirring, until vegetables are soft and turkey is no longer pink. Stir in mushrooms, rosemary, sage, thyme, water and chicken soup base. Lower heat, cover and simmer for 15 minutes. Add cream of chicken soup and milk, mix well and return to a simmer.

For the dumplings: Combine cornbread mix, pimentos, onion powder, milk and parsley. Drop 8 spoonfuls of cornbread mixture into simmering turkey ragout. Cover, lower heat and simmer until dumplings feel somewhat firm to the touch, but still springy, about 5-6 minutes.

*Note: This dish was originally created as a way to use leftover Thanksgiving turkey. To use pre-cooked turkey, reduce water to 1 cup and first simmering time (before adding dumplings) from 15 minutes to 5 minutes.

SKILLET CHICKEN STEW WITH HERB DUMPLINGS

Leigh Walter of Burnsville, Minnesota, won first prize in the HERB-OX Comfort Food Recipe Contest at the Minnesota State Fair in St. Paul, Minnesota. In 2003, fairgoers consumed 3,195,000 chocolate chip cookies, 184,000 foot-long hot dogs, 515,900 corn dogs and 181,000 ears of corn.

Makes 4 Servings

Chicken stew:
- ¼ cup vegetable oil
- 1 bunch green onions, whites only, finely sliced (reserve green tops for dumplings)
- ½ cup all-purpose flour
- 1 teaspoon salt
- 1 teaspoon pepper
- 1 teaspoon paprika
- ¾ pound boneless, skinless chicken breast, cubed
- 3 packets HERB-OX Instant Broth and Seasoning Chicken Flavored Bouillon
- 1 cup diced potato
- 1 cup diced carrot
- 1 cup frozen peas

Herb dumplings:
- 1½ cups all-purpose flour
- 2 teaspoons baking powder
- Dash of salt
- 3 tablespoons shortening
- ¾ cup milk
- ¼ cup finely chopped green onion tops only

For the stew: Heat oil in a large skillet (with a lid) over medium heat. Add green onions; cook for 2 minutes. In a bowl, combine flour, salt, pepper and paprika. Add chicken; turn to coat. Put chicken in skillet; cook until browned on all sides. Drain excess oil from pan. Dissolve bouillon in 2½ cups of hot water; add to skillet.

Raise heat to medium-high. Add potatoes and carrots. Cover and simmer for 10 minutes, stirring occasionally, until chicken and vegetables are almost cooked through. Add peas and return stew to a simmer. Add dumplings; simmer, uncovered, for 10 minutes. Cover and simmer for 10 minutes more, until dumplings are done.

For the dumplings: Mix flour, baking powder and salt. Cut in shortening until crumbly. Stir in milk (do not overmix). Stir in green onions. Shape into dumplings.

CREAMY CURRY CARROT SOUP

Lisa Renshaw of Kansas City, Missouri, was a runner-up in the USA Rice Federation's Rice to the Rescue recipe contest. This elegant soup highlights the versatility of rice, which adds texture and flavor to a creamy blend of carrots and onions.

Makes 6 to 8 Servings

2	tablespoons butter
2-3	teaspoons curry powder
1	teaspoon salt
1	medium onion, finely chopped
4	medium carrots, grated
3	(14½-ounce) cans chicken broth, divided
3	cups cooked long grain rice
1	cup whipping cream

Melt butter in a large pot over medium-high heat. Add curry powder and salt; cook, stirring constantly, for 30 seconds. Add onion and carrot; cook for 7-9 minutes, stirring frequently.

Transfer onion mixture to a blender or food processor. Add 1 can of broth and blend briefly (don't purée). Return mixture to pot; stir in remaining 2 cans of broth and rice. Heat over medium-high heat until hot, about 5 minutes. Remove from heat, stir in cream and serve.

SOUTH OF THE BORDER POTATO SOUP

Jan Shelton of Escondido, California, won the grand prize of a Viking stove and $3,000 at the Got Leche? Cook-off in Sacramento, California. "In California, Latin cuisine is mainstream, and the cook-off celebrated that influence," said Jeff Manning, California Milk Processor Board executive director.

Makes 6 to 8 Servings

½ stick butter
2 large onions, finely chopped
2 tablespoons all-purpose flour
3 cups chicken broth
5 medium potatoes, peeled and diced into small cubes
⅛ teaspoon saffron (optional)
⅛ teaspoon pepper, or more to taste
1 teaspoon salt
3 cups milk
½ cup frozen or canned peas
3 eggs
½ (8-ounce) package cream cheese, softened
1 large avocado, diced into small cubes
¼ cup chopped cilantro, for garnish

Melt butter in a large pot over medium heat. Add onions and cook until soft, but not browned. Stir in flour until smooth. Gradually add chicken broth and bring to boil, stirring constantly. Add potatoes, saffron, pepper and salt. Lower heat and simmer for 15 minutes. Add milk and peas; simmer for 5 minutes more.

In a medium bowl, beat eggs and cream cheese until fluffy. Gradually add 2 cups of hot soup to cream cheese mixture, beating constantly to avoid curdling. Add cream cheese mixture to soup and heat through (do not boil). Divide avocado among serving bowls. Pour soup over avocado. Garnish with cilantro to serve.

CHEESY CARROT & POTATO SOUP

Maxine Bonneau of Imperial, California, won first prize in the "miscellaneous" category at the 56th annual Holtville Carrot Festival in Holtville, California. The week-long festival is a celebration of this delicious vegetable. A carrot has just 30 calories and twice the recommended daily allowance of vitamin A.

Makes 6 to 8 Servings

8 medium baking potatoes, peeled and cubed
½ large onion, chopped
3 cups grated carrot, plus extra for garnish
2 sticks butter or margarine
3 tablespoons Johnny's Garlic Spread*
3 cloves garlic, minced
1 (15-ounce) can evaporated milk
2 tablespoons chopped parsley, plus extra for garnish
Salt and pepper, to taste
2 cups grated cheddar cheese
¾ cup sour cream
4 ounces deli ham, chopped

In a large pot, combine potatoes and onion with just enough water to cover potatoes. Bring to a boil, lower heat and simmer until potatoes are tender. Remove potatoes with a slotted spoon (reserve potato cooking water and onion in pot). Mash potatoes, then return to pot.

Stir carrots, butter, garlic spread, minced garlic and evaporated milk into potato mixture. Add parsley, salt and pepper. Bring to a boil, lower heat and simmer for 6-8 minutes. Stir in cheese, sour cream and ham; cook until cheese is melted. Serve soup garnished with grated carrot and chopped parsley.

*Note: Johnny's Garlic spread is a mixture of granulated garlic, Parmesan cheese, salt, oregano, basil and parsley. It is available at many groceries or from Johnny's Fine Foods (www.johnnysfinefoods.com). If you cannot find it, substitute any similar garlic spice blend.

THREE BEAN MEXISTRONE WITH CORNMEAL DUMPLINGS

Elaine Sweet of Dallas, Texas, won first prize for this soup in Mom!Mom!'s What a Crock Recipe Contest. One of Mom!Mom!'s regular entrants, Sweet never fails to send recipes that the judges fight over. This is her first time as the winner. For a vegetarian dinner, this just can't be beat.

Makes 4 to 6 Servings

Soup:
1   (15½-ounce) can red kidney beans, rinsed and drained
1   (15½-ounce) can black beans, rinsed and drained
1   (15½-ounce) can pinto beans, rinsed and drained
2   cups water
1½   cups Clamato juice or other spicy tomato juice
1   (14½-ounce) can Mexican-style stewed tomatoes
1   (10-ounce) package frozen corn, thawed
1   (4-ounce) can chopped mild green chilies
1   cup sliced carrots
1   yellow onion, chopped
3   cloves garlic, minced
2   tablespoons vegetable bouillon granules
2   teaspoons dried basil
1½   teaspoons dried oregano
1   teaspoon pepper

Cornmeal dumplings:
⅓   cup all-purpose flour
¼   cup yellow cornmeal
1   teaspoon baking powder
¼   teaspoon salt
¼   teaspoon pepper
1   egg white, beaten
2   tablespoons milk
1   tablespoon vegetable oil

For the soup: Put all soup ingredients in a large crockpot. Cover and cook on low for 7½ hours.

For the dumplings: In a medium bowl, combine flour, cornmeal, baking powder, salt and pepper. In a small bowl, combine beaten egg white, milk and vegetable oil; add to cornmeal mixture and mix well.

When soup has cooked for 7½ hours, drop dumpling mixture by teaspoonful (in 8 equal portions) into crockpot. Cover and cook for 30 minutes – no peeking!

THAI COCONUT CRAB SOUP

For more than 10 years, Chef Joey Altman has been at the forefront of the San Francisco culinary scene as a host for his award-winning cooking show, Bay Café, *and at restaurants here and abroad. Altman's won first prize at the 2003 Crab & Wine Marketplace's Challenge of the Masters cooking competition.*

Makes 4 Servings

3	tablespoons extra-virgin olive oil, divided
¼	cup chopped shallots
2	teaspoons minced ginger
2	teaspoons minced garlic
2	(14-ounce) cans coconut milk
2	cups chicken stock or broth
4	green onions, minced
12	ounces Dungeness crabmeat, cooked
Salt and pepper, to taste	
½	cup fresh lime juice
2	tablespoons Asian fish sauce
2	tablespoons sambal oelek*
4	fresh cilantro sprigs, for garnish

In a heavy, 4-quart saucepan over medium heat, combine 2 tablespoons of olive oil, shallots, ginger and garlic; cook, stirring frequently, for 2 minutes, or until shallots are tender. Add coconut milk and chicken stock. Lower heat and simmer for 10 minutes.

Heat remaining 1 tablespoon of oil in a small skillet over high heat. Add green onions and cook for 1 minute; transfer to a small bowl. Add crabmeat; stir to combine. Season with salt and pepper; set aside.

Stir lime juice, fish sauce and sambal oelek into soup. Season with salt and pepper. Divide soup among bowls. Top each bowl with ¼ of crabmeat mixture. Garnish with cilantro sprigs and serve immediately.

*Note: Sambal oelek is a blend of chiles, brown sugar and salt used in Malaysian, Indonesian and Indian cooking. It is available at Asian markets and in the Asian section of larger groceries.

CHICKEN, CORN & TORTILLA SOUP

At the 2003 America's Junior Miss National Finals, sponsor Tyson Foods, Inc. awarded seven scholarships for the best recipes in a range of categories. Georgia's Junior Miss 2003, Jillian Martin, went home with a $2,500 scholarship to use at the college of her choice for this healthy, Southwestern chicken soup.

Makes 4 Servings

2   tablespoons vegetable oil
1   cup chopped onion
4   cloves garlic, minced
1   tablespoon cumin
1½   cups corn
3   medium tomatoes, chopped
3½   cups chicken broth
1½   cups shredded cooked chicken
Salt and pepper, to taste
2   cups crushed tortilla chips,
     plus extra, for garnish
1   cup grated Monterey Jack
     cheese
Cilantro leaves, for garnish
Lime wedges, for serving

Heat oil in a large pot over medium heat. Add onion, garlic and cumin; cook, stirring constantly, for 5 minutes. Stir in corn, tomatoes, chicken broth, shredded chicken, salt and pepper. Bring to a boil, lower heat, cover and simmer for 10 minutes.

Divide crushed tortilla chips among serving bowls. Ladle soup over chips. Sprinkle with cheese, reserved tortilla chips and cilantro leaves. Serve with lime wedges.

SMOKED PORTOBELLO "CAPPUCCINO"

Sandy Ciarrocchi of Landenberg, Pennsylvania, won "best mushroom soup" and a trip to see Emeril Live *in New York City at the 17th annual Kennett Square Mushroom Festival's Fresh Mushroom Soup Cook-off in Historic Kennett Square, Pennsylvania. Ciarrocchi's elegant, rich soup is served in cappuccino cups, thus the name.*

Makes 4 Servings

1	tablespoon olive oil
1	clove garlic, minced
¼	cup chopped onion
¼	cup chopped carrot
¼	cup chopped celery
6	ounces smoked portobello mushrooms, chopped*
¼	pound white mushrooms, sliced
¼	cup dry sherry
1½	cups chicken stock or broth
1½	cups heavy cream
3	sprigs fresh thyme
Salt & pepper, to taste	

Heat olive oil in a large saucepan over medium heat. Add garlic, onion, carrot and celery; cook until soft. Add portobello and white mushrooms; cook until soft. Deglaze pan with sherry, stirring to scrape browned bits free. Lower heat and simmer for 10 minutes. Add chicken stock, cream and thyme. Purée soup in a blender or food processor. Return soup to pan and bring to a boil. Lower heat and simmer until reduced to desired consistency. Season with salt and pepper. Serve in cappuccino cups for an elegant flair.

*Note: Smoked portobello mushrooms are available at specialty food stores. If unavailable, you can also smoke your own or, use portobello mushrooms and add Liquid Smoke to taste.

GEARJAMMER'S CHILI VERDE

International Chili Society 2003 Chili Verde World Champion Robert Dyer of Canyon Lake, California, knows a thing or two about competition cooking, having taken second three times in the red chili championship. Dyer competed up and down the West Coast to qualify in all three categories at the 2003 World Championship.

Makes 8 to 10 Servings

2   pounds pork (loin preferred)
½   pound hot green New Mexico chiles, roasted, peeled, seeded and chopped, divided
¼   green bell pepper, finely chopped
6   medium green onions (white part only), finely chopped
5   medium tomatillos, husked and chopped*
7   large serrano chiles, seeded and finely minced
¼   cup minced garlic
12 ounces favorite green chile sauce
1   (14-ounce) can chicken broth
2   teaspoons salt, divided
¾   pound mild green chiles, roasted, peeled, seeded and chopped
White beans, for serving
Warm flour tortillas, for serving

In a large pot, brown pork, 1 pound at a time; drain any grease. Add half of hot green chiles, bell pepper, green onion, tomatillos, serrano chiles, garlic, green chile sauce, chicken broth and 1 teaspoon of salt. Bring to a boil, lower heat and simmer for 1½ hours.

Lower heat to low, add mild green chiles and remaining hot green chiles. Taste and add remaining 1 teaspoon of salt, if needed. Simmer for 30 minutes. Serve with white beans and warm flour tortillas.

*Note: Tomatillos are small, tart Mexican green tomatoes with a papery husk that is easily removed. They can be found in most larger groceries.

BRONCO BOB'S CHILI

For 30 years, wilderness guide Bob Wetzel of Manhattan, Montana, has led hunters, fishermen and horseback riders through the wilds of Montana and Wyoming. In 2003, he blazed a trail to the top of the world of competition chili. Wetzel won the $25,000 "red chili" category at the International Chili Society World's Championship.

Makes 6 to 8 Servings

1	cup chopped onion
1	canned Hatch green chile, chopped
1	tablespoon minced garlic
½	cup El Pato tomato sauce*
1	tablespoon tomato paste
8	tablespoons California chile powder, divided**
1-2	(14-ounce) cans chicken broth, divided
2	teaspoons salt, plus more to taste
1½	teaspoons Accent, divided (optional)***
1	teaspoon Tabasco sauce
2½	pounds tri-tip beef, cubed
¼	pound pork sausage
2	tablespoons mild New Mexico chile powder**
3	tablespoons cumin, divided
1	tablespoon hot New Mexico chile powder**
2	teaspoons lime juice

In a large pot, combine onion, green chile, garlic, tomato sauce, tomato paste, 6 tablespoons of California chile powder, 1 can of chicken broth, salt, 1 teaspoon of Accent and Tabasco sauce. Bring to a boil, lower heat and simmer for 1 hour.

Stir remaining 2 tablespoons of California chile powder into pot. In a skillet, brown beef and sausage; add to pot. Simmer for 30 minutes, adding more broth as needed. Add New Mexico chile powder and 2 tablespoons of cumin; simmer for 45 minutes longer.

Add remaining ½ teaspoon of Accent, hot chile powder, remaining 1 tablespoon of cumin and lime juice. Simmer for 30 minutes, adding more broth as needed. Add more salt to taste, if needed.

*Note: El Pato tomato sauce is a Mexican tomato sauce. It is available in the Mexican food section of most larger groceries.

**Note: Winner Bob Wetzel orders his spices from Sespe Creek Chili Potters (805-524-2078), run by former ICS champion Jim Beaty. Spices from Penzeys, Gebhardt or other favorite manufacturers can also be used.

***Note: Accent is a flavor enhancer also known as Monosodium Glutamate (MSG).

LITTLE ROCK BEEF CHILI

Al Jansen of Engine 21/Med 6, in Milwaukee, Wisconsin, won first prize at the 2003 World Beef Expo Firehouse Beef Chili Cook-off. Plan ahead – the chili should be refrigerated overnight for the best result.

Makes 6 to 8 Servings

1   pound ground beef
½   stick butter
1   pound sirloin steak, cubed
1   small onion, chopped
½   red bell pepper, chopped
½   green bell pepper, chopped
1   (10-ounce) can Frank's spiced
     tomatoes, diced, or other diced
     spiced tomatoes
1   (14-ounce) can hot chili beans
     (or kidney beans)
1   (23-ounce) bottle spicy V-8
     juice or spicy Bloody Mary mix
1½   teaspoons cumin
1½   tablespoons chili powder
1½   teaspoons salt
1   tablespoon pepper
Liquid Smoke, to taste
Hot sauce, to taste
1   cup chopped celery (optional)

In a skillet over medium heat, cook ground beef until no pink remains; drain grease and transfer beef to a large pot or Dutch oven. Melt butter in a skillet over medium heat. Add sirloin cubes and onion; cook until meat is browned on all sides and onion is soft; add to pot.

Add peppers to skillet and cook just until soft (add more butter, if needed); add to pot. Add tomatoes (undrained), beans, V-8 juice, cumin, chili powder, salt, pepper, Liquid Smoke and hot sauce to pot; stir to combine.

Bring chili to a boil, lower heat and simmer for 2 hours. Cool, then cover and refrigerate overnight. The next day, reheat and serve (if desired, skim grease off chili before reheating). If desired, add chopped celery during the last 20 minutes of reheating for some crunch.

TREE HUGGIN' HIPPIE CHILI

Alexander Tanalski of Petaluma, California, submitted this winning recipe for the Great Petaluma Chili Cook-off, Salsa & Beer Tasting. The cook-off benefits the children of Sonoma and Marin Counties. The event, which promotes child participation in the performing arts, has raised $100,000 since 1997.

Makes 8 Servings

1	tablespoon olive oil
3	pounds top sirloin, cut into ¼-inch squares (or use chili grind beef)
2-3	(14½-ounce) cans beef broth, divided
1	cup tomato sauce
1	white onion, finely chopped
1	tablespoon garlic powder
1	tablespoon onion powder
1	teaspoon salt, plus more, to taste
2	tablespoons cumin
7	tablespoons dried red chile powder, divided
4	tablespoons California light chile powder, divided
4	tablespoons New Mexico chile powder, divided
3	(6-ounce) cans diced mild green chiles
2	pounds pinto beans, cooked
½	teaspoon dried oregano
½	teaspoon cayenne pepper
	Sliced fresh or pickled jalapeño peppers, for serving

Heat oil in a large pot over medium heat. Add beef and cook until just done; drain fat. Add 1 can of broth, tomato sauce and onions. Stir, then add 1 more can of broth, garlic powder, onion powder, salt and cumin. Stir, then add 4 tablespoons dried chile powder, 2 tablespoons California chile powder and 2 tablespoons New Mexico chile powder. Mix well, bring to a boil, lower heat and simmer for 90 minutes, adding up to 1 more can of beef broth, if needed to reach desired consistency.

Stir in diced green chiles, beans, oregano, cayenne, 3 tablespoons dried red chile powder, 2 tablespoons California chile powder and 2 tablespoons New Mexico chile powder. Cook for 45-60 minutes longer. Add salt, if needed. To increase spiciness, add sliced or minced seeded fresh or pickled jalapeños, to taste. Serve with sliced pickled or fresh jalapeños.

WHITE CHICKEN CHILI WITH CHEDDAR HUSHPUPPY CRUST

Gaynell Lawson of Maryville, Tennessee, won first prize, $4,000 and a $2,500 Five Star stainless-steel gas range at the 2003 National Cornbread Festival's National Cornbread Cook-off. The hushpuppy crust adds a distinctly Southern flair to this savory dish.

Makes 6 to 8 Servings

White chicken chili:
1   tablespoon olive oil
1   cup finely chopped onion
2   cloves garlic, minced
1   green bell pepper, chopped
½   teaspoon cumin
1   tablespoon chili powder
2   tablespoons lime juice
1   (16-ounce) can cannellini beans (white kidney beans), drained
4   chicken breast halves, cooked and cut into bite-size pieces
2   (14-ounce) cans chicken broth
1   (4-ounce) can chopped mild green chiles, drained
Sour cream, for serving
Chopped fresh cilantro, for serving
Salsa, for serving

Cheddar hushpuppy crust:
1   (6-ounce) package Martha White Cotton Pickin' Cornbread Mix
¼   cup finely chopped onion
½   cup milk
1   egg
3   tablespoons butter, melted
1   cup grated cheddar cheese

For the chili: Heat oil in an 11-inch cast-iron skillet over medium heat. Add onion, garlic, green bell pepper, cumin and chili powder; cook until vegetables are tender. Add lime juice, beans, chicken, broth and chiles; simmer for about 10 minutes.

For the crust: Preheat oven to 425°F. Combine cornbread mix, onion, milk, egg, butter and cheese; pour over chili. Put skillet in oven and bake for 20-25 minutes, until cornbread crust is golden brown. Serve with sour cream, cilantro and salsa.

GULF-STYLE CAJUN GUMBO

The Medina Lake Cajun Festival in Lake Hill, Texas, began in 1981 as the Great Gumbo Cook-off, and gumbo remains the big draw today. Visitors can sample a wide variety of gumbos by amateur and professional chefs from Texas and Louisiana. Dainna Jurica and Debra Murphy of Canyon Lake, Texas, won first prize in 2003.

Makes 10 to 12 Servings

½   cup all-purpose flour
½   cup vegetable oil
¾   cup chopped onion
½   cup chopped green bell pepper
½   cup chopped celery
¾   cup chicken broth
½   ham hock
½   pound Andouille sausage, cubed
½   cup tomato sauce
½   (14-ounce) can diced tomatoes
1   tablespoon minced parsley
1   tablespoon Worcestershire sauce
1½   teaspoons Pickapeppa sauce
     (optional)
1   tablespoon minced fresh
     oregano (or 1 teaspoon dried)
1   bay leaf
1   tablespoon paprika
½   teaspoon garlic powder
Hot pepper sauce, to taste
1½   teaspoons salt
1   teaspoon pepper
½   (10-ounce) package frozen okra
½   pound peeled shrimp
3   ounces fresh crabmeat
½   pound small scallops
½   pound white fish, cubed
½   pint oysters
½   pound crawfish tails, peeled
¾-1 teaspoon filé powder*
Hot cooked rice, for serving

In a large pot (cast iron is best) over medium heat, mix flour and oil. Cook, stirring occasionally, for 20-30 minutes until mixture is dark brown (watch that mixture does not burn). Add onion, bell pepper and celery; cook, stirring constantly, until soft. Stir in broth. Stir in ham hock, sausage, tomato sauce, tomatoes (undrained), parsley, Worcestershire, Pickapeppa, oregano, bay leaf, paprika, garlic powder, hot pepper sauce, salt and pepper. Bring to boil, lower heat and simmer for 2 hours.

Remove ham hock, cool, then cut meat from bone and add meat to gumbo. Skim fat off gumbo. Add okra, shrimp, crab, scallops, fish, oysters and crawfish. Add water to cover (if there is not enough liquid in pot). Bring to boil, lower heat and simmer for 10-20 minutes, until seafood is cooked and tender. Remove gumbo from heat. Stir in filé powder and let stand for 5-10 minutes. Serve over hot cooked rice.

*Note: Filé powder is a seasoning from Louisiana used commonly in Creole cooking, especially gumbos. It is available in the spice section of larger groceries.

Seafood & Sausage Gumbo

John Noel won the title of "King Creole Gumbo VII" at the Gumbo Festival in Bridge City, Louisiana, the "Gumbo Capital of the World." Because Cajun folk traditions are rooted in an appreciation for food and competition, Cajun cooks challenge all comers in this annual gumbo cooking contest.

Makes 6 Servings

1	cup vegetable oil
2	cups all-purpose flour
1	cup chopped onion
½	cup chopped celery
½	cup chopped parsley
½	cup chopped green bell pepper
2	pounds raw shrimp, peeled
½	pint oysters
½	pound crabmeat
¾	pound bulk or sliced link smoked sausage
2	cups oyster water (or water)

Salt, pepper, Tabasco and cayenne pepper, to taste
Filé powder, to taste (optional)*
Hot cooked rice, for serving

Make a roux by heating oil in a large pot over medium heat. Whisk in flour and cook, stirring constantly at first, then frequently, until mixture is a medium brown color, about 30 minutes. Measure 1 cup of roux; discard the rest.

Add 2 quarts of water to roux; stir until roux is dissolved. Bring to a boil, lower heat and simmer for 30 minutes. Add onion, celery, parsley and bell pepper; simmer for 30 minutes. Add shrimp, oysters, crab, sausage and oyster water. Season generously with salt, pepper, Tabasco and cayenne. Simmer gently for 20 minutes, remove from heat and let stand for about 5 minutes. Skim excess fat. Stir in filé powder, if desired. Serve over hot rice.

*Note: Filé powder is a seasoning from Louisiana used commonly in Creole cooking, especially gumbos. It is available in the spice section of larger groceries.

SEAFOOD GUMBO

Carolyn Kass Falgout and Andy Galiano entered the 30th Bridge City Gumbo Festival as a mother-daughter team, the "Gumbo Girls," in memory of Lucy Kass, who taught them both how to cook. Lucy was Carolyn's mother and Andy's grandmother. Bridge City, Louisiana is "The Gumbo Capital of the World."

Makes 8 to 10 Servings

⅓	cup vegetable oil
½	cup all-purpose flour
1½	large onions, chopped
2	cups oyster water (or water)
2	tomatoes, chopped
1	small clove garlic, minced
½	teaspoon Worcestershire sauce
½	green bell pepper, chopped
1	stalk celery, chopped
2	small bay leaves
½	teaspoon liquid crab boil
½	teaspoon Tabasco sauce
1½	pounds Louisiana shrimp, peeled and deveined
1	gallon "Captain Pete" Louisiana oysters, or other fresh oysters
1½	pounds lump crabmeat

Salt and pepper, to taste
1   tablespoon filé powder, optional*
Hot cooked rice, for serving

Heat oil in a large pot over medium heat. Add flour and cook, stirring, until mixture turns golden brown. Add onions and cook until soft.

Add oyster water and tomatoes; bring to a boil. Add garlic, Worcestershire, bell pepper, celery, bay leaves, crab boil and Tabasco. Lower heat and simmer for 20 minutes.

Add shrimp, oysters and crabmeat; simmer for 15 minutes more. Season with salt and pepper. Remove from heat and stir in filé powder, if desired. Serve over hot rice.

*Note: Filé powder is a seasoning from Louisiana used commonly in Creole cooking, especially gumbos. It is available in the spice section of larger groceries.

Texas-Style Chile Cheese Crab Chowder

Linda Morten of Katy, Texas, won Phillips Seafood's fifth annual crabmeat recipe contest with this Lone Star State take on a Yankee chowder. Seafood is one of Morten's favorite things to cook – she uses crabmeat in a wide variety of dishes.

Makes 6 Servings

½	stick butter or margarine
½	cup finely sliced green onion
⅓	cup all-purpose flour
2½	cups chicken broth
4	cups grated Monterey Jack cheese
1	(4-ounce) can chopped mild green chilies
½	teaspoon cumin
½	teaspoon dried oregano
½	teaspoon cayenne pepper
1	cup half & half
1	pound Phillips crabmeat (lump or claw recommended)
6	tortilla (taco) salad bowls
2	tablespoons seeded and chopped tomato
1	tablespoon chopped cilantro
6	tortilla chips

Melt butter in a large saucepan or Dutch oven over medium heat. Add onion; cook for 2-3 minutes. Add flour and cook, stirring constantly, for about 2 minutes. Gradually add broth and cook, stirring constantly, for 4 minutes, or until thickened.

Stir in cheese, chilies, cumin, oregano and cayenne. Lower heat to medium-low and simmer, stirring often, for 10 minutes. Stir in half & half and crabmeat (reserve ¼ cup of crabmeat). Simmer, stirring often, for 6-8 minutes, or until heated through.

Ladle chowder into tortilla salad bowls. Mix tomatoes, reserved ¼ cup of crabmeat and cilantro. Spoon some crabmeat mixture onto each tortilla chip and float in center of chowder. Serve immediately.

THREE FISH TRAWLER CHOWDER

Frances Benthin of Scio, Oregon, won second prize at the Agri-Business Council of Oregon's 2003 chowder cook-off. The council consists of more than 750 agricultural businesses, including growers, manufacturers, suppliers, government entities and retailers, among others.

Makes 6 to 8 Servings

1	pound fresh cod
1	pound fresh snapper
1	bouquet garni*
10	tablespoons butter, divided
1	cup chopped onion
3	cups diced peeled potatoes
½	cup chopped celery
5	tablespoons all-purpose flour
1	cup heavy cream
1½	cups milk
1	pound shrimp, cooked
½	cup dry white wine
1	cup clam juice
1	tablespoon dried dill
2	tablespoons Worcestershire sauce

Salt and cayenne pepper, to taste
Paprika, for garnish
Fresh parsley, for garnish

Put cod and snapper in a large pot. Cover with cold water (5-6 cups), add bouquet garni and bring to a boil over high heat. Lower heat and simmer, covered, for 15 minutes. Strain fish broth into a 2-3 quart saucepan and reserve. Remove any bones from fish and set fish aside; discard fish bones and bouquet garni.

Melt 5 tablespoons of butter in a 4-5 quart Dutch oven over low heat. Add onion; cook for 5 minutes. Add potatoes and celery; cook for 10 minutes more, stirring occasionally. Add remaining 5 tablespoons of butter and flour; stir to combine well. Add cream and milk. Cook, stirring, until thickened. Stir in reserved fish broth. Cover and simmer until potatoes are tender.

Break cod and snapper into bite-sized pieces; stir into chowder. Add shrimp, wine, clam juice, dill weed and Worcestershire sauce. Season with salt and cayenne. Ladle chowder into bowls. Sprinkle with paprika and garnish with a small sprig of parsley.

*Note: To make a bouquet garni, wrap 4 parsley sprigs, 2 bay leaves, 2 fresh rosemary sprigs, 2 cloves of garlic, 1 teaspoon of salt and 6 peppercorns in a cheesecloth and tie closed.

PIGEON COVE LOBSTER COMPANY CLAM CHOWDER

Essex, Massachusetts is famous for its clams, and the Essex Division of the Cape Ann Chamber of Commerce pays homage to the bicuspid at the annual Clamfest. In 2003, 14 restaurants offered their clam chowders to over 1,000 patrons. The winner of the 21st edition was the Pigeon Cove Lobster Company of Rockport, the first time a non-Essex restaurant won!

Makes 6 to 8 Servings

2	slices bacon
1½	sticks butter
¾	cup all-purpose flour
½	cup chopped onion
¼	bunch celery, chopped
2	tablespoons chopped garlic
1	bay leaf
1	tablespoon minced thyme
3	cups chopped clams with juice
1½	cups clam juice
2	cups cream
Salt, pepper, Worcestershire sauce and cayenne pepper, to taste	
2	cups chopped potatoes

Freeze bacon slightly, then chop finely. Cook bacon in a large pot over low heat so fat melts but bacon does not get crispy, about 20 minutes. Add butter. When butter sizzles, remove from heat and stir in flour. Return to heat and add onions, celery, garlic, bay leaf and thyme; cook over low heat until onion is soft (the slow cooking infuses all the flavor into the butter).

Add clams and clam juice. Raise heat to medium and bring to a simmer, stirring constantly. Lower heat and simmer gently for 1½-2 hours, stirring frequently (do not scrape bottom of pan too hard). In a separate pot of highly salted boiling water, cook potatoes until tender; drain. In a saucepan, simmer cream for a few minutes.

Remove chowder from heat and let stand for 10 minutes, then stir in cream, salt, pepper, Worcestershire and cayenne. Add potatoes, mix well and serve.

Tip: This chowder is best made a day ahead, covered and refrigerated to allow the flavors to blend. Reheat and serve the next day.

SMOKED CORN & CRAB CHOWDER WITH MOUNT GAY RUM

The 23rd annual Schweppes Great Chowder Cook-off featured over 3,000 gallons of chowder served up by 30 of the nation's best restaurants and chefs who competed for over $6,500 in prizes. Mark Bolton of the Smokehouse Cafe at The Mooring Restaurant in Newport, Rhode Island, won second prize in 2003.

Makes 4 to 6 Servings

6	Jonah crabs
1	cup (¼-inch) diced potatoes
½	stick butter
½	cup finely diced onion
¼	cup finely diced celery
2	tablespoons finely diced red bell pepper
2	tablespoons finely diced green bell pepper
½	cup all-purpose flour
4	cups half & half
1	cup hickory smoked corn (from 2-3 ears of corn)*
1	tablespoon sherry pepper sauce (Outerbridges Sherry Pepper Sauce recommended)
1	tablespoon Mount Gay rum

Paprika, for garnish

Bring 2 quarts of water to a boil in a large pot. Add crabs and cook until tender and cooked through; remove crabs and set aside to cool (reserve liquid in pot).

Over high heat, make a crab stock by reducing crab cooking liquid to 2 cups of liquid; transfer to a bowl. When crabs are cool enough, pick shells from crabmeat (should yield about ½ pound of meat); set aside.

Put potatoes in a large saucepan with enough cold water to cover. Bring to a boil and cook potatoes until al dente. Drain and transfer potatoes to a bowl of ice water to stop the cooking. Drain again and set aside.

In a large pot, melt butter over medium-low heat. Add onion, celery and red and green bell pepper; cook until tender. Add flour and cook, stirring, for 2-3 minutes. Add crab stock, potatoes, half & half, smoked corn, sherry pepper sauce, rum and crabmeat; cook until heated through. Sprinkle with paprika to serve.

*Note: If you do not have a smoker, grill the corn to give it a smoky flavor or, use steamed fresh corn or canned corn and add Liquid Smoke to taste.

PATRICK HOGAN'S CLAM CHOWDER

Chef Patrick Hogan of O'Neill's Irish Pub & Restaurant in Norwalk, Connecticut, won the ninth annual Norwalk Harbor Splash! Clam Chowder Cook-off. Chef Hogan also won the event in 2002 and tied for first prize in 2000 and 2001.

Makes 6 Servings

1½ tablespoons extra-virgin olive oil
1   medium onion, diced
4-5 stalks celery, diced
5   green onions, chopped
3   cups chopped clams (8-10 ounces of clams)
¼   cup all-purpose flour
2-4 tablespoons Harvey's Bristol Cream sherry, to taste
2-4 tablespoons Bailey's Irish Cream, to taste
1½ cups clam juice
4   cups milk
2   medium potatoes, diced
1½ cups heavy cream
Salt and pepper, to taste

Heat oil in a large pot over medium heat. Add onion, celery, green onions and clams; cook until onion is beginning to brown. Stir in flour. Stir in sherry, Irish Cream and clam juice; bring to a boil, lower heat and simmer for 3-5 minutes.

Add milk and potatoes; simmer for about 20 minutes, until potatoes are cooked but still firm. Add cream and return to a simmer. Season with salt and pepper. Stir to combine and serve.

CHOWDER OF SCALLOPS, CELERIAC & POTATO WITH CARAMELIZED PEAR & ROASTED CHESTNUTS

Chef Casey Riley of the Castle Hill Inn & Resort in Newport, Rhode Island, won third prize at the 23rd annual Schweppes Great Chowder Cook-off.

Makes 6 to 8 Servings

4-6 tablespoons butter, divided
2 medium Spanish onions, sliced
2-3 cloves garlic, minced
1 (750-ml.) bottle Sakonnet Fumé Vidal wine (or fumé blanc)
7 celery roots, peeled and divided
7 medium Yukon gold potatoes, peeled and divided
Chicken broth or water
1¼ cups heavy cream
Salt and white pepper, to taste
Lemon juice, to taste
2-3 tablespoons vegetable oil
2 pounds medium dry-packed sea scallops
3-4 Bartlett pears, peeled and diced
2 pounds chestnuts, roasted and coarsely crushed or chopped
Pinch of nutmeg
1 pound feta or blue cheese, crumbled
Crusty bread or toast, for serving

In a large pot, melt 2-3 tablespoons butter over medium heat. Add onions and garlic; cook until softened, but not browned. Add wine; cook until liquid is reduced by half. Quartered 6 celery roots and 5 potatoes; add to pot and cover with broth or water by 1-inch. Bring to a boil, lower heat and simmer until potatoes are very tender. Using an immersion (hand) blender (or in a blender or food processor), purée vegetables until very smooth. Add cream and return to a simmer, stirring constantly (be careful, soup can burn easily). Season with salt, white pepper and lemon juice.

Dice remaining 1 celery root and 2 potatoes; place in a large saucepan and cover with cold water. Season with salt. Bring to a boil, lower heat and simmer until just tender. Drain and set aside.

Heat oil in a large skillet over high heat. Add scallops; sear until golden brown on both sides. Remove scallops with a slotted spoon; set aside. Ladle some soup into skillet, deglaze pan, stirring to scrape browned bits free; transfer scrapings into soup. Add scallops to soup and keep warm over low heat.

In a skillet, melt remaining 2-3 tablespoons of butter over medium heat. Add pears and chestnuts; cook until pears are just beginning to brown. Season with nutmeg.

Divide chopped potato and celery root among soup bowls. Ladle soup into bowls and sprinkle with pears, chestnuts and cheese. Serve with crusty bread or toast.

SALADS & SANDWICHES

FENNEL APPLE SALAD WITH MUSTARD SEED VINAIGRETTE

Executive Chef Peter Halikas of Dean & Deluca in St. Helena, California, won the "Executive Chef of the Year" title for this dish at the seventh annual Napa Mustard Festival World-Wide Mustard Competition in Napa Valley, California.

Makes 4 Servings

Fennel apple salad:

2	tablespoons butter, divided
1½	cups chopped onion, divided
4	cups chopped fennel bulb, divided
3	cups water, divided
2	cups blanched fennel fronds
Salt and pepper, to taste	
1	cup chopped apple
1	cup julienned fennel
1	cup julienned apple
1	tablespoon chopped fennel fronds (the lacy top part)

Mustard seed vinaigrette:

2	teaspoons Dijon mustard
1	tablespoon rice vinegar
¼	cup olive oil
2	teaspoons water
1	tablespoon mustard seed
Salt and pepper, to taste	

For the salad: In a skillet over medium heat, melt 1 tablespoon of butter. Add ½ cup of chopped onion; cook until translucent. Add 1 cup of chopped fennel; cook until tender. Add ¾ cup of water; cook until most of water is absorbed. Remove and cool. When cool, put mixture in blender with blanched fennel fronds and ¼ cup of water; purée. Season with salt and pepper.

Melt remaining 1 tablespoon of butter in a skillet over medium heat. Add remaining 1 cup of chopped onion; cook until translucent. Add apple and remaining 3 cups of chopped fennel; cook until fennel is tender. Add remaining 2 cups of water; cook until most of water is absorbed. Remove and purée in a blender. Season with salt and pepper.

For the vinaigrette: Whisk together all ingredients.

To serve: Put some fennel purée (first purée) in center of each plate. Surround fennel purée with 3 mounds of apple purée (second purée). Toss julienned fennel and apple with half of vinaigrette; season with salt and pepper. Put a mound of julienned fennel on each plate. Drizzle some of remaining vinaigrette around each plate. Garnish with chopped fennel fronds.

Apple & Arugula Salad with Almond Brittle

Rebecca Ludwig, chef and owner of Place in Ketchum, Idaho, won the $2,500 first prize in the "regional American recipe" category at the 2003 Almond Board of California's Almond Inspirations Recipe Contest. Ludwig's almond brittle is delicious in the salad and on its own as a sweet snack.

Makes 6 Servings

Almond brittle:
¾   cup sliced almonds
¼   cup corn syrup
2½ teaspoons honey, warmed
     slightly (aids mixing)
1⅓ tablespoons butter, melted
2½ teaspoons all-purpose flour
¾   teaspoon salt
⅛   teaspoon pepper

Apple cider vinaigrette:
2   tablespoons white wine vinegar
1   tablespoon apple cider vinegar
¾   teaspoon minced shallot
2   tablespoons apple cider
½   cup olive oil
Salt and pepper

Apple and arugula salad:
12   ounces arugula
1½ pounds apples, julienned
1½ cups crumbled goat cheese

For the almond brittle: Preheat oven to 300°F. Combine all almond brittle ingredients. Spread mixture onto a parchment paper-lined baking sheet; press to form a ¼-inch thick layer. Bake for 30-40 minutes. Cool on a wire rack, then break into 2-inch pieces. Store in an airtight container at room temperature.

For the vinaigrette: Combine white wine and apple cider vinegar and shallots; let stand for 30 minutes. In a small, non-reactive saucepan, simmer apple cider until reduced to 1 tablespoon. Whisk cider and olive oil into vinegar mixture until combined. Season with salt and pepper.

For the salad: For each salad, toss 2 cups of arugula and 1 cup of julienned apples with 1 tablespoon of vinaigrette, or more to taste. Mound salad on a plate and sprinkle with ¼ cup of goat cheese. Garnish with almond brittle.

SAVORY CHICKEN SALAD

Lynn Vezina of Cortlandt Manor, New York, tied for first prize in the Delicious Living *recipe contest. Each bite of this perfect-for-summer salad bursts with a different fresh, crisp flavor. Serve it with a slightly dry, fruity white wine and a sourdough baguette.*

Makes 4 Servings

1	cup uncooked soft red wheat berries
1	cup finely diced celery
½	cup finely diced parsley
2	green onions, finely diced
½	cup dried cranberries
3	cups (¾-inch) cubes cooked chicken breast meat
½	cup finely chopped pecans, toasted and divided
¼	cup cranberry sauce
½	cup Hain Pure Mayonnaise
½	cup low-fat sour cream

Herb salt and pepper, to taste

¼	cup Spectrum Naturals Organic Canola Oil
2	tablespoons Spectrum Naturals Organic Golden Balsamic Vinegar
¼	cup crumbled blue cheese
1	head butter or Bibb lettuce, leaves washed and dried

Soak wheat berries overnight in water to cover. Drain, cover with fresh water and bring to a boil. Lower heat, cover and simmer for 1 hour, or until tender. Drain excess liquid; cool wheat berries to room temperature.

In a large bowl, combine celery, parsley, green onions and dried cranberries. Add chicken, wheat berries and ¼ cup of pecans; stir to combine. In a small bowl, combine cranberry sauce, mayonnaise and sour cream; add to chicken mixture and stir lightly until combined. Season with herb salt and pepper.

In a small bowl, whisk together oil and vinegar until smooth. Stir in crumbled blue cheese. Divide lettuce among serving plates. Top with chicken mixture. Drizzle with blue cheese dressing. Sprinkle with remaining ¼ cup of pecans.

NAPOLI CHICKEN PASTA SALAD

More than 26 million chickens are produced in Oregon each year. Amanda Stanko of Lebanon, Oregon, won second prize in the 2003 Oregon Fryer Commission Recipe Contest. Her Mediterranean salad with Oregon grown chicken makes a great, light supper.

Makes 6 to 8 Servings

Chicken pasta salad:

2	tablespoons salt
1	(12-ounce) package gemelli, rotini or penne pasta
3	cups diced cooked Oregon grown chicken (or 4 boneless, skinless chicken breast halves, grilled and sliced)
3	slices prosciutto, diced small
1	cup cherry tomato halves
1	(6-ounce) jar marinated artichoke hearts, drained and halved
1	cup julienned bell pepper (mix of colors)
¾	cup pitted kalamata olives
1	cup diced fresh buffalo mozzarella cheese
½	cup julienned red onion
½	cup julienned fresh basil
¼	cup drained capers

Lemon slices, for garnish
Basil leaves, for garnish

Dressing:

2	tablespoons Dijon mustard
2	tablespoons yogurt
2	tablespoons mayonnaise
1	clove garlic, minced
¼	cup red wine or sherry vinegar
⅔	cup olive oil

Salt and pepper, to taste

For the salad: In a large pot, bring 5 quarts of water to a boil. Add salt and pasta. Cook until al dente, about 8 minutes. Drain pasta and rinse with cold water. Put pasta in a large bowl; add remaining salad ingredients, except lemon slices and basil leaves. Add dressing to salad; toss to combine. Season with salt and pepper. Garnish with lemon slices and basil leaves to serve.

For the dressing: Whisk together all dressing ingredients.

GRILLED RASPBERRY CHICKEN & SPINACH SALAD

America's Junior Miss provides over 63 million dollars in college scholarships each year. The program's goal is to honor young women and encourage them to go to college and assume leadership roles in their communities and professions. Kentucky's Junior Miss 2003, Mary Ellen Fortney, won the "salad" category in 2003.

Makes 6 to 8 Servings

Raspberry chicken:
1 cup red raspberry seedless preserves
⅓ cup red wine vinegar
8 boneless, skinless Tyson chicken breast halves

Spinach salad:
1 (10- to 16-ounce) bag baby spinach
¾-1 pound fresh strawberries, halved or sliced
1 bunch red seedless grapes, halved
1 cup crumbled feta cheese
½ cup sliced almonds, toasted, if desired

Poppy seed dressing:
½ cup sugar
2 tablespoons sesame seeds
1 tablespoon poppy seeds
1½ teaspoons minced onion
¼ teaspoon Worcestershire sauce
¼ teaspoon paprika
¼ cup apple cider vinegar
½ cup vegetable or canola oil

For the chicken: Preheat grill. Whisk together preserves and vinegar. Brush chicken with preserve mixture; grill for 30 minutes, or until done, turning often and basting each time. (Or, bake chicken in a preheated 350°F oven for 30-40 minutes, until done, basting often.)

For the spinach salad: In a large bowl, combine salad ingredients. Just before serving, pour dressing over salad and toss to combine. Slice chicken and serve with or on top of salad.

For the dressing: Combine all dressing ingredients, except oil. Whisk in oil until combined.

SMOKED TROUT SALAD

Cynthia Taines of Madison, Wisconsin, won first prize in the "wild foods" category at the Food For Thought recipe contest in Madison. Taines said of her recipe, "I made this as a summer dinner from ingredients purchased at local Farmers' markets. It's excellent served with a chilled Sauvignon Blanc."

Makes 2 to 4 Servings

Dressing:
1 tablespoon minced fresh dill
1 large clove garlic, minced
1 shallot, minced
1 teaspoon Dijon mustard
½ teaspoon salt
Pinch of black pepper
Finely grated zest of 1 lemon
2 tablespoons fresh lemon juice
3 tablespoons champagne or
   white wine vinegar
1 tablespoon crumbled soft
   sheep or goat's milk cheese
   (such as goat cheese)
¾-1 cup extra-virgin olive oil

Salad:
2 tablespoons kosher salt or
   1 tablespoon table salt
4 medium red potatoes
Salt and pepper, to taste
8-12 cups mixed baby greens,
   rinsed and dried
1 large or 2 small fennel bulbs,
   with tops
1 medium red onion, thinly sliced
1 tablespoon minced flat-leaf
   parsley
1 tablespoon minced fresh dill
2 green onions, thinly sliced
⅓ pound smoked rainbow trout,
   boned and crumbled

For the dressing: In a bowl, whisk together all dressing ingredients, except olive oil. Slowly whisk in 3/4 cup of olive oil. Add more oil, lemon or salt, to taste.

For the salad: In a large pot, bring 3 quarts of water and salt to a boil. Add potatoes; cook over medium-high heat for 10-15 minutes, until tender. Drain and cool for 15 minutes. Cut potatoes into quarters, then slice quarters in half. Put potatoes in a small bowl and toss with 5-7 tablespoons of dressing. Season with salt and pepper.

Put greens in a large bowl. Trim tops off fennel bulbs; mince enough of the leaves to yield 1 tablespoon. Cut bulbs in half, remove core, cut bulb into quarters and thinly slice the quarters. Add sliced fennel and minced fennel leaves to greens. Add red onion, parsley, dill, green onions and crumbled trout. Toss gently with remaining dressing, top with potatoes and serve immediately.

Green Goddess Oyster & Artichoke Salad

Jackie Horridge of Nashville, Tennessee, won the grand prize at the 36th annual National Oyster Cook-off.
The cook-off is part of the St. Mary's County Oyster Festival, one of the Eastern Seaboard's leading
festivals, which celebrates the opening of the oyster season on the Chesapeake Bay.

Makes 4 Servings

Green goddess dressing:

1	clove garlic, minced
½	teaspoon salt
½	teaspoon dry mustard
⅛	teaspoon pepper
1	teaspoon Worcestershire sauce
2	tablespoons anchovy paste
1	cup mayonnaise
½	cup sour cream
2	tablespoons tarragon wine vinegar
3	tablespoons chopped chives
⅓	cup chopped fresh parsley
⅓	cup chopped fresh spinach

Oyster & artichoke salad:

1	cup olive oil, plus more as needed
½	teaspoon pepper
1½	cups panko or dry bread-crumbs*
½	cup grated Parmesan cheese
24	fresh Maryland oysters, shucked
2	egg whites, lightly beaten
4	cups baby field greens
1	cup grated carrot
4	fresh artichokes, steamed

For the dressing: Blend all dressing ingredients in a blender until smooth. If time allows, cover and refrigerate for at least 24 hours to blend flavors.

For the salad: Heat 1 cup of olive oil in a skillet over medium heat. In a bowl, combine pepper, breadcrumbs and Parmesan cheese. Dip oysters into egg whites, then dredge in breadcrumb mixture to coat. Cook oysters in batches until golden brown, adding more oil as needed. Drain oysters on paper towels.

Combine field greens and carrots; divide among salad plates. Remove leaves and chokes from artichokes; discard chokes and save leaves for another use. Put 1 artichoke bottom on top of field greens on each plate. Put 6 oysters on each artichoke bottom. Drizzle about ¼ cup of dressing over oysters. Serve with remaining dressing.

*Note: Panko is a coarse Japanese breadcrumb that gives fried foods a light, crunchy crust. It is available in larger groceries, Asian markets and specialty food stores.

Summer Fruit Salad with Mint Honey Lime Dressing

Randy Teeuwen of Denver, Colorado, won the "medium honey" category in the National Honey Board's Viva Variety Recipe Contest with this delicious mix of melons, tropical fruit and strawberries, tossed with a healthy dressing of mint honey, lime and yogurt.

Makes 8 Servings

Dressing:
- ⅓ cup fresh lime juice
- ⅓ cup mint honey, warmed slightly (aids mixing)
- ½ cup plain low-fat yogurt
- 2 teaspoons grated lime zest

Fruit salad:
- 4 cups cantaloupe balls
- 4 cups honeydew melon balls
- 3 cups seedless red grapes
- 3 cups diced pineapple
- 1 medium papaya, sliced
- 1½ cups fresh strawberries halves
- 1 tablespoon high quality balsamic vinegar
- 8 fresh mint sprigs, for garnish

For the dressing: Whisk together lime juice and honey until smooth. Stir in yogurt and lime zest. Cover and chill until serving.

For the fruit salad: Combine all fruit, except strawberries, in a large glass bowl. Sprinkle strawberries with balsamic vinegar, then lightly mix into fruit in bowl. Cover and chill until serving.

When ready to serve, mix dressing into fruit. Let stand for 15 minutes to blend flavors. Divide salad among salad plates. Garnish with mint sprigs to serve.

The Spicy Rascal

Mike Fabrizio of Rhinebeck, New York, was a finalist at the 2003 Finlandia Cheese Great Sandwich Recipe Contest. Judges came from Deli Business Magazine, Ladies Home Journal, Newsday, *The Carnegie Deli,* Bon Appetit *and* Time.

Makes 1 Serving

1   sesame seed hero roll, sliced
3   ounces rare deli roast beef
2   ounces Finlandia Swiss Cheese, sliced
3   ounces pepper ham
Black olive tapenade, to taste*
Hot sauce, to taste
Grilled onions

Heat a small skillet over medium heat. Spray skillet with non-stick cooking spray. In shape of hero roll, create a stack in the following order: roast beef, then cheese, then ham; put in skillet, roast beef-side-down, and cook for about 2 minutes. Turn stack ham-side-down and cook for 1 minute, until cheese is melted.

Spread tapenade on both sides of roll. Splash hot sauce over tapenade. Put grilled onions on roll. Top with roast beef stack. Close sandwich and cut in half.

*Note: Black olive tapenade is a thick, often slightly chunky purée. Tapenades are often available in the olive section of larger groceries and specialty food stores.

BBQ PORK SMOKEHOUSE CUBAN-STYLE SANDWICH

Each year, five chefs are selected for their culinary excellence to serve as a National Pork Board Celebrated Chef. Steven Jayson, a 2003 Celebrated Chef, is vice president, corporate executive chef for Universal Studios Worldwide. In 2000, Jayson was selected as the American Culinary Federation's National Chef of the Year.

Makes 6 Servings

Mango barbecue sauce:
½ cup puréed mango
2 cups barbecue sauce

BBQ pork sandwich:
1 stick unsalted butter
1 yellow onion, chopped
2 pounds hickory-smoked BBQ pork butt, thinly sliced for sandwiches*
2 (2-foot) loaves Cuban or French bread, halved lengthwise
1 whole kosher pickle (or kosher pickle chips)
1 clove garlic, minced (optional)
12 slices smoked Gouda cheese

For the barbecue sauce: Thoroughly combine mango purée and barbecue sauce.

For the sandwich: Melt butter in a skillet over medium-low heat. Add onion; cook slowly until deep golden brown and sweet, about 20 minutes. Put 1 pound of sliced barbecued pork on bottom half of each loaf of bread. Spread 1 cup of mango barbecue sauce over pork on each loaf. Spread onions over sauce. Slice pickles into chips (round or lengthwise slices), about ⅛-inch thick. Put pickles on top of onions. Sprinkle with garlic, if desired. Put 6 slices of cheese on top of pickles. Place top half of bread loaves on top.

Cut each sandwich into thirds. Put sandwiches on a Cuban or panini sandwich press set at 325°F for about 5 minutes, or until bread is crisp. If you do not have a sandwich press, put sandwiches in a lightly buttered skillet over medium heat. Cover with foil. Weigh down with a heavy skillet. Cook for 3 minutes. Uncover pan, turn sandwiches, re-cover with foil and weigh down again. Heat until very hot and cheese begins to melt, about 3 minutes more.

*Note: Barbecued pork butt is available by the pound at most barbecue restaurants. Or use another favorite sliced barbecued meat – the result will still be delicious!

JIF TROPICAL FANTASY

Twelve-year-old Stephanie Wieseler of Burnsville, Minnesota, won the grand prize in the J. M. Smucker Company's Jif's Most Creative Peanut Butter Sandwich Contest for Kids. The contest encourages kids ages 6 to 12, to use their imagination to create their ultimate peanut butter sandwich.

Makes 1 Serving

2   slices cinnamon bread
2   tablespoons Jif peanut butter
1   banana, sliced
Canned pineapple chunks, drained
Canned mandarin orange sections, drained
Grated peeled ginger (optional)
Pomegranate seeds (optional)

Toast bread. Spread peanut butter on 1 slice of bread. Place banana slices, pineapple chunks and mandarin oranges on other slice of bread. Sprinkle with ginger, if desired. Add pomegranate seeds, if desired (for a tart, crunchy touch). Put bread slices together. Decorate top of sandwich with additional pomegranate seeds, if desired. Decorate plate with mandarin orange sections.

CUBAN REUBEN WITH MOJO MAYO

Susan Asanovic of Wilson, Connecticut, won over the judges at the 2003 Finlandia Cheese Great Sandwich Recipe Contest at New York City's famed Carnegie Deli. Fittingly, the event took place on National Sandwich Day, November 3rd.

Makes 4 to 6 Servings

1   cup mayonnaise
2   tablespoons lime juice
Grated zest of ½ lime
2   tablespoons orange juice
     concentrate, thawed
1   teaspoon cumin
¼   teaspoon pepper
1–2 teaspoons hot pepper sauce,
     to taste
2   (10- or 11-inch) loaves French
     or Italian bread
1¼   cups canned black beans,
     drained
6   slices Finlandia Sandwich
     Naturals Swiss cheese
6   ounces thinly sliced corned
     beef
1⅓   cups sauerkraut, rinsed
6   slices Finlandia Sandwich
     Naturals Muenster cheese

Combine mayonnaise, lime juice, lime zest, orange juice concentrate, cumin, pepper and hot sauce.

Cut each loaf of bread nearly all the way through, leaving a "hinge." Mash black beans with a fork and combine with ¼ cup of mayonnaise mixture. Spread remaining mayonnaise mixture equally on cut sides of breads.

Layer bottom half of each loaf with 3 slices of Swiss cheese, black bean mixture, corned beef, sauerkraut and 3 slices of Muenster cheese. Close breads.

Place loaves top-side-down on a preheated, well-oiled griddle or large skillet (or use a sandwich or panini press). Cover with foil and weigh down with a heavy skillet. Cook for 5-6 minutes. Uncover loaves, turn, re-cover loaves with foil and weigh down again. Heat until very hot and cheese begins to melt. Cut each loaf in halves or thirds to serve.

THE ADULT GRILLED CHEESE SANDWICH

Linda Frieden of Vista, California, won $500 for her crunchy sandwich creation at the 2003 French's Taste Toppers Crunchy Creations Recipe Contest. To win, contestants had to incorporate 1⅓ cups of French's Original French Fried Onions in an original entrée, side dish, sandwich or garnish.

Makes 4 Servings

4 teaspoons mayonnaise
½ teaspoon French's Mustard (any flavor)
Pinch of allspice (or cinnamon)
8 slices onion rye bread
8 slices sharp cheddar cheese (or Swiss, provolone, etc.)
1⅓ cups French's Original French Fried Onions
Olive oil

Combine mayonnaise, mustard and allspice. Preheat griddle. Lightly oil griddle and put 4 slices of bread on griddle. Top each slice of bread with 1 slice of cheese.

Spread 1 teaspoon of mayonnaise mixture on each remaining slice of bread. As cheese just begins to melt, place ⅓ cup of French's Fried Onions on top of each slice of cheese, pressing gently to stick to cheese.

Top with remaining bread slices (with mayonnaise on inside). Brush tops of sandwiches with a little olive oil, carefully turn and continue grilling until bread is toasted and cheese is melted.

Finlandia Fresca Crab Panini

Matthew S. Kozak of Hauppauge, New York, won second prize and $500 in the 2003 Finlandia Cheese Great Sandwich Recipe Contest. One of four finalists chosen from over 4,000 entries, Kozak appeared on NBC's Today Show *for creating this delicious panini.*

Makes 4 Sandwiches

¼	cup plus 1 tablespoon mayonnaise
½	small habanero chile pepper, seeded
1	ripe avocado, divided
½	teaspoon lemon pepper
½	teaspoon Old Bay seasoning
3	tablespoons chopped onion, divided
1½	teaspoons chopped red bell pepper
1½	teaspoons chopped green bell pepper
1½	teaspoons chopped yellow bell pepper
1	pound crabmeat, roughly chopped
8	slices ciabatta bread or crusty country-style bread or roll
Olive oil	
4	leaves red leaf lettuce
16	slices Finlandia Swiss cheese
1	ounce alfalfa sprouts

Put mayonnaise, habanero, ½ avocado, lemon pepper, Old Bay seasoning and 1½ tablespoons of onion in a blender; purée, then transfer to a bowl. Add red, green and yellow bell pepper, crabmeat and remaining 1½ tablespoons of onion; cover and chill for 15-20 minutes.

Spray or brush both sides of panini bread slices with olive oil. Slice remaining ½ avocado very thinly. Layer half of bread slices as follows: 1 leaf of lettuce, 2 slices of Swiss cheese, ½ cup of crab mixture, 2-3 slices of avocado, 2 slices of Swiss cheese, sprouts and a second slice of bread.

Put sandwiches on a preheated, well-oiled griddle or a large skillet (or use a sandwich or panini press). Cover with foil and weigh down with a heavy skillet. Cook for 5-6 minutes. Uncover sandwiches, turn, re-cover with foil and weigh down again. Heat until bread is toasted well and cheese is melted through. Cut in half and serve.

SENSATIONAL SMOKED SALMON B.L.T. SANDWICH

Patsy Rankin of Bethany Beach, Delaware, won the monthly Just Smoked Salmon recipe contest. Hall N' Wright Distributing, the producer of Just Smoked Salmon, was started in 1999 by Jim Hall and Victor Wright with the goal of bringing regional products, such as Olympic Peninsula alder smoked salmon, to worldwide markets.

Makes 1 Serving

B.L.T.:
Favorite bread or roll
1-2 leaves lettuce
Vine ripened tomatoes, sliced
3-4 ounces smoked salmon
3   slices applewood smoked
     bacon, cooked crisp

Horseradish dill aioli:
1   cup mayonnaise
1   tablespoon horseradish sauce
Juice of ½ lemon
1   tablespoon dried dill

Spread some horseradish dill aioli on bread or roll. Place lettuce on roll. Top with tomato slices. Arrange smoked salmon on top of tomatoes. Lay strips of bacon on top of salmon. Drizzle aioli on top of bacon.

For the aioli: Mix all ingredients. Put aioli in a squeeze bottle, if available.

SIDE DISHES

YAM PONE

Jonas Hubbard of Opelousas, Louisiana, won second prize at the Yambilee Festival in Opelousas, Louisiana. One medium yam supplies more than the recommended daily allowance of vitamin A and one-third of the vitamin C. The yam's golden color indicates a high content of beta carotene, an important antioxidant.

Makes 6 to 8 Servings

½   stick butter, softened
¼   cup brown sugar
2   eggs
½   cup evaporated milk
½   cup all-purpose flour
¼   teaspoon nutmeg
¼   teaspoon cinnamon
1½ teaspoons baking powder
½   cup cane syrup*
¼   cup honey, warmed slightly
1   teaspoon vanilla extract
2   cups grated yam

Preheat oven to 350°F. In a large bowl, cream butter and sugar. Beat in eggs and milk. Sift together flour, nutmeg, cinnamon and baking powder into a medium bowl. Add flour mixture to butter mixture; mix well. Add cane syrup, honey, vanilla and grated yam. Mix well and pour into a greased baking dish or casserole. Bake for 1 hour.

*Note: Cane syrup is a thick sweetener. If unavailable, substitute 2 parts dark corn syrup and 1 part molasses.

Tip: This is also delicious with the addition of 1 cup of raisins.

ITALIAN POTATO TORTE

Each year, the Old Farmer's Almanac *holds a recipe contest highlighting one ingredient. In 2003, the potato took center stage and Deborah Coberly Goranflo of La Grange, Kentucky, took first prize with this torte.*

Makes 8 to 10 Servings

3	pounds white potatoes, peeled and chopped
1½	cups milk
½	stick butter
3	tablespoons olive oil
3	cloves garlic, minced
2	teaspoons dried parsley
1	teaspoon dried basil
1	teaspoon salt
½	teaspoon pepper
½	cup grated Asiago cheese

Put potatoes in a large pot with water to cover. Bring to a boil over medium-high heat; lower heat and simmer until tender. Drain potatoes and set aside.

Heat milk and butter in a small saucepan over medium heat until milk begins to steam and butter is melted. Add to potatoes and mash.

Preheat oven to 350°F. In a small skillet over medium heat, warm olive oil just until fragrant. Add garlic; cook until it begins to brown. Add oil and garlic to potatoes. Stir in parsley, basil, salt, pepper and Asiago cheese. Spoon potatoes into a casserole dish lightly greased with olive oil. Bake until lightly browned, about 20 minutes.

EGGPLANT & GORGONZOLA-STUFFED PORTOBELLO MUSHROOMS

Kay Schroeder won third prize in the "appetizer" category at the 2003 Eggplant Fest in Loomis, California. Loomis has been known for its fruit and vegetable production for over 100 years.

Makes 6 Servings

6	(5- to 6-inch) portobello mushrooms, stemmed
¼	cup olive oil
4	Japanese eggplants (unpeeled), finely chopped
6	tablespoons chopped, drained oil-packed sun-dried tomatoes
3	cloves garlic, minced
¼	cup dry red wine
6	ounces Gorgonzola cheese, crumbled
2	tablespoons chopped fresh basil, divided

Salt and pepper, to taste
¼   cup freshly grated Parmesan cheese

Preheat oven to 375°F. Arrange mushrooms, round-side-down, on a baking sheet. Heat oil in a medium skillet over medium heat. Add eggplant, sun-dried tomatoes and garlic; cook until eggplant is soft, about 8 minutes. Stir in red wine; simmer until liquid evaporates. Remove from heat. Stir in Gorgonzola cheese and 1 tablespoon of basil. Season with salt and pepper. Spoon eggplant mixture into mushroom caps. Sprinkle with Parmesan cheese.

Cover mushrooms with foil and bake for 15 minutes. Remove foil and continue baking until cheese is melted and mushrooms are tender, about 10 minutes longer. Sprinkle with remaining basil. Serve warm.

Vidalia Onion & Apple Casserole

Hannah Hanford won "best side dish" in Adirondack Life's *Apple Recipe Contest. Hanford said of her recipe, "My husband's family owns an apple orchard in Peru, New York. We enjoy entertaining, and I try to feature apples in every course. I could probably write a cookbook of apple recipes — it was difficult narrowing down the choices!"*

Makes 6 Servings

1	stick butter
4	medium Vidalia onions, thinly sliced (or other sweet onion)
3	medium McIntosh apples, peeled and sliced ¼-inch thick
15-20	saltine crackers, crushed
1	(10¾-ounce) can cream of mushroom soup, stirred
1½	cups grated Gruyère cheese, divided
½	cup grated Parmesan cheese
2	eggs, beaten
½	cup milk

Melt butter in a large skillet over medium heat. Add onions; cook, stirring frequently, for 10 minutes. Add apples and cook until onions are golden brown and sweet, about 10-15 minutes longer.

Preheat oven to 350°F. Spread cracker crumbs in the bottom of a lightly greased 2-quart casserole dish (reserve 3 tablespoons of cracker crumbs for topping). Layer with half the soup, ½ cup of Gruyère cheese, ¼ cup of Parmesan cheese and half of apple mixture; repeat layers.

Combine eggs and milk; pour over layers in dish. Top with remaining ½ cup of Gruyère and the reserved 3 tablespoons of cracker crumbs. Bake for 20-30 minutes, until bubbly and golden brown.

Note: This side dish is delicious with any pork recipe or grilled steaks or chicken. For a vegetarian entrée, add 2-3 large, sliced portobello mushrooms to the onions with the apples.

CRAB & CORN PUDDING WITH RED PEPPER CREAM SAUCE

Marrita Blatchley of Shrewsberry, Pennsylvania, won the grand prize at the annual National Hard Crab Day Derby & Fair Crab Cooking Contest. Held in Crisfield, Maryland, this three-day event includes a crab-cooking contest, crab-picking contest, country music and the ever-popular crab race.

Makes 4 Servings

Crab and corn pudding:
1½ cups frozen corn
⅓   cup heavy cream
1   large egg
2   large egg yolks
1   pound crabmeat, divided and
    shells picked out
1   tablespoon all-purpose flour
1   teaspoon salt
½   teaspoon sugar
⅛   teaspoon cayenne pepper
1   tablespoon flat-leaf parsley,
    chopped
Dash of Tabasco sauce
2   tablespoons chopped chives
Sliced red bell pepper, for garnish

Red pepper cream sauce:
1   tablespoon vegetable oil
1   red bell pepper, diced
1   tablespoon chopped garlic
¼   teaspoon cayenne pepper
Pinch of red pepper flakes
1   tablespoon dry white wine
1½ cups heavy cream
Salt and pepper, to taste

For the pudding: Preheat oven to 350°F. Purée corn, cream, egg, egg yolks and half of crabmeat in a blender or food processor. Add flour, salt, sugar and cayenne; process for a few seconds to blend. Transfer purée to a bowl. Stir in remaining crabmeat, parsley and Tabasco. Divide mixture among 4 buttered individual ramekins.

Cover ramekins with foil and place in a baking pan. Add enough water to baking pan to come halfway up sides of ramekins. Bake for 30-40 minutes, until set. Remove ramekins. Drizzle warm red pepper cream sauce over each pudding. Garnish with slices of red pepper to serve.

For the red pepper cream sauce: Heat oil in a small saucepan or skillet over medium heat. Add bell pepper; cook until soft (do not brown). Stir in garlic, cayenne and red pepper flakes. Add wine and deglaze pan, stirring to scrape browned bits free. Stir in cream.

Bring to a boil, lower heat and simmer for 2-3 minutes, until mixture thickens. Purée sauce in a blender or food processor. Season with salt and pepper. Return to pan and keep warm until serving.

Texas Cowboy Skillet

Debra Brooks of Byron, Georgia, won second prize in the Georgia National Fair's Grits Anytime Recipe Contest. Hundreds of recipes are submitted each year and this one, with a decidedly Southwestern flair, is an excellent way to spice up your grits!

Makes 4 Servings

4	cups cooked grits
1½	sticks butter, melted
¼	cup half & half
2	cups grated colby Jack cheese, divided
½	pound bulk hot sausage, crumbled and cooked
½	(14-ounce) can Mexicorn, drained
½	cup yellow hominy
Salt and pepper, to taste	
6	whole canned mild green chilies
6	finger-length pieces Monterey Jack cheese
Salsa, for serving (optional)	

Preheat oven to 350°F. Combine grits, butter, half & half, 1 cup of colby Jack cheese, sausage, corn, hominy, salt and pepper; pour mixture into a 10-inch cast-iron skillet or other oven-proof skillet.

Cut a seam in each chile; stuff with 1 piece of Monterey Jack cheese. Put chiles on top of grits mixture in a spoke-like fashion, with tips in center of grits. Sprinkle with remaining 1 cup of colby Jack cheese. Bake until cheese is melted, about 20 minutes. Serve with salsa, if desired.

BAKED LENTILS & CHEDDAR

This savory dish, by Rita Iverson of Moscow, Idaho, won third prize in the "entrée" category at the 15th annual National Lentil Festival cook-off in Pullman, Washington. Lentils are a highly nutritious grain with 20 grams of carbohydrates, 4 grams of fiber, 9 grams of protein and only 115 calories per serving.

Makes 8 to 10 Servings

2	cup dry lentils
2	tablespoons vegetable oil
1	cup chopped onion
2	cloves garlic, minced
½	cup chopped green bell pepper
1	(16-ounce) can chopped tomatoes
1	(8-ounce) can tomato sauce
½	teaspoon marjoram
½	teaspoon thyme
½	teaspoon sage
2	teaspoons salt
2	cups grated medium or sharp cheddar cheese

Bring 8 cups of water to a boil in a large pot. Add lentils, lower heat, cover and simmer for 20-30 minutes, until tender; drain and spread into a 9x13-inch baking dish.

Preheat oven to 375°F. Heat oil in a skillet over medium heat. Add onion and garlic; cook until onion is soft. Stir bell pepper, tomatoes, tomato sauce, marjoram, thyme, sage and salt into onion mixture; spread on top of lentils.

Cover baking dish with foil and bake for 1 hour. Remove foil, sprinkle with cheese and bake for 10-15 minutes longer, until cheese melts.

FARROTTO WITH PECORINO & PEARS

Italian Cooking & Living's *recipe competition featured delectable concoctions of fresh, affordable ingredients that require less than an hour to prepare. This winning recipe from executive chef Patrizio Siddu of Pepolino in New York, New York features the Tuscan grain farro.*

Makes 6 Servings

2½ cups pearl farro*
¼ cup extra-virgin olive oil
2 pears, peeled and cubed
8 cups vegetable stock, warmed
¾ cup freshly grated Parmigiano-Reggiano cheese
Salt and pepper, to taste
2 tablespoons butter
4 ounces aged pecorino cheese, grated
1 pear, sliced, for garnish

Bring a large pot of salted water to a boil. Add farro, lower heat, cover and simmer for 20 minutes. Meanwhile, heat oil in a large, heavy skillet over medium heat. Add pears; cook until a pale golden color.

Drain farro; add to pears and cook for about 2 minutes. Add ½ cup of stock. When stock has been absorbed, stir in Parmigiano cheese. Continue adding broth in ½-cup increments until farro is tender.

Season with salt and pepper. Stir in butter and pecorino cheese until melted and combined. Transfer to a serving platter and garnish with sliced pear, if desired.

*Note: Farro, which has been a mainstay of northern Italian cooking since the days of the Roman Empire, can be found in some larger groceries and specialty food stores. If farro is unavailable, substitute wheat berries or arborio rice (see note on page 110).

FRUITED WILD RICE SALAD WITH TOASTED HICKORY NUTS

J.D. Thorne of Milwaukee, Wisconsin, won second prize in the "wild foods" category at the Food For Thought recipe contest in Madison, Wisconsin. Thorne said, "This is a simple, yet gourmet salad. I've made it to bring along for weekend grouse hunts 'with the boys' and served it as a fancy side dish at our 25th wedding anniversary party."

Makes 6 to 8 Servings

1¼	cups wild rice
2	cups hickory nuts or pecans
½	cup fresh orange juice
6	tablespoons chopped shallots
2	tablespoons balsamic vinegar
4	teaspoons Dijon mustard
2	teaspoons minced garlic
1	cup extra-virgin olive oil

Salt and pepper, to taste

1¼	cups chopped flat-leaf parsley
¾	cup thinly sliced dried apricots
¾	cup dried cranberries
½	cup golden raisins

Rinse wild rice in a sieve with cold water. Put wild rice in a saucepan with cold water to cover by 2 inches. Bring to a boil, lower heat, cover and simmer for 45-60 minutes, until tender; drain. While rice is cooking, preheat oven or toaster oven to 350°F. Place nuts on foil and toast lightly until fragrant and lightly colored.

Make a vinaigrette by whisking together orange juice, shallots, vinegar, mustard and garlic in a large bowl. Gradually whisk in olive oil until thickened. Season with salt and pepper. Rinse cooked rice under cold water and drain well; stir into vinaigrette. Stir in nuts, parsley, dried apricots, cranberries, raisins and salt and pepper to taste. Serve at room temperature.

Greek Garden Rice Salad

Sharyn Hill of Organ, New Mexico, was a runner-up at the USA Rice Federation's Rice to the Rescue recipe contest. Rice is cultivated in more than 100 countries and on every continent except Antarctica. It is grown from sea level to altitudes of over 9,000 feet and sustains two-thirds of the world's population.

Makes 4 to 6 Servings

½ cup chopped oil-packed
   sun-dried tomatoes
3 tablespoons oil from sun-dried
   tomatoes
3 cups cooked medium grain rice
1 small red onion, chopped
½ cup halved kalamata olives
2 (4-ounce) packages crumbled
   feta cheese with garlic and herbs
¼ teaspoon salt
¼ teaspoon pepper
½ (6-ounce) bag baby spinach
   leaves, thinly sliced

Combine sun-dried tomatoes, sun-dried tomato oil and rice. Stir in onion, olives, feta cheese, salt and pepper. Add spinach; toss gently to combine.

SPINACH, GORGONZOLA & LEMON RICE

Kelly Mapes of Fort Collins, Colorado, was a runner-up at the USA Rice Federation's Rice to the Rescue Recipe Contest. Pairing savory Gorgonzola cheese with tart lemon, this recipe will delight and intrigue your palate. And, it is as easy as it is good!

Makes 6 Servings

2   tablespoons olive oil
2   cups coarsely chopped fresh mushrooms
1   (4-ounce) package crumbled Gorgonzola cheese
½   cup heavy cream
2   tablespoons fresh lemon juice
½   teaspoon salt
¼   teaspoon pepper
3   cups cooked rice
2   cups lightly-packed torn fresh spinach leaves
2   teaspoons grated lemon zest

Heat oil in a large saucepan over medium heat. Add mushrooms; cook until soft, about 4 minutes. Lower heat to medium-low. Add cheese and cook, stirring frequently, until cheese melts, about 3 minutes. Stir in cream, lemon juice, salt and pepper. Stir in rice and heat until hot, about 5 minutes. Stir in spinach just before serving. Sprinkle with lemon zest to serve.

Fabian's Apricot & Almond Dressing

Fabian Robles of Highland Park, California, took first prize in Mrs. Cubbison's Thanksgiving Stuffing Cook-off, held each year at Los Angeles Trade Technical College's Culinary School.

Makes 8 to 10 Servings

- 1 cup chopped dried apricots
- 1 cup white wine
- 1 stick butter, divided
- ½ cup chopped onion
- ½ cup chopped celery
- 1 (15-ounce) can apricot halves, divided
- ¼ cup brown sugar, divided
- 1 tablespoon minced fresh tarragon
- 1 tablespoon chopped fresh rosemary
- ½ cup sliced almonds
- 1 (12-ounce) package Mrs. Cubbison's Dressing
- 1 cup chicken or turkey stock or broth
- Salt and pepper, to taste
- 1 tablespoon minced parsley

Soak dried apricots in white wine for 1 hour. Melt 2 tablespoons of butter in a skillet over medium heat. Add onion and celery; cook until soft. Chop 4 apricots halves; add to onion mixture along with 2 tablespoons of brown sugar, dried apricots and dried apricot soaking liquid. Cook until onions are soft and golden brown. Add tarragon, rosemary and almonds; stir until well mixed.

In a large bowl, combine dressing and chicken stock. Season with salt and pepper. Mix apricot mixture into dressing mixture.

Preheat oven to 325°F. In a skillet, melt remaining 6 tablespoons of butter over medium heat. Add remaining 2 tablespoons of brown sugar; stir until combined. Add remaining apricots. Cook until apricots are browned. Remove apricots and set aside. Stir butter mixture in skillet into dressing mixture.

Put dressing in a baking dish, cover and bake for 25-30 minutes. Uncover baking dish, put apricot halves on top of dressing, re-cover dish and bake for 15 minutes more. Garnish dressing with parsley to serve.

HAM & CHIPOTLE DRESSING

David Martinez of Long Beach, California, won third prize in Mrs. Cubbison's Thanksgiving Stuffing Cook-off. Sophie ("Mrs.") Cubbison's culinary career began on her father's lima bean ranch in San Diego County, California, where she cooked for her family and the ranch workers to pay for college.

Makes 12 to 14 Servings

1	cup apple cider vinegar
1	teaspoon cinnamon
1	teaspoon coriander seeds
2	whole cloves
½	teaspoon dry mustard
1	bay leaf
⅓	cup packed brown sugar
1	cup chicken or turkey stock or broth
2	sticks butter
1	cup diced white onion
1	cup diced celery
1	pound baked ham, diced
1	Granny Smith apple, peeled and diced
1	cup chopped walnuts
1	tablespoon minced canned chipotle chile (or more for a spicier dressing)*
1	cup raisins
1	cup dried cranberries
1	(12-ounce) package Mrs. Cubbison's Dressing

Salt and white pepper, to taste

In a saucepan, combine vinegar, cinnamon, coriander seeds, cloves, dry mustard, bay leaf and brown sugar. Add chicken stock. Bring to a boil, lower heat and simmer until liquid is reduced by half.

Melt butter in a skillet over medium heat. Add onion and celery; cook until crisp-tender. Add ham and apple; cook until apple is softened. Add walnuts, chipotle, raisins and dried cranberries; cook for a 3-4 minutes. Remove from heat.

Preheat oven to 325°F. In a large bowl, combine apple mixture and dressing. Strain chicken stock mixture through a fine sieve; add to dressing mixture. Season with salt and pepper. Stir gently and put dressing in a greased baking dish. Cover and bake for 40-45 minutes. For a crisper top, uncover dish during last 10-15 minutes of baking time.

*Note: Chipotle chiles are smoked jalapeño peppers canned in a spicy adobo sauce. They can be found in the Mexican food section of most larger groceries.

PASTA & VEGETARIAN ENTREES

Black Japonica Ravioli with Blue Cheese Cream

Norita Solt, a Bettendorf, Iowa homemaker, won the Lundberg Family Farms' Rice Recipe Contest with this sophisticated but simple ravioli. Wonton wrappers are an excellent time-saving substitute for traditional ravioli pasta in the recipe, and Black Japonica rice adds effortless elegance to the dish.

Makes 6 to 8 Servings

Ravioli:
1   tablespoon butter
¼   cup chopped walnuts
1   cup Lundberg Black Japonica
    rice
2½ cups water
2   teaspoons vegetable bouillon
    granules (or 2 cubes)
1   tablespoon minced parsley
2   tablespoons minced green
    onion plus 2 tablespoons finely
    sliced green onions, for garnish
½   teaspoon dried Italian herb mix
1   clove garlic, minced
48 refrigerated wonton wrappers
    (a 14-ounce package has 50)
Egg wash (1 egg yolk mixed with
    1 tablespoon of water)
Parsley sprigs, for garnish
1   tablespoon minced red bell
    pepper or pimento, for garnish

Blue cheese cream sauce:
2   tablespoons butter
1   cup whipping cream
½   (8-ounce) package cream
    cheese
2   tablespoons crumbled blue
    cheese

For the ravioli: Melt butter in a 2-quart saucepan over medium-low heat. Stir in walnuts; cook until nuts are lightly toasted. Remove nuts with a slotted spoon and set aside. Add rice, water, bouillon, parsley, minced green onion, Italian herbs and garlic. Bring to a boil over high heat. Stir, cover and lower heat to medium-low. Simmer for 45-50 minutes, until grains "bloom" and water is absorbed. Stir in toasted walnuts. Remove from heat and let stand for 15 minutes (mixture may be made ahead to this point and refrigerated).

Bring 4 quarts of salted water to a boil in a large pot. Brush wonton wrappers with egg wash. Put 1 heaping tablespoon of rice mixture in center of half of wonton wrappers. Cover with remaining wrappers, pressing edges together well to seal and force out as much air as possible. Slide wontons into boiling water, a few at a time. Cook for 3 minutes, then remove and drain; keep warm.

For the sauce: Melt butter in a saucepan over low heat. Stir in whipping cream, cream cheese and blue cheese; heat until cheese is melted and combined.

To serve: Divide ravioli among serving plates. Spoon cream sauce over and around them. Sprinkle with sliced green onion, parsley and minced sweet red pepper.

BACON N' BASIL RAVIOLI

Priscilla Yee of Concord, California, won first prize in the Farmer John Meats' Everything's Better Wrapped in Bacon Recipe Contest. In 1931, two brothers, Francis and Bernard Clougherty, started Farmer John Meats, now the largest pork producer on the West Coast.

Makes 4 Servings

1	(9-ounce) package refrigerated cheese ravioli
12	strips Farmer John Bacon, cut into 1-inch pieces
2	tablespoons extra-virgin olive oil
3	cups diced Roma tomatoes
1	teaspoon minced thyme
½	cup thinly sliced fresh basil plus basil sprigs, for garnish
1	cup grated Parmesan cheese

Salt and pepper, to taste

⅓	cup chopped hazelnuts, toasted

Cook ravioli according to package directions. In a large, heavy skillet over medium heat, cook bacon until crisp; drain on paper towels.

Pour off all but 2 tablespoons of bacon drippings. Add olive oil, tomatoes and thyme to skillet; cook, stirring, until heated through. Stir in sliced basil, Parmesan and bacon. Season with salt and pepper.

Divide ravioli among plates. Top ravioli with bacon mixture. Sprinkle with hazelnuts. Garnish with basil sprigs to serve.

PASTA WITH MEATLESS MEATBALLS & SOUR CREAM DILL SAUCE

Gardenburger offers all-natural products made with wholesome ingredients. Gardenburger products can be enjoyed on their own or used to create delicious recipes. Diane Nemitz of Ludington, Michigan, won first prize in the "ethnic specialties" category in the first annual Best of Gardenburger Recipe Contest with her vegetarian take on this classic pasta dish.

Makes 4 to 6 Servings

2 tablespoons butter, margarine or vegetable oil
2 medium onions, thinly sliced
1 cup dry white wine
2 (12-ounce) packages Gardenburger Meatless Meatballs
1 cup low-fat sour cream
1 tablespoon all-purpose flour
3 tablespoons minced fresh dill
8 ounces medium or wide noodles, cooked

Melt butter in a large skillet over medium-low heat. Add onions; cook until golden brown, about 10-15 minutes. Add white wine and bring to a boil. Boil for 1 minute. Lower heat to medium, add meatballs and cook until meatballs are heated through.

In a small bowl, combine sour cream and flour. Stir in a little sauce from the skillet, then stir sour cream mixture and dill into skillet. Cook until mixture just simmers. Serve over noodles.

CRAB CANNELONI WITH ROASTED RED PEPPER SAUCE

Kerin Lee Lewis, executive chef and co-owner of Villa Italia Restaurant in Shelton, Washington, won gold medals for "best professional entrée" and "best overall" in the Shelton OysterFest. Lewis said of her dish, "Though unorthodox in a traditional Italian recipe, egg roll wrappers have a good consistency for canneloni."

Makes 6 Servings

Crab canneloni:

½ tablespoon butter
1 large shallot, minced
1 pound Dungeness crabmeat, shells picked out
½ pound cooked shrimp, minced
2 egg yolks
1 cup ricotta cheese
⅔ cup grated Parmesan cheese
⅓ teaspoon nutmeg
2 tablespoons chopped flat-leaf parsley
Grated zest of 1 lemon
12 egg roll wrappers

Roasted red pepper sauce:

4 large red bell peppers
2 cups heavy cream
½ stick butter
2 cloves garlic, minced
¼ cup grated Parmesan cheese

For the canneloni: Preheat oven to 475°F. Melt butter in a small skillet over medium heat. Add shallots and cook until soft; set aside. Break up crabmeat into small pieces. Add shallots and remaining ingredients, except egg roll wrappers; mix well.

Fill a piping bag (or a ziplock plastic bag with a corner cut off) with crab mixture; pipe onto egg roll wrappers. Fold in edges of wrapper and roll. Seal ends with water. Put canneloni in a baking dish and cover with roasted red pepper sauce. Bake for 8 minutes.

For the sauce: Roast or grill red peppers until skin is blackened all over. Seal in a paper bag and let steam for a few minutes. Remove peppers from bag; peel and seed pepper. Purée peppers in a food processor or blender. Combine red pepper purée, cream, butter and garlic in a saucepan over medium heat. When mixture begins to boil, lower heat, add Parmesan cheese and cook, stirring, until cheese is melted and combined.

PECAN RISOTTO WITH SMOKED GOUDA & CARAMELIZED ONIONS

The I Can Use Pecans in THAT? Recipe Contest is hosted by the National Pecan Shellers Association, a trade association committed to educating the public about the nutritional benefits, uses and great taste of pecans. Karla V. Boetel, a student at the Culinary Institute of America, won first prize in the "professional" category with the savory rice dish.

Makes 8 Servings

1	tablespoon butter
1	tablespoon olive oil
1	medium onion, sliced
1	cup Arborio rice*
8	cups chicken stock or broth, heated
¾	cup chopped pecans, toasted
2	tablespoons chopped flat-leaf parsley
1	cup grated smoked Gouda cheese

Salt and pepper, to taste

Melt butter and oil in a saucepan over low heat. Add onion; cook slowly, stirring constantly until golden brown and sweet, about 20-30 minutes. Raise heat to medium-high. Add rice and cook, stirring, for 1 minute.

Add 2 cups of stock and cook, stirring constantly, until absorbed. Add remaining stock, ½ cup at a time, stirring until each ½ cup is absorbed, until rice is tender but firm and mixture is creamy, about 20 minutes.

Stir in pecans, parsley and cheese. Season with salt and pepper. Serve immediately with chicken, fish or pork.

*Note: Arborio rice is an Italian rice used in risotto. It can be found in the rice section of most groceries.

PECAN FOUR-CHEESE PIZZA

Pecans are good for you and they taste great, too — which is evidenced by the hundreds of recipes entered in the first I Can Use Pecans in THAT! Recipe Contest. Consumers, food professionals, culinary students and even kid cooks developed some tantalizing pecan recipes, such as this winner from Kerri Levine of Longwood, Florida.

Makes 2 to 3 Servings

1 (12-inch) pre-baked pizza crust
1 tablespoon olive oil
2 large onions, sliced
3 tablespoons goat cheese, softened
3 tablespoons cream cheese, softened
½ cup crumbled feta cheese
1 cup grated mozzarella cheese
⅔ cup coarsely chopped pecans
Chopped parsley, for garnish

Preheat oven to 450°F. Put pizza crust on a cookie sheet. Heat oil in a skillet over low heat. Add onions and cook slowly until golden brown, soft and sweet, about 20-30 minutes; cool slightly.

In a small bowl, combine goat cheese and cream cheese; spread on crust. Spread onions over goat cheese mixture. Sprinkle feta and mozzarella cheese over onions. Top with pecans. Bake for about 5 minutes, or until cheeses melt. Sprinkle with parsley. Cut into 6 wedges to serve.

QUESO BLANCO PIZZA WITH FRESH SALSA

Leah Lyon of Ada, Oklahoma, won the grand prize for "best traditional pizza" in the Mama Mary's Pizza Creations Contest. Tom Baliker, creator of Mama Mary's, uses top-quality ingredients so his crusts taste better longer. Today his crusts are sold in 10,000 grocery stores in 48 states.

Makes 8 to 10 Servings

Pizza:

1	Mama Mary's 12-inch Gourmet Pizza Crust
	Olive oil
1	tablespoon unsalted butter
¼	cup chopped onion
1	clove garlic, minced
1	teaspoon salt
1	(10-ounce) package frozen spinach, thawed and drained
½	cup grated Parmesan cheese
½	cup crumbled queso fresco cheese*
½	cup shredded Parmesan cheese
¼	pound asadero cheese, cut into strips or cubes**
3	large poblano chiles, roasted, peeled, seeded and sliced into thin strips
2	cups grated mozzarella cheese

Salsa:

¼	sweet onion, chopped
2-3	jalapeños, seeded and chopped
1	teaspoon salt, or more to taste
2	tablespoons fresh lime juice
1-2	large tomatoes, cut in sixths

For the pizza: Preheat oven to 425°F. Line a vented pizza pan or a large baking sheet with parchment paper; trim paper so edges do not hang over pan or touch oven wall. Put pizza crust on pan. Mist or brush crust, including crust edges, with olive oil.

Melt butter in a small skillet over medium heat. Add onion and garlic; cook until softened. Add salt. Squeeze excess liquid from spinach; stir into onion mixture and cook for about 1 minute. Stir in grated Parmesan cheese.

Layer ingredients on pizza in the following order: queso fresco cheese, spinach mixture, shredded Parmesan cheese, asadero cheese, roasted poblano pepper strips, mozzarella cheese. Bake pizza for 12 minutes. To crisp the crust, put pizza directly on oven rack for 90 seconds more. Slice and serve with fresh salsa.

For the salsa: Put onion, jalapeños and salt in a food processor; pulse until finely chopped. Add lime juice and tomatoes; pulse until chopped but still chunky. Drain salsa before serving, if desired.

*Note: Queso fresco cheese is a white, hard cheese from Mexico with a somewhat salty flavor. It is available in larger groceries.

**Note: Asadero is a white cow's milk cheese from Mexico similar to Monterey Jack. It is available in larger groceries.

TOFU WITH GINGER & GARLIC SAUCE

Akira Otani of College Park, Maryland, won Yoyoga's Simple Vegetarian Recipe Contest with this entrée that takes just 10 minutes to prepare. Joan Budilovsky, creator of Yoyoga, has been studying and practicing yoga for 20 years. Her healthy lifestyle focuses on maintaining body and mind, which inspired her vegetarian diet and vegetarian recipe contest.

Makes 2 to 4 Servings

1	pound soft or firm tofu
2	tablespoons olive oil
1	clove garlic, minced
1	tablespoon minced peeled ginger
2	red Chinese peppercorns or red pepper flakes, to taste (optional)
2	tablespoons light or regular soy sauce
2	tablespoons rice wine or red wine vinegar
1	tablespoon miso paste
1	tablespoon brown sugar
2	teaspoons chopped green onion
1	teaspoon sesame oil

Cooked noodles or rice, for serving (optional)

Drain tofu for 20-30 minutes on a cutting board tipped at an angle or in a colander. Cut tofu into ½-inch cubes. Heat olive oil in a wok or skillet over medium heat until it smokes. Add garlic, ginger and red peppercorns; stir-fry for 2 minutes, until it starts to color. Add tofu; stir-fry until tofu browns.

Combine soy sauce, rice wine vinegar, miso and brown sugar; add to tofu mixture. When sauce comes to a boil, remove from heat and stir in sesame oil. Serve tofu over noodles or rice, if desired. Garnish with green onions.

"Fish, to taste right,

must swim three times –

in water, in butter,

and in wine."

Polish Proverb

FISH & SEAFOOD

GRILLED CANDIED GARLIC SALMON ON BABY ASIAN GREENS & CRISPY RICE NOODLES

Joann Donangelo of Salinas, California, won first prize in the Gilroy Garlic Festival's Great Garlic Cook-off, one of the America's best-known cooking contests.

Makes 6 Servings

Salmon:
2	tablespoons Asian fish sauce
3	tablespoons lime juice
2	cloves garlic, minced
2	teaspoons minced peeled ginger
2	teaspoons curry paste
6	(6- to 8-ounce) salmon fillets

Candied garlic:
10	cloves garlic, very thinly sliced
½	cup water
½	cup white wine
½	cup sugar
2	tablespoons butter

Crispy rice noodles and shallots:
Vegetable oil, for frying
8	ounces dried rice noodles (mai fun or rice sticks)
½	cup thinly sliced shallots

All-purpose flour

Greens and dressing:
½	cup snap peas, julienned
2	green onions, sliced, plus extra for garnish
8	cups baby Asian greens
1	clove garlic, minced
⅓	cup soy sauce
2	tablespoons lime juice

Salt and pepper, to taste

For the salmon: Combine fish sauce, lime juice, garlic, ginger and curry paste in a ziplock plastic bag. Add salmon, toss to coat and refrigerate for about 1 hour.

For the candied garlic: In a small saucepan, combine garlic, water, wine, sugar and butter; simmer for 10 minutes until syrupy (garlic should not be mushy). Remove garlic with a slotted spoon and cool (reserve 2½ tablespoons of candied garlic syrup for dressing).

For the noodles and shallots: Heat oil and fry noodles according to package directions, a few at a time. Drain noodles on paper towels (they'll look like styrofoam); set aside. Coat shallots with flour and fry until golden and crisp. Drain on paper towels; set aside.

For the greens and dressing: In a large bowl, combine snap peas, green onions and baby Asian greens. Make a dressing by combining minced garlic, the reserved 2½ tablespoons of candied garlic syrup, soy sauce and lime juice. Thin with a little water, if needed.

To serve: Remove salmon from marinade; discard marinade. Grill salmon for about 5 minutes per side, or until done. Add dressing to Asian greens; toss to combine.

Divide salad among serving plates. Top with noodles, then with a salmon fillet. Top salmon with some fried shallots, candied garlic and sliced green onion. Season with salt and pepper.

FISH & SEAFOOD

SEARED ROCKFISH FILLET WITH OYSTER & CORN STEW

Rich Hoffman of Rudy's 2900 in Finksburg, Maryland, won the grand prize at the 2003 Maryland Rockfish Celebration Cooking Contest. Rockfish, commonly known as striped bass, was named Maryland's state fish in 1965.

Makes 4 Servings

Oyster and corn stew:
2   tablespoons butter
2   tablespoons chopped red bell pepper
¼   cup minced celery
¼   cup minced onion
¼   cup minced leeks
¼   cup minced shallot
¼   cup finely chopped fresh wild mushrooms
1   cup roasted or grilled corn
¾   cup all-purpose flour
¼   cup dry vermouth
1   cup oyster liquor (oyster water)
2   cups half & half
Salt and pepper, to taste
12 large plump fresh oysters
¼   cup chopped peeled tomatoes
1   tablespoon minced parsley
1   tablespoon minced fresh tarragon
1   tablespoon minced fresh basil

Seared rockfish fillet:
2   pounds rockfish fillets, cut into 4 (8-ounce) portions
Dry mustard, to taste
Salt and pepper, to taste
1-2 tablespoons clarified butter*
Lemon juice, to taste

For the stew: Melt butter in a saucepan over medium heat. Add bell pepper, celery, onions, leeks, shallots, wild mushrooms and corn; cook until vegetables are tender. Add flour; cook, stirring, until flour is a very light brown.

Deglaze pan with vermouth, stirring to scrape browned bits free. Cook off alcohol. Add half & half and oyster liquor. Bring to a boil, lower heat and simmer for 25 minutes, until sauce coats the back of a spoon. Season with salt and pepper. Remove from heat. Stir in oysters, tomatoes, parsley, tarragon and basil. Cook for about 2-3 minutes, until edges of oysters begin to curl. Set aside and keep warm.

For the rockfish: Preheat oven to 350°F. Season rockfish with dry mustard, salt and pepper. Heat clarified butter in an oven-proof skillet over medium heat. Add rockfish and cook until golden brown on both sides. Transfer to oven and bake for 8 minutes, or until done. Sprinkle with lemon juice. Serve oyster stew topped with rockfish.

*Note: Clarified (drawn) butter is butter that is slowly melted, the foam skimmed off and the remaining clear liquid used for cooking. Start with ½ stick of butter to yield 2 tablespoons of clarified butter.

Sauteed Sea Bass with Mediterranean Bean Salad

Chef Melissa Shaffer of the Colonial Williamsburg Foundation in Williamsburg, Virginia, won the $1,500 second prize at the Northarvest Bean Growers Association's Chefs Say Bean Appétit Recipe Contest. Recipes were required to include dry or canned pinto, navy, kidney and/or black beans.

Makes 6 Servings

Bean salad:
½   pound dry navy beans
6   ounces small green beans, halved
¾   cup (¼-inch) diced Yukon gold potatoes
1   tablespoon olive oil
½   large yellow onion, diced
1   tablespoon minced garlic
1   cup red grape tomatoes, halved
¾   cup walnuts, toasted and coarsely chopped
¼   cup chopped kalamata olives

Sea bass:
6   (7-ounce) sea bass fillets
2   tablespoons chopped parsley
2   tablespoons chopped thyme
Salt and pepper, to taste
1   tablespoon olive oil
Shaved Parmesan cheese, for garnish
Fresh thyme sprigs, for garnish
Bruschetta, for serving

Whole grain mustard vinaigrette:
¾   cup olive oil
¼   cup sherry vinegar
2¼   teaspoons whole grain mustard
¾   teaspoon sugar
¾   teaspoon minced garlic
¾   teaspoon minced shallot
½   teaspoon hot pepper sauce
½   teaspoon Worcestershire sauce

For the bean salad: Put navy beans in a large saucepan; add cold water to cover by 2 inches. Bring to a boil and boil for 2 minutes. Remove from heat, cover and let stand for 1 hour; drain. Return beans to saucepan and add cold water to cover by 2 inches. Bring to a boil. Lower heat, cover and simmer for 40-50 minutes, until tender. Drain and cool.

Cook green beans and potatoes separately in simmering water in large saucepans until crisp-tender; drain, cool in ice water and drain again. Heat olive oil in a skillet over medium heat. Add onion and garlic; cook until tender, about 5 minutes, then let cool. In a large bowl, combine Navy beans, potatoes, onions, tomatoes, green beans, walnuts and olives. Add mustard vinaigrette and toss to combine. Season with salt and pepper.

For the sea bass: Preheat oven to 450°F. Sprinkle sea bass with parsley, thyme, salt and pepper. Heat olive oil in a large skillet over high heat. Add sea bass and cook until browned on both sides, about 5 minutes. Put fish on a baking sheet; bake until fish is tender and flakes with a fork, about 10 minutes.

To serve: Put 1 cup of bean salad on a large plate or in a shallow pasta bowl. Top with a fish fillet. Garnish with Parmesan cheese and thyme sprigs. Serve with bruschetta.

For the vinaigrette: Whisk together vinaigrette ingredients.

GRILLED RAINBOW TROUT ADOBO WITH ROASTED CORN SALSA

Wayne Oden of Hartford, Connecticut, won second prize in the Clear Springs Foods' Clear-Cuts Recipe Challenge. This dish appeals to the eye while the robust flavors delight the palate. And the ease of preparation makes this dish popular with the chef!

Makes 6 Servings

Trout:

6	(8-ounce) Clear Springs Clear Cuts butterflied rainbow trout fillets
1½	cups dry white wine
¾	cup fresh lime juice
1½	tablespoons adobo sauce (from canned chipotle chiles)*
1½	tablespoons minced garlic

Coarse salt, to taste
Olive oil
Field greens, for serving
Grated lime zest, for garnish
Grated lemon zest, for garnish

Roasted corn salsa:

1½	cups roasted corn
¾	cup diced roasted green chilies
¾	cup diced plum tomatoes
3	tablespoons diced red onion
¼	cup plus 2 tablespoons fresh lemon juice
3	tablespoons chopped fresh cilantro
1½	tablespoons adobo sauce (from canned chipotle chiles)*
1½	tablespoons minced seeded jalapeño pepper
1	teaspoon coarse salt
¼	teaspoon red pepper flakes

For the trout: Put trout in a glass baking dish. In a small bowl, combine wine, lime juice, adobo sauce, garlic and salt; pour over trout. Turn trout to coat. Cover and refrigerate for 2 hours.

For the salsa: Combine salsa ingredients and let stand for at least 20 minutes to blend flavors. Heat salsa in a little olive oil; keep warm.

On a well-oiled grill, preferably wood-fueled, grill trout, flesh-side-down, for 2 minutes. Turn and cook just until firm, about 1 minute more.

To serve: Arrange a small bed of field greens on each plate. Put 1 trout fillet on greens. Spoon warm salsa over and alongside trout. Garnish with lime and lemon zest.

*Note: Chipotle chiles are smoked jalapeño peppers canned in a spicy adobo sauce. They can be found in the Mexican food section of most larger groceries.

Southeast Asian Spiced Grilled Rainbow Trout with Lime Ginger Dipping Sauce

Malley Sisson, a Kansas State University student, won the grand prize in the Clear Springs Foods' Clear-Cuts Recipe Challenge.

Makes 6 Servings

Asian spiced grilled trout:

¼ cup yogurt
¼ cup minced peeled ginger
4 teaspoons turmeric
4 teaspoons sugar
4 teaspoons rice vinegar
1 tablespoon grated lime zest
2 teaspoons coarse salt
6 (4-ounce) Clear Springs Clear Cuts Rainbow Trout natural fillets, each cut lengthwise into 4 strips
24 lettuce leaves, torn into strips
1½ cups jasmine rice, cooked

Lime ginger dipping sauce:

1½ cups fish sauce
1 cup sugar
1 cup water
¾ cup fresh lime juice
⅔ cup chopped peeled ginger
⅓ cup chopped cilantro
4 cloves garlic, chopped
6 chopped seeded Thai bird chiles, or other small green chiles

For the trout: In a glass baking dish, combine yogurt, ginger, turmeric, sugar, rice vinegar, lime zest and coarse salt. Add trout and toss to coat. Cover and refrigerate for 30 minutes.

Preheat grill. Grill trout, flesh-side-down, for 1 minute. Turn and grill just until firm, about 30 seconds more.

To serve: On each plate, make 2 nests with 3 pieces of lettuce. Put 1 tablespoon of rice into each nest. Drizzle nests with 1 teaspoon of dipping sauce. Put 2 pieces of trout in each nest, cutting to fit in nest. Drizzle with 1 teaspoon of dipping sauce. Serve with 3 tablespoons of dipping sauce on the side.

For the dipping sauce: In a blender or food processor, purée all dipping sauce ingredients.

Parmesan-Battered Rainbow Trout with Sherried Beurre Blanc & Vegetable Risotto

Walter Miller of Columbus Country Club in Hillard, Ohio, won third prize in the Clear Springs Foods' Clear-Cuts Recipe Challenge.

Makes 6 Servings

Vegetable risotto:
1¼ cups chopped asparagus
1½ cups diced zucchini
½   cup halved snow peas
5   cups chicken stock or broth
1½ tablespoons olive oil
1   cup chopped onion
1½ cups Arborio rice
1   cup chopped Roma tomatoes
½   cup grated Parmesan cheese
¾   teaspoon chopped parsley
¾   teaspoon minced fresh thyme

Parmesan-battered rainbow trout:
6   (6-ounce) Clear Springs Clear Cuts Rainbow Trout fillets
Coarse salt and pepper, to taste
4   large eggs, lightly beaten
1½ cups grated Parmesan cheese
All-purpose flour
Clarified butter (see note, page 117)

Sherried beurre blanc:
1½ tablespoons olive oil
½   cup finely chopped shallot
2   cloves garlic, minced
¾   cup sherry
1½ cups fish stock
Arrowroot slurry*
2   tablespoons fresh lemon juice
¾   stick unsalted butter

For the risotto: Separately steam asparagus, zucchini and snow peas until barely crisp-tender; set aside. Bring chicken stock to a boil; keep warm over low heat. Heat oil in a large saucepan over medium heat. Add onion; cook until golden. Stir in rice; cook, stirring constantly, until rice is lightly browned. Add 1 cup of chicken stock to rice at a time, cooking until stock is absorbed. Repeat until rice is tender, about 15 minutes. Stir in blanched vegetables, tomatoes, Parmesan cheese, parsley and thyme. Cover and keep warm.

For the trout: Season both sides of trout with salt and pepper. Combine eggs and Parmesan cheese. Dredge trout in flour, then spread egg mixture over flesh side of trout. Heat butter in a skillet over medium heat. Brown trout, flesh-side-down, about 2 minutes. Turn and cook just until firm to the touch, about 1 minute more.

For the beurre blanc: Heat oil in a saucepan over medium heat. Add shallots and garlic; cook until soft. Deglaze pan with sherry. Add fish stock; reduce liquid by half. Lightly thicken mixture with arrowroot slurry. Stir in lemon juice. Remove from heat and whisk in butter, 1 tablespoon at a time, until melted and combined. Keep warm.

To serve: Put ½ cup risotto on each plate. Top with a trout fillet. Drizzle with ¼ cup of warm beurre blanc.

Note: Arrowroot slurry is used like cornstarch. Mix with a little water to make a slurry and use to thicken sauces.

HARVEST-STYLE TROUT CAKES WITH CHIPOTLE REMOULADE

Elaine Sweet of Dallas, Texas, won second prize in the Shuckman's Fish Company & Smokery recipe contest. Shuckman's, founded in 1919 in Louisville, Kentucky, is now in its fourth generation of family ownership, producing smoked catfish, salmon, trout and bass, as well as American Kentucky Spoonfish caviar.

Makes 6 Servings

Trout cakes:

2	teaspoons plus ¼ cup extra-virgin olive oil
1	onion, diced
3	green onions, sliced
2	red bell peppers, diced
4	cloves garlic, minced
1	jalapeño, seeded and minced
3	stalks celery, chopped
½	cup chopped cilantro, divided
1	tablespoon minced fresh thyme
2	(16-ounce) packages Shuckman's Smoked Kentucky Rainbow Trout
4	eggs, beaten
3	cups panko or dry breadcrumbs, divided*

Chipotle remoulade:

¼	red onion, diced
3	tablespoons chopped capers
1	chipotle pepper in adobo sauce, chopped**
¾	cup mayonnaise
1	tablespoon whole grain mustard

Juice of 1 lime
½ teaspoon lemon pepper
8 dashes of Tabasco sauce

For the trout cake: Heat 2 teaspoons of olive oil in a skillet over medium heat. Add onion, green onion, bell pepper, garlic, jalapeño, celery, cilantro and thyme; cook for 4 minutes, then transfer to a bowl and cool.

Add smoked trout to onion mixture. Add eggs and 2 cups of breadcrumbs; mix well and shape into 12 cakes. Dip trout cakes into remaining breadcrumbs to coat.

Heat the ¼ cup of olive oil in a skillet over medium heat. Cook trout cakes until golden brown on both sides.

Put 2 trout cakes on each plate. Drizzle remoulade over cakes and around edges of plates.

For the remoulade: Combine remoulade ingredients. Cover and refrigerate until using.

*Note: Panko is a coarse Japanese breadcrumb that gives fried foods a light, crunchy crust. It is available in larger groceries, Asian markets and specialty food stores.

**Note: Chipotle chiles are smoked jalapeño peppers canned in a spicy adobo sauce. They can be found in the Mexican food section of most larger groceries.

NUT-CRISPED MAHI WITH MANGO SAUCE & COCONUT CURRY RICE

C. Patricia Cruz of Miami, Florida, won first prize in the "entrée" category at Fairchild Tropical Garden's International Mango Festival Cook-off in Coral Gables, Florida. The contest is held each July, to coincide with the mango harvest.

Makes 4 to 6 Servings

Nut-crisped mahi-mahi:
Canola or vegetable oil, for frying
1½ cups pecans, finely chopped
¾ cup pine nuts, finely chopped
1½ teaspoons salt
2½ cups dry breadcrumbs
6 (6-ounce) mahi-mahi fillets
4 eggs, beaten
Chives, for garnish

Warm mango sauce:
2 tablespoons butter
½ onion, finely chopped
1 (9-ounce) jar Major Grey's Mango Chutney
Juice of ½ lime
¼ teaspoon curry powder
Pinch of white pepper (optional)
1 cup finely chopped mango

Coconut curry rice::
2 cups white rice
2¾ cups water
2¼ teaspoons salt
1½ teaspoons curry powder
1 (15-ounce) can garbanzo beans, drained
⅓ cup chopped onion
1 cup coconut or vegetable oil
2 tablespoons grated coconut or coconut milk (optional)

For the mahi-mahi: Heat oil for frying in a large skillet. Mix pecans, pine nuts, salt and breadcrumbs in a shallow dish. Cut each mahi-mahi fillet into 3 lengthwise strips; dip in egg, then in breading, pressing down to be sure pecan pieces stick to it. Cook until golden brown on both sides and crisp; drain on paper towels. Serve mahi-mahi over coconut curry rice with individual ramekins of warm mango sauce. Garnish with chives to serve.

For the mango sauce: Melt butter in a saucepan over medium-low heat. Add onion; cook until translucent. Stir in chutney and lime juice. Stir in curry powder and white pepper. Stir in mango. If desired, purée sauce to desired consistency. Keep warm until serving.

For the rice: Combine all ingredients in a large saucepan. Stir, bring to a boil, lower heat to low, cover and simmer until all water is absorbed and rice is tender, about 15-20 minutes. Remove from heat.

TORTILLA CRUSTED MAHI-MAHI WITH HABANERO CORN SAUCE

Chef Jack Lewis of Jake's in Tyler, Texas, won the "entrée" category in Mission Tortilla's Think Outside the Tortilla Recipe Contest. This dish is a Hawaiian favorite with a spicy kick. Mahi-Mahi is seasoned with smoky chipotles and crusted with red, yellow and blue corn tortilla crumbs, then served over a fiery sauce.

Makes 6 Servings

Tortilla crusted mahi-mahi:
2   (7-ounce) cans chipotle peppers in adobo sauce*
5   tablespoons Southwestern seasoning
3   pounds mahi-mahi fillets, cut into 6 (8-ounce) portions
8   Mission red corn tortillas
10 Mission yellow corn tortillas
8   Mission blue corn tortillas
All-purpose flour, for coating fish
3   eggs, beaten
2   tablespoons vegetable oil
1   bunch cilantro, chopped
2   lemons, cut into wedges

Habanero corn sauce:
2   tablespoons vegetable oil
⅔   cup pine nuts
3   habanero peppers, seeded, ribbed and sliced into thin strips
1   cup roasted corn (cut from cob)
3   cups heavy cream
3   tablespoons Southwestern seasoning
2   teaspoons salt

For the mahi-mahi: Purée chipotle peppers with adobo sauce. Put purée in a bowl (reserve 2 tablespoons for the corn sauce) with Southwestern seasoning and mahi-mahi; thoroughly coat fish with chipotle mixture.

Preheat oven to 350°F. In a food processor or blender, grind tortillas to almost a fine crumb. Dredge fish in flour, then eggs, then ground tortillas. Heat 2 tablespoons of oil in a large skillet over medium heat. Add fish and cook until lightly browned on both sides. Transfer to oven and finish cooking to desired doneness. Serve mahi-mahi over habanero corn sauce. Garnish with cilantro, lemon wedges and a sprinkle of Southwestern seasoning.

For the sauce: Heat 2 tablespoons of oil in a saucepan over medium heat. Add pine nuts, habanero peppers and roasted corn; cook for about 2 minutes. Add heavy cream, Southwestern seasoning, salt and the reserved 2 tablespoons of chipotle purée. Simmer until reduced by a third; serve warm.

*Note: Chipotle chiles are smoked jalapeño peppers canned in a spicy adobo sauce. They can be found in the Mexican food section of most larger groceries.

Grilled Lemon Herb Shrimp

Featuring eucalyptus honey, this "dark honey" category winner in the National Honey Board's Viva Variety Recipe Contest was created by food editor Andi Bidwell of Bloomington, Minnesota. The dish is a delicious mix of honey, fresh herbs and shrimp that is sure to have grills fired-up year round.

Makes 3 to 4 Servings

¼   cup finely sliced green onion
¼   cup vegetable oil
2   teaspoons grated lemon zest
2   tablespoons fresh lemon juice
½   cup eucalyptus honey
3   tablespoons chopped fresh parsley
2   tablespoons chopped fresh thyme leaves
¼   teaspoon salt
1   pound (21-25 count) medium shrimp, peeled and deveined, with shells left on tails

In a medium bowl, combine all ingredients except shrimp. Stir in shrimp. Cover and chill for 1 hour.

Preheat grill. Remove shrimp from marinade and thread on 3-4 skewers; discard marinade. Grill shrimp for 5-7 minutes, turning once, until opaque. Serve warm.

Note: The shrimp may also be broiled. After removing shrimp from marinade, place shrimp on a broiler pan. Broil in a preheated oven, 4 inches from heat, for 6-8 minutes, turning once, until opaque.

Tip: For added tartness, add an additional 1 tablespoon of lemon juice and an additional dash of salt.

PICANTE SHRIMP BURRITOS WITH FRUIT SALSA

Helen Belichko of Kansas City, Missouri, won second prize in Mealtime.org's Celebration of Food Recipe Contest. Mealtime.org, part of the Canned Food Alliance, holds this recipe contest to showcase the versatility of canned foods. This light and fresh burrito is delicious on a summer evening.

Makes 8 Servings

Salsa:
1   (11-ounce) can mandarin oranges, drained
1   (8-ounce) can pineapple tidbits, drained
¼   cup thinly sliced green onion
1   tablespoon chopped canned mild green chiles (or chopped seeded fresh jalapeño)
1   tablespoon chopped cilantro
1   tablespoon lemon or lime juice

Burritos:
1   tablespoon olive oil
1   cup thinly sliced yellow bell pepper
1   cup thinly sliced red onion
1   clove garlic, minced
1½ pounds medium shrimp, peeled and deveined (thawed, if frozen)
1   (14-ounce) can diced tomatoes, well drained
½   teaspoon cumin
½   teaspoon chili powder
½   teaspoon pepper
¼   teaspoon salt
8   (10-inch) flour tortillas, warmed
2   cups grated Monterey Jack cheese

For the salsa: Combine all salsa ingredients.

For the burritos: Heat oil in a large skillet over medium heat. Add bell pepper, red onion and garlic; cook until crisp-tender, about 4 minutes. Add shrimp, tomatoes, cumin, chili powder, pepper and salt. Cook, stirring, until shrimp are firm and opaque.

To serve: Divide shrimp mixture among tortillas. Top with salsa and cheese. Fold in edges of tortillas and roll up.

Tip: This dish is also excellent served as shrimp soft tacos in mini flour tortillas – serve 2-3 tacos per person.

CRUNCHY COCONUT SHRIMP WITH MANGO DIP

The makers of Crisco recently invited people from across America to submit their favorite festive recipes to the Crisco Celebrates the Flavor of the Holidays Recipe Contest. This shrimp recipe, from Jasmina Shane of Bayside, New York, won first prize.

Makes 4 to 6 Servings

Mango dip:

2	cups coarsely chopped mango
1	tablespoon lime juice
1½	teaspoons minced seeded Scotch bonnet chile pepper
2	teaspoons Crisco Pure Canola Oil
¼	teaspoon salt
½	teaspoon pepper
½	cup finely chopped red onion

Crunchy coconut shrimp:

	Crisco All-Vegetable Shortening, for frying
½	cup all-purpose flour
¼	cup cornstarch
1	teaspoon paprika
1	teaspoon jerk seasoning
1	cup unsweetened coconut milk
1¾	cups unsweetened shredded wheat cereal, crushed
½	cup shredded coconut
25	large shrimp (about 1 pound), peeled, with tail left on

For the dip: Put all dip ingredients, except red onion, in a food processor; pulse until almost smooth (or mash with a potato masher). Stir in red onion. Put mixture in a small serving bowl and set aside.

For the shrimp: Melt enough shortening in a deep skillet to equal 2 inches (or fill a deep fryer half-full with shortening). Heat shortening to 350°F (or 365°F in a fryer).

In a shallow bowl, combine flour, cornstarch, paprika and jerk seasoning. Pour coconut milk into a second bowl. In a third bowl or shallow plate, combine crushed shredded wheat and flaked coconut.

Hold shrimp by the tail, coat with flour mixture, dip in coconut milk, then coat with crushed wheat mixture. Put shrimp on a wire rack with wax paper beneath to catch drippings.

Fry 6-8 shrimp at a time for 1-2 minutes, or until golden brown and crisp. Reheat oil to 350°F (365°F for a deep fryer) before frying each batch. Drain shrimp on paper towels, then transfer to a serving platter. Serve hot or warm with mango dip.

Note: Shrimp may be prepared in advance and frozen for up to 2 weeks. To serve, defrost slightly and re-crisp in a preheated 375°F oven.

GRILLED JUMBO SHRIMP WITH SPICY CRAWFISH POTATO SALAD

Chef John Franke, a Dallas, Texas concept chef, won the $10,000 grand prize and the title of "Tabasco's Hottest Chef" in the annual Tabasco's Hottest Chef Recipe Contest. The contest challenged entrants to give traditional, all-American comfort food recipes a new "Tabasco twist."

Makes 8 Servings

Peppery citrus glaze:

¾ cup pineapple juice
¾ cup fresh orange juice
1 tablespoon fresh lime juice
2 small bay leaves
Pinch of ground ginger
2 tablespoons soy sauce
1½ teaspoons balsamic vinegar
1 tablespoon Tabasco Green Pepper Sauce
1½ teaspoons kosher salt
1½ teaspoons black peppercorns
1½ teaspoons honey
3 tablespoons unsalted butter, cut into ½-inch cubes

Grilled jumbo shrimp:

¼ cup minced mixed fresh herbs (such as basil, oregano, etc.)
½ cup olive oil
2½ pounds shrimp, peeled and deveined
Kosher salt and coarsely ground black pepper
Tabasco Pepper Sauce
8 whole crawfish, for garnish
2 tablespoons chopped parsley
24 (4-inch) chives, for garnish
8 sprigs parsley, for garnish

For the glaze: Put all glaze ingredients, except butter, in a small saucepan over high heat. Bring to a boil. Boil until syrupy, about 15 minutes. Remove from heat and whisk in butter, a little at a time, until melted and combined. Strain mixture through a fine mesh strainer. Let stand at room temperature until using.

For the shrimp: In a small bowl, combine herbs and olive oil. Add shrimp, cover and refrigerate for 30 minutes. Preheat grill over medium heat. Season shrimp with salt and pepper. Grill shrimp on both sides until opaque. Bring a small saucepan of water to a boil. Add Tabasco and crawfish; boil for 3 minutes. Drain and set aside.

To serve: Put about 1 cup of potato salad (recipe follows on next page) on each plate. Top with 6 grilled shrimp, piled high. Drizzle about 1 tablespoon of citrus glaze over shrimp and plate. Sprinkle chopped parsley over entire plate. Add 3 chives to shrimp, poking out of top of shrimp. Garnish with 1 sprig of fresh parsley and 1 boiled crawfish for a fun flair. Serve immediately.

Spicy crawfish potato salad:

3½ pounds baby red potatoes
3   quarts water
½   pound crawfish tails
1½ stalks celery, finely diced
½   medium red onion, finely diced
½   green bell pepper, finely diced
½   red bell pepper, finely diced
1½ cups mayonnaise
2   tablespoons red wine vinegar
1   tablespoon chopped parsley
1½ teaspoons coarse black pepper
1   tablespoon kosher salt
1   tablespoon plus 2 teaspoons
    Tabasco Pepper Sauce

For the potato salad: Wash potatoes under cold water. In a large pot, bring potatoes and water to a boil. Lower heat and simmer for 30-35 minutes, until fork tender. Remove from heat, drain and let potatoes cool at room temperature for 30 minutes. When cool, chop potatoes into 1-inch cubes and transfer to a large bowl. Add remaining ingredients; mix well with a rubber spatula. Cover and chill for at least 1 hour to let flavors blend. Bring to room temperature before serving.

STUFFED MAUI ONIONS

Nearly 10,000 onion lovers gathered at the 14th annual Whalers Village Maui Onion Festival in 2003 to honor one of Maui's most esteemed agricultural products. Denise Espinosa of Lahaina, Maui, Hawaii, won first prize in the "amateur" category with this intriguing Hawaiian/Southwestern fusion.

Makes 2 Servings

2	large Maui onions
2	tablespoons

Pinch of red pepper flakes

13	large tiger prawns, peeled
1	chicken breast half, cooked and shredded
½	cup crabmeat
¼	cup chopped macadamia nuts
1½	cups grated pepper Jack cheese
12	pimento-stuffed Spanish green olives
½	cup crumbled lime-flavored tortilla chips
2	cups red enchilada sauce
2	large avocados, each cut into 8 slices

Preheat oven to 375°F. Butter an 8x8-inch baking dish. Cut off tops and root buttons of onions and remove first thick layer of skin. Scoop out centers of onions with a melon baller, leaving a ¼-inch thick shell. Make 3 equally-spaced vertical slices about halfway through each onion to create a "flower" look; set aside.

Melt 2 tablespoons of butter with red pepper flakes in a skillet over medium heat. Add prawns; cook until done. Chop 3 prawns and mix with chicken, crab, macadamia nuts (reserve 2 teaspoons of nuts for garnish), cheese, olives and tortilla chips. Stuff onions generously with crab mixture. Put onions in baking dish; bake for 35-40 minutes, until onions are browned and cheese is bubbly.

While onions are baking, heat enchilada sauce. Put sliced avocado on serving plates in a circular fashion. Pour some enchilada sauce in center of plates. Place onions on enchilada sauce. Drizzle some enchilada sauce over onions and sprinkle with reserved nuts. Decorate plates with remaining prawns placed between avocado slices.

THREE CHEESE, MANGO & KING CRAB QUESADILLAS

Donna Hurley of Kodiak, Alaska, won second prize at the Kodiak Crabfest's Wild About Kodiak Seafood Cook-off. The five day festival, held to celebrate one of the nation's largest fishing ports, draws over 15,000 people each year and includes the cook-off, a dog show, the "Shrimp Parade" and a halibut filleting contest, among other events.

Makes 1 to 2 Servings

1	large flour tortilla
1	tablespoon butter
1	tablespoon low-fat cream cheese
2	tablespoons finely chopped mango
1	cup shredded king crab (or other crabmeat)
2	teaspoons sliced green onion
½	cup grated sharp cheddar cheese
¼	cup grated cotija cheese*

Chopped fresh cilantro, for garnish
Warmed salsa, for serving

Preheat broiler. Put tortilla in a skillet over medium-low heat. Spread tortilla generously with butter. Turn tortilla over and brown lightly (be careful, tortillas burn easily), then remove from heat.

Spread cream cheese over tortilla. Sprinkle with mango, crab and green onions. Top with cheddar and cotija cheese. Return to skillet and heat until toppings are warmed. Broil for 1 minute, or until cheese is bubbly (watch carefully). Fold tortilla in half and cut into triangles. Sprinkle with chopped cilantro and serve with warmed salsa.

*Note: Cotija cheese is a hard Mexican cheese with a mild, slightly salty flavor. It can be found in the Mexican food or cheese sections of larger groceries.

SAFFRON LOBSTER GRATINEE WITH PUFF PASTRY TOP

Margo Bartelho of Biddeford, Maine, won first prize at the 2003 Maine Lobster Fest. One highlight of the festival is the firing of the world's largest lobster cooker, in which well over ten tons of lobster is prepared each year.

Makes 8 Servings

12 ounces lobster meat, cut into chunks
1½ teaspoons Old Bay seasoning
½ teaspoon dry mustard
1½ teaspoons sea salt
½ teaspoon white pepper
1 stick unsalted butter
½ shallot, chopped
2 tablespoons minced garlic
¼ cup chopped fresh parsley
½ cup chopped stemmed portobello mushrooms
¼ cup plus 2 tablespoons sherry
1 egg yolk
2 cups heavy cream
A few threads of saffron, finely crushed (optional)
1 cup grated Monterey Jack cheese
Puff pastry sheets
Egg wash (1 egg beaten with 1 teaspoon of water)

Preheat oven to 350°F. Lightly rub lobster with Old Bay seasoning, dry mustard, salt and white pepper. Melt butter in a skillet over medium heat. Add shallots, garlic, parsley and mushrooms; cook until shallots and garlic are translucent and mushrooms are browned. Stir in lobster meat. Add sherry; cook until liquid is reduced. Remove from heat and set aside, stirring occasionally.

Put egg yolk in a stainless steel bowl. In a saucepan, heat cream until hot. Add a little cream to egg yolk. Stir to combine, then whisk egg yolk mixture into remaining cream in saucepan. Add saffron and cook until cream is reduced by half. Whisk in Monterey Jack cheese until melted and combined. Remove from heat and fold cream mixture into lobster mixture.

Fill 8 individual ramekins to top with lobster mixture. Cut puff pastry to fit ramekin tops and place on top of ramekins. Brush puff pastry with egg wash. Bake until tops are browned and bubbly, about 20 minutes.

FISH & SEAFOOD

POULTRY

CHICKEN STRIPS WITH MANGO AVOCADO SALSA

Ten-year-old Lauren Assayag of Los Angeles, California, won Dole's 5-A-Day Kid's Recipe Contest. "Mangos and avocados are two of my favorite foods, so I liked combining them," said Assayag. She likes art projects, and sees cooking as a kind of art, combining colors and tastes. She would like to be a chef when she grows up.

Makes 4 Servings

Chicken:

4	boneless, skinless chicken breast halves, cut into strips
1	teaspoon garlic powder
¾	cup Dole pineapple-orange juice
1	teaspoon chopped cilantro, plus extra for garnish
2	tablespoons olive oil

Mango avocado salsa:

1	Dole mango, diced
1	small Dole avocado, diced
1	tomato, diced
¼	jicama, peeled and diced
3	tablespoons diced green onion
2	tablespoons chopped cilantro
2	tablespoons Dole pineapple-orange juice
2	teaspoons olive oil

For the chicken: Sprinkle chicken with garlic powder and place in a ziplock plastic bag. Add pineapple-orange juice and cilantro; toss to mix. Seal bag and refrigerate for 30-60 minutes.

Heat oil in a large, non-stick skillet over medium heat. Remove chicken from marinade; discard marinade. Add chicken to skillet and cook, stirring, until cooked through and lightly browned, about 4-5 minutes. Top with mango avocado salsa. Garnish with cilantro to serve.

For the salsa: Combine all salsa ingredients.

PISTACHIO CHICKEN TENDERS WITH COUNTRY MUSTARD

Nick Sparrow of Osage, Iowa, won third prize at Gold Kist Farms' Winning Taste Recipe Contest. Sparrow comes from a cooking family – his mother, Diane, was the "Winning Taste" grand prize winner in 2000. Sparrow created this dish for his wedding reception for his new bride who loves pistachios.

Makes 4 Entrée or 8 Appetizer Servings

Chicken:

8	Gold Kist Farms chicken tenders (about 1 pound)
2	tablespoons olive oil
3	tablespoons fresh lemon juice
1	tablespoon Worcestershire sauce
1	tablespoon honey
2	cloves garlic, minced
2	tablespoons minced thyme
8	(9x13-inch) sheets phyllo dough, defrosted according to package directions
½	stick butter, melted
½	cup finely chopped pistachio nuts

Country mustard:

¼	cup mayonnaise
2	tablespoons country-style mustard
1	tablespoon honey
2	teaspoons minced thyme

For the chicken tenders: Rinse chicken tenders, pat dry and place in a non-metallic dish or ziplock plastic bag. Whisk together olive oil, lemon juice, Worcestershire sauce, honey, garlic and thyme; pour over tenders. Cover dish or seal bag and refrigerate for 1 hour.

Preheat oven to 400°F. Lightly butter a shallow baking pan or line with parchment paper. Brush 1 sheet of phyllo dough with melted butter. Top with another sheet; brush with butter. Repeat with 2 more sheets, creating 2 stacks of 2 sheets of phyllo. Cut each phyllo stack lengthwise into 4 strips. Sprinkle with pistachio nuts.

Remove chicken from marinade; discard marinade. Put 1 chicken tender at one end of each phyllo strip (tenders will extend beyond phyllo). Tightly roll up each tender in phyllo. Put phyllo rolls seam-side-down in pan.

Bake rolls for 20 minutes, or until chicken is cooked through and phyllo is golden brown. Serve rolls with country mustard.

For the mustard: In a small serving bowl, thoroughly combine all mustard ingredients. Cover and refrigerate until serving.

Note: Tenders may be prepared ahead, covered and refrigerated or frozen. When ready to serve, thaw in refrigerator and bake as directed.

PACIFIC RIM CHICKEN BURGERS WITH GINGER MAYONNAISE

Kristine Snyder of Kihei, Hawaii, won the $25,000 grand prize at the National Chicken Cooking Contest with this innovative take on the hamburger. Judges praised the winning dish as a "new twist on an old favorite," for using Asian-spiced ground chicken in place of beef.

Makes 4 Servings

Chicken burgers:

- 1¼ pounds ground chicken
- ⅔ cup panko or dry breadcrumbs*
- 1 egg, lightly beaten
- 2 green onions, thinly sliced
- 3 tablespoons chopped cilantro, plus extra for garnish
- 1 clove garlic, minced
- 1 teaspoon Asian hot chile sauce
- 1 teaspoon salt
- ½ cup bottled teriyaki glaze
- 4 teaspoons honey, warmed slightly (aids mixing)
- 1 tablespoon vegetable oil
- 4 sesame buns, split and toasted
- 4 red lettuce leaves
- 1 cucumber, peeled, seeded, halved and thinly sliced lengthwise

Ginger mayonnaise:

- ½ cup mayonnaise
- 2 teaspoons sweet pickle relish
- 2 teaspoons minced peeled ginger
- 2 teaspoons lime juice
- 1 clove garlic, minced
- ¼ teaspoon salt

For the chicken burgers: In a large bowl, mix chicken, breadcrumbs, egg, onions, cilantro, garlic, chili sauce and salt. With oiled hands, form mixture into 4 patties. In a small bowl, combine teriyaki glaze and honey; set aside.

Heat oil in a large non-stick skillet over medium-high heat. Add chicken patties and cook, turning and brushing with teriyaki mixture, for about 10 minutes, until done. Put burgers on buns. Top with lettuce, cucumber and ginger mayonnaise. Garnish with cilantro and cucumber slices to serve.

For the ginger mayonnaise: Combine all mayonnaise ingredients.

*Note: Panko is a coarse Japanese breadcrumb that gives fried foods a light, crunchy crust. It is available in larger groceries, Asian markets and specialty food stores.

Chicken Cakes with Chipotle Mayonnaise

Kathleen L. Boulanger of Williston, Vermont, won the grand prize in the Gold Kist Farms 15th annual Winning Taste Recipe Contest, taking home over $10,000 in cash and prizes. Boulanger learned to cook when she married. She now enters cooking contests as a hobby.

Makes 6 Entrée Servings or 24 Bite-Sized Appetizers

Chipotle mayonnaise:
1	cup mayonnaise
1	tablespoon lime juice
2	teaspoons minced shallot
1	teaspoon minced garlic
1	teaspoon chipotle chili pepper*
Salt, to taste	

Chicken cakes:
1½	pounds Gold Kist Farms boneless, skinless, split chicken breasts
½	cup panko or dry breadcrumbs
½	cup minced shallots
1	egg, lightly beaten
2	tablespoons jalapeño pepper jelly, melted and cooled
2	tablespoons minced cilantro
Salt and pepper, to taste	

Coating:
¼	cup all-purpose flour
1	egg, lightly beaten
½	cup panko or dry breadcrumbs
2	tablespoons olive oil
Cilantro leaves, for garnish	

For the chipotle mayonnaise: Combine mayonnaise ingredients. Set aside 6 tablespoons for chicken cakes. Put remaining chipotle mayonnaise in a dish, cover and refrigerate until ready to serve.

For the chicken cakes: Put chicken in single layer in a large saucepan. Add water to cover by ½-inch. Bring to a boil, lower heat, cover and simmer for 12-15 minutes, until chicken is no longer pink inside. Drain and cool.

When chicken is cool, finely chop to yield about 3 cups. Combine chicken, reserved 6 tablespoons of chipotle mayonnaise and remaining chicken cake ingredients; mix gently until well combined. For entrée servings, make 12 (¼-cup) cakes. To make appetizer servings, form small patties with about 1 tablespoon per patty.

For the coating: Using 3 pie plates or shallow dishes, put flour in one, beaten egg in a second and breadcrumbs in a third. Lightly coat both sides of each chicken cake with flour, then egg, then breadcrumbs. Heat oil in a large non-stick skillet over medium-high heat until very hot, but not smoking. Cook chicken cakes in a single layer, without crowding. Cook until golden brown, about 3 minutes per side; drain on paper towels. Serve with chipotle mayonnaise. Garnish with cilantro.

*Note: Chipotle chile pepper can be found in the spice aisle of some groceries or at www.penzeys.com. Or use about 1 teaspoon adobo sauce from canned chipotles.

PHYLLO TART WITH CALIFORNIA NECTARINES & SMOKED CHICKEN

Chef Mark Salter won first prize in the "lunch" category at the Eat California Fruit Make It Special With California Peaches, Plums and Nectarines Recipe Contest. These tarts, stuffed with juicy, ripe California nectarines, smoked chicken and vegetables, are perfect for a light lunch or appetizer.

Makes 6 Servings

Tart:
3   sheets phyllo dough
¾   stick unsalted butter, melted
½   cup grated Parmesan cheese

Filling:
2   California nectarines, cut into ¼-inch cubes
2   ounces snow peas, blanched
1   stick celery, julienned
2   (4-ounce) breasts of smoked chicken, shredded
Juice of 1 lime
4   tablespoons light olive oil
Salt and pepper, to taste
1   teaspoon chopped cilantro
1   teaspoon chopped mint
1   cup arugula

Dressing:
1   tablespoon plus 1 cup light olive oil
2   shallots, chopped
1   teaspoon cumin
2   egg yolks (pasteurized is best)
Juice of 1 lime
Salt and pepper to taste

Garnish:
2   California nectarines, sliced thin
6   sprigs fresh cilantro
Light olive oil

For the tarts: Preheat oven to 375°F. Brush 1 sheet of phyllo with ⅓ of melted butter and sprinkle with ⅓ of Parmesan cheese. Repeat with next 2 sheets, layering sheets. Cut phyllo stack into 6 squares, then lay in fluted (6x¾-inch) molds; put same size mold on top and press down. With molds in place, bake for 3-5 minutes, until golden. Cool slightly, then remove top mold and turn out pastry from bottom mold. Cool.

For the filling: Mix nectarines, snow peas, celery and chicken. Stir in lime juice and olive oil. Season with salt and pepper. Stir in cilantro and mint. Put some arugula in bottom of each tart. Top with chicken mixture.

For the dressing: Heat 1 tablespoon of olive oil in a small skillet over medium-low heat. Add shallots; cook until soft. Add cumin and cook for 1 minute more. Transfer mixture to a food processor. Add egg yolks and process until smooth. Add 1 cup of olive oil, lime juice, salt and pepper; process to form a fairly thick dressing.

To assemble: Put a spoonful of dressing onto each plate. Put tart on top of dressing (to keep it from moving). Spoon dressing over tart and filling. Garnish plates with nectarine slices and a sprig of cilantro. Drizzle olive oil around outside of plate and serve.

Twisted Roast Chicken

Michael Messmer won the $10,000 grand prize in the "student" category in the Tabasco's Hottest Chef Recipe Contest. Messmer is a culinary arts student at the Florida Culinary Institute.

Makes 6 Servings

3   roasting chickens, cut into serving pieces
Salt and pepper, to taste
1½   tablespoons vegetable oil
1½   carrots, finely chopped
1½   celery stalks, finely chopped
1   leek, finely chopped
1   large clove garlic, minced
1½   tablespoons all-purpose flour
4   cups chicken broth
Juice of ½ lemon
1   tablespoon honey
1   teaspoon cumin
1½   tablespoons Tabasco Pepper Sauce
2   teaspoons Tabasco Chipotle Pepper Sauce
1   tomato, seeded and chopped
Chopped parsley or cilantro, to taste

Rinse and dry chicken parts (except breasts; reserve them for another use). Season chicken with salt and pepper. Heat oil in a large roasting pan or Dutch oven over medium heat. Add chicken and brown evenly on all sides. Remove chicken; leave oil in pan.

Preheat oven to 325°F. Add carrot, celery and leeks to pan; cook until leeks and celery are translucent. Add garlic and cook lightly (do not brown). Dust with flour and cook slightly, stirring constantly. Add broth and bring to a simmer. Return chicken to pan and simmer for 5-10 minutes. Add lemon, honey, cumin and Tabasco Pepper and Chipotle Sauce. Cover and bake for about 30 minutes, until chicken is cooked through.

Remove chicken from pan and set aside. Add tomatoes to sauce in pan. Reduce sauce, if desired. Skim sauce to remove excess oil. Add parsley or cilantro. Put most of sauce in a serving dish. Put chicken to serving dish. Drizzle chicken with remaining sauce.

Smoky BBQ Chicken

Each year, the Oregon Fryer Commission's recipe contest draws some of the most mouth-watering chicken recipes in the country. John Billups of Portland, Oregon, took second prize with a traditional barbecue sauce that blends the perfect amounts of chile powder, onions, molasses and brown sugar.

Makes 2 to 4 Servings

Barbecue rub:
1   cup paprika
½   cup chili powder
¼   cup cumin
1   teaspoon pepper
½   cup packed brown sugar
2   tablespoons garlic powder
2   tablespoons onion powder
2   tablespoons Chinese five-spice powder
1   Oregon grown chicken

Barbecue sauce:
1   cup ketchup
½   cup water
¼   cup packed brown sugar
3   tablespoons dark molasses
½   cup rice wine vinegar
2   tablespoons minced garlic
2   tablespoons minced onion
3   tablespoons onion powder
3   tablespoons garlic powder
1   tablespoon chile powder
⅛   teaspoon ground cloves
2   tablespoons Worcestershire sauce
1½ teaspoons paprika
½   teaspoon turmeric
1   teaspoon Liquid Smoke

For the barbecue rub: Preheat grill. Mix all ingredients well, except chicken. Rub spice mixture under skin of chicken. Slowly grill chicken using indirect heat.

When chicken is almost done (internal temperature of 120-130°F degrees), begin basting with barbecue sauce. Continue cooking and basting chicken until done. Warm remaining barbecue sauce and serve with chicken.

For the barbecue sauce: Combine all sauce ingredients.

SMOTHERED WITH LOVE CHICKEN

Edwina Gadsby of Great Falls, Montana, won the grand prize in the "Original" Louisiana Hot Sauce Black History Month Recipe Contest. Bruce Foods, maker of the sauce, processes 1 million pounds of hot peppers per day and is also America's leading producer of canned yams – about 40 million cans annually!

Makes 4 Servings

½	cup all-purpose flour
2	teaspoons seasoned salt
2	teaspoons pepper
1	teaspoon garlic powder
4	chicken breast halves
¼	cup vegetable oil
1	small onion, diced
1	cup assorted wild mushrooms, stemmed and sliced
¼	cup finely diced red bell pepper
2	teaspoons minced garlic
1	cup sour cream
½	cup chicken broth
2	teaspoons "Original" Louisiana Hot Sauce

In a large ziplock plastic bag, combine flour, seasoned salt, pepper and garlic powder. Add chicken and toss to coat; shake off excess coating.

Heat oil in a large skillet over medium-high heat. Add chicken; brown on both sides. Remove chicken from skillet and set aside. Pour off all but 2 tablespoons of oil from skillet.

Add onion, mushrooms, bell pepper and garlic to skillet; cook until soft. Add sour cream, broth and hot sauce; mix well. Return chicken to skillet and smother with sauce. Bring to a simmer, cover, lower heat and simmer for 25-35 minutes, until chicken is cooked through.

Jerk Chicken Thighs on Sweet Potato Pancakes

Linda Miranda of Wakefield, Rhode Island, won third prize at the National Chicken Cooking Contest. The contest is sponsored by the National Chicken Council and the U.S. Poultry & Egg Association with the goal of uncovering new trends in chicken cooking and encouraging the development of new chicken recipes.

Makes 4 Servings

Jerk chicken thighs:
1 pound boneless, skinless chicken thighs
2 tablespoons jerk seasoning
2 tablespoons butter
2 tablespoons vegetable oil

Sweet potato pancakes:
2 cups shredded sweet potato
2 tablespoons finely chopped red onion
¼ teaspoon salt
⅛ teaspoon cayenne pepper
⅓ cup all-purpose flour
1 egg, slightly beaten
1 (12-ounce) bottle mango chutney
1 mango, diced
2 tablespoons chopped flat-leaf parsley, for garnish
Rosemary sprigs, for garnish

For the chicken: Preheat oven to 350°F. Rub chicken with jerk seasoning. Heat butter and oil in an oven-proof skillet over medium-high heat. Add chicken and cook for about 2 minutes per side to brown. Put skillet in oven; bake chicken for about 45 minutes, or until fork-tender. Remove chicken from pan and shred.

For the potato pancakes: In a large bowl, combine sweet potato, onion, salt, cayenne, flour and egg; mix well. Spray a skillet with non-stick cooking spray. Heat over medium heat. Add sweet potato mixture, 2 tablespoons at a time, to make small pancakes. Cook pancakes until lightly browned on both sides.

To serve: Top a potato pancake with some shredded chicken and a small dollop of chutney. Top chicken with a second pancake. Put pancake stacks on serving plates and garnish with diced mango and parsley. Pierce each potato pancake stack with a sprig of rosemary.

MOROCCAN CHICKEN & SQUASH TAGINE

Jamie Miller of Maple Grove, Minnesota, won second prize at the National Chicken Cooking Contest. First held in 1949 at a poultry festival, the contest is now one of the nation's leading food events, having held more national cook-offs than any other culinary competition.

Makes 4 Servings

2	tablespoons olive oil
1	whole chicken, cut-up
1	teaspoon salt
½	teaspoon pepper
1	(14-ounce) can low-sodium chicken broth, divided
2	cups chopped onion
4	cloves garlic, minced
1	small jalapeño, seeded and minced
1	teaspoon cinnamon
½	teaspoon ground ginger
1	(1½-pound) butternut squash, peeled, seeded and cut into ¾-inch chunks
⅓	cup chopped dried apricots
⅓	cup minced parsley, divided
¼	cup sliced almonds

Parsley sprigs, for garnish

Heat olive oil in a Dutch oven or large saucepan over medium-high heat. Season chicken with salt and pepper. Add half of chicken to pot and cook, turning, for about 6 minutes, to brown. Remove and repeat with remaining chicken; set aside.

Add ¼ cup of chicken broth and deglaze pan, stirring to scrape browned bits free. Add onion; cook until soft. Add garlic, jalapeño, cinnamon and ginger; cook, stirring, for 1 minute. Add squash, apricots, remaining broth and 2 tablespoons of minced parsley. Bring to a boil. Return chicken to pot, lower heat, cover and simmer for about 35 minutes, until chicken is done and squash is tender.

Remove chicken to a serving dish. Raise heat; boil squash mixture until slightly thickened, about 5 minutes. Pour squash mixture over chicken. Sprinkle with remaining parsley and almonds. Garnish with parsley sprigs.

CITRUS-SEARED CHICKEN WITH ORANGE OLIVE SAUCE

Priscilla Yee of Concord, California, took first prize in the "consumer" category in the Florida's Natural Growers' Citrus Recipe Cook-off. The tangy-sweet orange and grapefruit juices used in this recipe give the sauce a fabulous citrus flavor, and give the chicken coating an extra-special crunch.

Makes 4 Servings

1   cup Florida's Natural Premium Orange Juice
¼   cup Florida's Natural Ruby Red Grapefruit Juice
1   tablespoon Jamaican jerk seasoning, divided
¾   teaspoon cumin
¼   cup all-purpose flour
4   boneless, skinless chicken breast halves
2   tablespoons olive oil
½   cup diced red bell pepper
¼   cup coarsely chopped pimento-stuffed green olives
¼   cup coarsely chopped kalamata olives
1   tablespoon honey
Orange slices, for garnish
Basil sprigs, for garnish

In a medium non-reactive bowl, combine orange juice, grapefruit juice, 2 teaspoons of jerk seasoning and the cumin; mix well. In a shallow bowl, combine flour and remaining 1 teaspoon of jerk seasoning. Dip chicken in orange juice mixture, then coat with flour mixture. Reserve remaining orange juice and flour mixtures.

Heat olive oil in a large non-stick skillet over medium heat. Add chicken; cook for 5 minutes per side, or until golden on outside and no longer pink in center. Transfer chicken to a serving plate and cover with foil to keep warm; reserve oil in skillet.

Add reserved flour mixture to oil in skillet; stir until flour is absorbed. Raise heat to medium. Stir in reserved orange juice mixture, bell pepper, olives and honey. Cook until sauce is thickened and bubbly, about 3-4 minutes.

Serve chicken with sauce. Garnish with orange slices and basil sprigs, if desired.

ARROZ CON POLLO

Patty Knighton of San Diego, California, won first prize in the HERB-OX Comfort Food Recipe Contest at the California State Fair in Sacramento, California. American state fairs can trace their start to Elkanah Watson, a New England farmer and businessman who showcased his sheep in a public square in 1807.

Makes 4 Servings

2	tablespoons vegetable oil
2	chicken breasts, each cut into 6 pieces
½	pound hot Italian sausage, cut into 2-inch pieces
1	small onion, chopped
4	cloves garlic, minced
1	green bell pepper, chopped
1	teaspoon cumin
½	teaspoon paprika
½	teaspoon chili powder
1	teaspoon turmeric
¼	teaspoon red pepper flakes
1	cup canned diced tomatoes
1	bay leaf
2	cups long grain white rice
3	HERB-OX Chicken Flavored Bouillon Cubes

Chopped cilantro, for garnish
Sliced or chopped olives, for garnish

Heat oil in a large, deep skillet over medium heat. Add chicken; cook for 7-10 minutes, until browned on both sides. Remove chicken to a plate. Add sausage to pan and cook until browned; remove to plate with chicken.

Drain all but 2 tablespoons of oil from skillet. Add onion, garlic and bell pepper; cook for 5 minutes. Return chicken and sausage to skillet. Add cumin, paprika, chili powder, turmeric and red pepper flakes. Cook, stirring, for 1 minute. Stir in tomatoes and bay leaf.

Dissolve bouillon in 3¼ cups of boiling water. Add bouillon mixture and rice to skillet. Bring to a boil, lower heat and simmer for about 25 minutes, until rice is tender. Remove bay leaf. Garnish with cilantro and olives to serve.

HOISIN BLACK-EYES & CHICKEN STIR-FRY

This chicken dish won first prize in the 16th annual California Dry Bean Festival. In its inaugural year, the festival's menu featured Basque garbanzos, Portuguese bean soup and baby lima beans con chiles con queso, among other dishes. The versatility of beans continues to amaze festival-goers today.

Makes 4 Servings

2	boneless, skinless chicken breast halves, thinly sliced
2	tablespoons low-sodium soy sauce, divided
1	tablespoon dry sherry
½	cup low-sodium chicken broth
2	tablespoons hoisin sauce
1½	teaspoons sugar
1	teaspoon cornstarch
2	tablespoons vegetable oil, divided
2	cloves garlic, minced
1	jalapeño, seeded and minced
1	small red bell pepper, cut into 1-inch dice
1	stalk celery, sliced diagonally
1	(15-ounce) can black-eyed peas, drained and rinsed
3	cups hot cooked rice

In a medium bowl, combine chicken, 1 tablespoon of soy sauce and sherry. In a small bowl, combine chicken broth, remaining 1 tablespoon of soy sauce, hoisin, sugar and cornstarch.

Heat 1 tablespoon of oil in a wok or large skillet over medium-high heat. Add chicken and stir-fry for about 2 minutes, or until chicken is cooked through; set aside.

Heat remaining 1 tablespoon of oil in wok. Add garlic, jalapeño, bell pepper and celery; stir-fry for 1 minute. Lower heat to medium-low and return chicken to wok along with hoisin mixture and black-eyed peas; stir gently and cook until mixture is heated through and sauce is thickened. Serve over hot rice.

CHERRY CHA CHA CHIPOTLE CHICKEN WITH BASMATI RICE

Margee Berry of White Salmon, Washington, won first prize and a year's supply of Oregon Chicken in the 2003 Oregon Fryer Commission recipe contest. Berry impressed the judges with her creative use of smoky chipotle chilies and tart dried cherries.

Makes 4 Servings

Basmati rice:

2	cups low-sodium chicken broth
1	teaspoon olive oil
1	cup basmati rice
⅓	cup pine nuts, toasted

Cherry cha cha chicken:

4	Oregon grown boneless, skinless chicken breast halves
Salt and pepper, to taste	
2	tablespoons unsalted butter, divided
½	cup chopped shallots
1	tablespoon minced garlic
1	teaspoon cumin
2	bay leaves
2	tablespoons balsamic vinegar
⅓	cup Merlot or other red wine
1	tablespoon minced canned chipotle chilies in adobo sauce*
½	cup cherry preserves
½	cup chopped dried tart cherries

For the rice: In a large saucepan over medium heat, bring chicken broth, oil and rice to a boil. Cover, lower heat to low and cook 20 minutes. Add toasted pine nuts and fluff with a fork just before serving.

For the chicken: Season chicken on both sides with salt and pepper. Melt 1 tablespoon of butter in a large skillet over medium-high heat. Add chicken and cook until golden brown on both sides, about 4 minutes per side; transfer to a plate and keep warm.

Melt remaining 1 tablespoon of butter in skillet. Add shallots and cook until golden brown, about 3-4 minutes. Add garlic and cumin; cook for 1 minute more. Add bay leaves, vinegar, wine, chipotle chilies, cherry preserves and dried cherries; cook for 5 minutes.

Remove bay leaves. Return chicken to skillet and heat through. Divide rice among serving plates. Top with 1 chicken breast and some of the pan sauce.

*Note: Chipotle chiles are smoked jalapeño peppers canned in a spicy adobo sauce. They can be found in the Mexican food section of most larger groceries.

BASIL GRILLED CHICKEN WITH TOMATO BASIL BUTTER

Molly Pardo of Jupiter, Florida, won second prize at Gold Kist Farms' 15th annual Winning Taste Recipe Contest. "While on vacation, I created this dish for my husband's family with ingredients my sister-in-law had on hand. I usually serve it with garlic mashed potatoes and steamed asparagus," said Pardo, a first-time cooking contest entrant.

Makes 6 Servings

Chicken:
6   Gold Kist Farms boneless, skinless, split chicken breasts
¾   cup olive oil
½   cup chopped fresh basil
3   tablespoons grated Romano cheese
¾   teaspoon minced garlic
½   teaspoon Italian seasoning
¾   pound mozzarella cheese, sliced

Tomato basil butter:
1½ sticks unsalted butter, softened
½   cup oil-packed sun-dried tomatoes, drained and chopped
⅓   cup chopped fresh basil
3   tablespoons grated Romano cheese
Salt and pepper, to taste

For the chicken: Rinse chicken and pat dry; place in a non-metallic dish or ziplock plastic bag. Combine olive oil, basil, Romano cheese, garlic and Italian seasoning; pour over chicken, tossing to coat all sides. Cover dish or seal bag; refrigerate for several hours, turning occasionally.

Preheat charcoal or gas grill to medium-high heat. Lightly coat grill grate with oil or non-stick cooking spray. Remove chicken from marinade; discard marinade. Grill chicken about 4-6 inches from heat source for about 7 minutes per side, or until no longer pink inside (160°F on a meat thermometer).

Lower grill heat to low. Top chicken with mozzarella cheese. Close grill and let cheese melt. Put chicken on a platter and top with some tomato basil butter. Serve chicken with remaining tomato basil butter on the side.

For the tomato basil butter: Put softened butter in a small bowl. Add remaining ingredients and blend well. Season with salt and pepper; set aside.

HERB-GRILLED CHICKEN WITH KUMQUAT CHIPOTLE CHUTNEY

This fragrant, light chicken dish with a delightfully flavored kumquat chutney from Angela Pasko of New Port Richey, Florida, won first prize in the "youth entrée" category at the sixth annual Kumquat Festival Cooking Contest in Dade City, Florida. Use fresh herbs for the best result.

Makes 2 Servings

Herb grilled chicken:

2	boneless, skinless chicken breast halves
1	cup golden sherry
1	teaspoon chopped fresh dill
1	teaspoon chopped fresh basil
1	tablespoon chopped garlic
½	cup puréed kumquat
½	teaspoon minced fresh oregano
Dash of curry powder	

Kumquat chipotle chutney:

½	cup puréed kumquat plus ½ cup coarsely chopped kumquat
¼	cup chopped celery
1	tablespoon chopped red onion
½	teaspoon sugar
Dash of salt	
Dash of pepper	
1	teaspoon adobo sauce from canned chipotle peppers, more or less to your taste*

For the chicken: Pound both sides of chicken breast halves with a tenderizing mallet until flat. In a large, stainless steel bowl, combine sherry, dill, basil, garlic, kumquat, oregano and curry powder. Add chicken, cover and refrigerate for at least 4 hours (preferably overnight). Bring chicken to room temperature and preheat grill to high. Grill chicken for 2 minutes per side, or until cooked through. Serve with warm kumquat chutney.

For the chutney: In a small saucepan, combine puréed and chopped kumquat, celery, onion, sugar, salt and pepper. Bring to a boil, lower heat and simmer gently for 30 minutes. Stir in adobo sauce; simmer for 2 minutes more. Cool until warm.

*Note: Chipotle chiles are smoked jalapeño peppers canned in a spicy adobo sauce. They can be found in the Mexican food section of most larger groceries.

Stuffed Roasted Quail with Wild Grains, Broccoli Rabe & a Port Wine Reduction

Carmine Peluso of Kings Beach, California, won the grand prize and a $70,000 scholarship to Johnson & Wales University in the 14th annual National High School Recipe Contest.

Makes 4 Servings

Wild grains:
- ½ cup plus 2 tablespoons extra-virgin olive oil, divided
- 2 cups pecans, coarsely chopped
- ½ cup chopped shallots
- 8 ounces wild rice
- 8 ounces wheat berries
- 2 cups water
- 2 cups chicken stock
- ¼ cup plus 2 tablespoons fresh orange juice
- ¼ cup champagne vinegar
- 1 teaspoon grated orange zest
- ⅔ cup quinoa

Dried fig and chestnut stuffing:
- 10 ounces chestnuts
- 8 ounces dried figs, stemmed and coarsely chopped

Broccoli rabe:
- ½ cup extra-virgin olive oil
- 4 cloves garlic, thinly sliced
- ½ teaspoon red pepper flakes
- 2 pounds broccoli rabe, washed and drained*

Port wine reduction:
- 32 ounces Ruby Port wine, preferably Ramos Pinto

For the grains: Heat ¼ cup plus 2 tablespoons of olive oil in a medium saucepan over medium heat. Add pecans and shallots; cook until shallots are translucent. Add wild rice and wheat berries; stir until coated with oil. Add water and chicken stock. Bring to a boil, cover, lower heat and simmer for 40 minutes.

Add quinoa and stir briefly. Cover and simmer for 15-20 minutes more, or until all liquid is absorbed. Put grains in a bowl. Whisk together remaining ¼ cup of olive oil, orange juice, champagne vinegar and orange zest in a bowl; cover and set aside. Stir orange juice mixture into rice mixture until grains are well coated. Cool to room temperature (uncovered).

For the stuffing: Bring a pot of water to a boil. Make a small cut in chestnuts. Put chestnuts in boiling water, lower heat and simmer for 15 minutes. Remove chestnuts, peel and coarsely chop. In a bowl, combine chestnuts and figs; cover and chill until needed.

For the broccoli rabe: Heat olive oil in a large skillet over medium heat. Add garlic and red pepper flakes; cook until fragrant. Add broccoli rabe; cook until tender, about 10 minutes. Season with salt and pepper. Set aside and keep warm.

For the port wine reduction: Put port in a heavy, medium saucepan. Bring to a boil over high heat and reduce to about 1 cup; pour into a small bowl and set aside.

Roasted quail:

4   (5-ounce) quail, boned except
     for thigh and wing bones*
Salt and pepper, to taste
12 fresh sage leaves, for garnish
3   fresh figs, sliced, for garnish
¼   cup extra-virgin olive oil
Grated orange zest, for garnish

For the quail: Preheat oven to 425°F. Bone quail by cutting through shoulder joints at the tendon, pulling from the top or bottom and removing carcass without cutting skin. Pat quail dry with paper towels. Season with salt and pepper. Put quail on a dish and drizzle with olive oil.

Stuff quail with chestnut stuffing. Heat a large oven-proof skillet over medium heat. Add quail, breast-side-up, and cook for 3 minutes. Put pan in oven and roast quail for 10 minutes. Brush quail with ¼ cup of port wine reduction, then broil for 5 minutes, or until skin is dark.

To serve: Drizzle about 2 tablespoons of port reduction onto each of 4 heated dinner plates. Put 1 cup of grains on plate in the shape of an X. Put 1 cup of broccoli rabe between grains, also in the shape of an X. Put 1 quail in center of each plate. Put 3 leaves of sage on outer part of plate with a slice of fig on top each leaf. Top quail with a little orange zest and serve.

*Note: This recipe would also be delicious with boned Cornish game hens. You can ask your butcher to bone the quails or hens.

PEAR-GLAZED CORNISH HENS WITH APPLE & PEAR STUFFING

Brian Goldsack of Milford, Pennsylvania was the "youth" category grand prize winner in the fourth annual Pear Blossom Cook-off in Milford, Pennsylvania. Cooks of all ages take their pear tarts, pies, cakes, breads and casseroles for judging by a team of well-seasoned pear connoisseurs.

Makes 2 Servings

2   Cornish game hens
Salt and pepper, to taste
Olive oil
1   pear, peeled and chopped
1   apple, peeled and chopped
¼   stick butter
1   (12-ounce) package stuffing
    mix
1   cup water

Preheat oven to 400°F. Wash hens thoroughly, inside and out. Put hens in a deep roasting pan. Season with salt and pepper and brush with oil. Add pear and apple to pan. Roast hens for 60-75 minutes, basting often with pan juices, until done.

Remove hens from pan; set aside. Transfer pan sauce, apples and pears to a saucepan over medium heat; reduce liquid by half. Prepare stuffing according to package directions. Stir half of apple mixture into stuffing.

Place 1 hen on each plate. Serve hens with stuffing and remaining apple mixture. Drizzle pan sauce over hens and stuffing.

EASTERN WILD TURKEY ROULADE WITH ORANGE SAUCE

The White Marsh and Lower Cape Fear River Chapters of Wildlife Action sponsor the annual North Carolina Wildlife Action Wild Game Cook-off and Sportsman's Expo. Cooks compete in the categories of "fin, fur or fowl." Bill White's turkey roulade won the "fowl" category in 2003.

Makes 4 Servings

Turkey:
2 tablespoons butter
1 shallot, finely chopped
1 clove garlic, minced
2 wild turkey breasts, deboned (or domestic turkey breasts)
1 pound thick bacon
2 (10-ounce) packages frozen chopped spinach, thawed and squeezed dry
Salt and pepper, to taste
1 teaspoon dried thyme
½ pound prosciutto, thinly sliced

Orange sauce:
½ cup red wine vinegar
¼ cup sugar
1¼ cups fresh orange juice
1 cup chicken or turkey stock or broth
1 teaspoon grated orange zest

For the turkey: Melt butter in a skillet over medium heat. Add shallots and cook for 2 minutes, or until soft. Add garlic and cook for 1 minute. Add spinach and cook until almost dry. Remove to a bowl and set aside.

Butterfly turkey breasts, place between plastic wrap and pound to ¼-inch thick. Lay bacon on parchment or wax paper, with slices overlapping one another. Top bacon with turkey. Sprinkle with salt, pepper and thyme. Layer with prosciutto, then spread half of spinach mixture in a thin layer on each turkey breast, leaving a ½-inch border. With the parchment or wax paper, roll up breasts jelly-roll style; secure with toothpicks or kitchen twine.

Grill turkey slowly for 30-45 minutes, turning once halfway through cooking time, until done (juices run clear and internal temperature is 150°F). Remove turkey from grill; let stand for 5 minutes. Remove toothpicks or twine. Slice ½-inch thick. Serve with warm orange sauce.

For the sauce: In a saucepan over low heat, combine vinegar and sugar; cook, stirring, until sugar dissolves. Raise heat and boil until mixture starts to brown and caramelize, about 5 minutes. Add orange juice and chicken stock. Boil mixture until reduced to 1 cup. Add orange zest; simmer until reduced to ¾ cup. Keep warm.

TACCHINO DI PERLA

Student Chef Ming-Chu "Pearl" Lin and her Tacchino di Perla (Turkey by Pearl) won the National Turkey Federation's Turkey For All Seasons Recipe Contest. Lin graduated from the Culinary Institute of America (CIA) and then entered "Cucina e Cultura," a CIA-sponsored, 15-week study of Italian cuisine and culture that inspired this recipe.

Makes 2 Servings

Spicy tomato sauce:
¼   cup extra-virgin olive oil, divided
2   cloves garlic, chopped
2   cups cherry tomatoes, washed
½   cup turkey or chicken stock or broth
2   tablespoons minced fresh basil
Salt, pepper and red pepper flakes, to taste

Turkey:
2   (7-ounce) boneless, skinless turkey breast, butterflied
Salt and pepper, to taste
2   very thin slices prosciutto
3   ounces fontina cheese, cut into strips
6   fresh sage leaves
½   cup breadcrumbs
½   cup chopped toasted hazelnuts
½   cup all-purpose flour
2   large eggs, beaten
¼   cup olive oil

Arugula salad:
2   cups arugula, chilled
Extra-virgin olive oil
Juice of ½ lemon
Salt and pepper, to taste
2   tablespoons chopped parsley, for garnish

For the tomato sauce: Heat 2 tablespoons of oil over medium heat. Add garlic and cherry tomatoes; cook until softened. Add turkey stock; cook for 10 minutes. Coarsely purée in a food processor or blender. Return to saucepan and simmer for 5 minutes. Add basil. Season with salt, pepper and red pepper flakes. Finish with 1-2 tablespoons of remaining olive oil, as needed.

For the turkey: Pound turkey breasts between pieces of plastic wrap to ¼-inch thick; trim each breast into a 6x6-inch square. Season with salt and pepper. Cover each turkey square with a layer of prosciutto. Put cheese and sage leaves in an even line on bottom edge of each turkey square. Roll up from bottom, so cheese and sage are in the middle of the rolls.

Preheat oven to 400°F. Mix breadcrumbs and hazelnuts. Dip turkey in flour, coat with egg and then roll in bread-crumb mixture. Heat oil in an oven-proof skillet over medium heat. Cook turkey until golden brown on both sides. Transfer to oven and bake for 10-15 minutes, or until internal temperature is 170°F. Remove from oven and let stand for 5 minutes. Slice each roll diagonally into 3 pieces that can stand upright.

For the salad and to serve: Toss arugula with oil, lemon juice, salt and pepper. Divide salad among plates. Stand turkey roll slices on end atop salad. Sprinkle with spicy tomato sauce. Garnish with parsley.

SEARED DUCK BREASTS WITH CHERRY SALSA & DRIED CHERRY POLENTA

This sophisticated, yet simple duck won the Northwestern Michigan College Culinary Arts' National Cherry Festival Taste of Cherries Recipe Contest.

Makes 4 Servings

Duck:

2	cups cherry Riesling wine
1	cup soy sauce
4	star anise
2	cardamom pods
½	teaspoon coarse black pepper
4	boneless duck breast halves
2	tablespoons vegetable oil

Cherry brandy

Cherry salsa:

2	cups fresh or frozen pitted cherries
2	oranges, peeled, membranes removed
4	teaspoons grated orange zest
1	cup sugar
¼	cup finely chopped onion
1	tablespoon ground coriander
1	tablespoon minced peeled ginger
1-2	jalapeños, seeded and minced

Salt, to taste
Cherry Riesling wine, as needed

Dried cherry polenta:

2	cups water
2	cups chicken stock or broth
1½	cups polenta (or cornmeal)
2	egg yolks
1	cup grated Parmesan cheese
½	cup coarsley chopped dried cherries

For the duck: Combine cherry Riesling, soy sauce, star anise, cardamom pods and pepper. Warm mixture over a low heat until hot (about 140°F). Cool completely, add duck breasts, cover and refrigerate for 1 hour to marinate.

Preheat oven to 400°F. Remove duck from marinade and pat dry; discard marinade. Heat oil in a skillet over medium-high heat until almost smoking. Sear duck, skin-side-down, for 1 minute; turn and sear the other side. Remove duck to a roasting pan; drain fat. Deglaze skillet with cherry brandy. Reduce sauce slightly and set aside. Roast duck for 10-12 minutes (medium-rare to medium). Remove from oven and let stand for 5 minutes.

To serve: Put 2 triangles of polenta on a plate. Spoon some pan sauce over polenta. Slice duck diagonally and fan over polenta. Top with a spoonful of salsa.

For the salsa: Chop cherries and oranges coarsely; put in a saucepan with remaining salsa ingredients and enough cherry Riesling to moisten ingredients. Bring to a boil, lower heat and simmer for about 30 minutes or until thickened. Cool and serve at room temperature.

For the polenta: In a saucepan, bring water and chicken stock to a boil. Whisk in polenta, cover, lower heat and simmer slowly for about 20 minutes. Add cherries, egg yolks and cheese; spread mixture about 1/2-inch thick on an oiled baking sheet. Cover and refrigerate until firm. Cut into squares, then into triangles. Heat a little butter or oil in a skillet over medium heat. Add polenta and cook until golden brown on both sides.

DUCK BREAST WITH POTATO CRISP & BLACK PEPPER CRANBERRY SAUCE

Chef Sean Griffin of the Four Seasons Hotel in Los Angeles, California, won the grand prize in the Maple Leaf Farms' Culinary Chefs Recipe Contest. Maple Leaf Farms, a family-run business that began in 1958, has grown into the nation's leading duck producer.

Makes 6 Servings

Duck:
6 (6-ounce) Maple Leaf Farms boneless duck breasts
Salt and pepper

Black pepper cranberry sauce:
8 ounces duck demi-glace*
¾ cup cranberries, cooked
1 tablespoon freshly cracked black pepper

Potato crisp:
2 large Idaho potatoes, peeled and julienned
¼ cup canola oil
Salt and pepper, to taste

For the duck: Preheat oven to 375°F. Score duck breast skin at ¼-inch intervals, being careful not to cut into breast meat. Rotate breasts and score again making a criss-cross pattern. Season with salt and pepper.

Heat an oven-proof skillet over medium-low heat. Add duck breasts, skin-side-down; cook for 8-12 minutes, or until fat is rendered and skin is crisp and brown. Turn and cook for 1-2 minutes more. Put skillet in oven for 8-10 minutes, or until internal temperature of duck is 160°F. Let duck cool for 2-3 minutes, then slice thinly.

For the cranberry sauce: Heat together duck demi-glace and enough cranberries to form a sauce-like consistency. Stir in pepper.

For the potato crisp: Toss potatoes in oil; season with salt and pepper. In a skillet over medium-high heat, add 1/6 of potatoes; spread very thinly and loosely. Cook until browned; turn and cook until crisp. Drain potato crisp on paper towels. Repeat with remaining potatoes to make 6 potato crisps.

To serve: Fan slices of duck on each plate. Drizzle sauce around plate. Serve with potato crisp.

*Note: Duck demi-glace is a rich stock base used to make sauces. It is available in the meat or sauce sections of some groceries. If duck demi-glace is unavailable, substitute chicken demi-glace.

PORK

Spicy Sweet Sticky Summertime Ribs

Christine Erickson of Madison, Wisconsin, won second prize in the "international" category at the Food For Thought Recipe Contest. She said, "This recipe was inspired by a Korean friend who makes great ribs. These are Asian-style, not the barbeque sauce-type common here in America. I call them 'Four-S Ribs' for they are spicy, sweet, sticky summertime ribs!"

Makes 2 Servings

Ribs:

2½ pounds pork spare ribs, cut into 3 portions
4   small hot chile peppers (Thai Dragon, Mexi-Hot or Fire Cracker recommended), seeded and sliced
4-5 cloves garlic, chopped
3-4 tablespoons chopped mint
1-2 stalks fresh lemon grass (the tender bottom part), finely chopped, or 1½ teaspoons dried lemon grass
Soy sauce
2   tablespoons fresh lemon juice
2   tablespoons wildflower honey, warmed slightly (aids mixing)

Glaze:

2   tablespoons chopped mint
2-3 tablespoons grated peeled ginger
2   tablespoons soy sauce
3   tablespoons garlic chili sauce
¼   cup honey, warmed slightly
Juice of 1 lime

For the ribs: With a mortar and pestle (or in a blender), pulverize chile peppers, garlic, mint and lemon grass (the peppers can squirt – protect your eyes); put mixture in a measuring cup. Add enough soy sauce to reach the ⅔-cup mark. Add lemon juice. Add honey and mix well. Taste and adjust seasonings, if needed (the mixture should be pretty hot for it to infuse the meat well – it should have a nice balance of salty, tart, hot and minty).

Put ribs in a shallow bowl or dish. Pour soy sauce mixture over ribs; turn ribs to coat. Cover and refrigerate for 8-24 hours (the longer the better), turning ribs occasionally.

About 90 minutes before serving, put ribs in a roasting pan. Pour some marinade over ribs and add ½ cup of water; discard marinade. Cover with foil. Preheat oven to 375°F. Bake for 30-40 minutes; remove from oven.

For the glaze: Preheat grill to medium-low heat. Combine mint, ginger, soy sauce, garlic chili sauce and honey. Add lime juice. Taste; add more lime juice and soy sauce as needed to balance flavors. Put ribs on grill meat-side-up; brush with glaze. Grill, turning and glazing every 3-5 minutes, for about 40 minutes. When done, the ribs should be sticky and shiny looking, with a few crispy charred parts, and the meat will have come away from the bone on the edges. Remove ribs and slice into individual ribs to serve.

BLUEBERRY RHUBARB PORKCHOPS

Maine blueberries have been found to have considerable nutritional value. The berries are harvested in August and are celebrated each year with the Machias Wild Blueberry Festival on the third weekend in August. Suzanne Plaisted of Jonesboro, Maine, won first prize in the "entrée" category with these pork chops.

Makes 4 Servings

4	pork chops
¼	cup all-purpose flour
	Salt and pepper
2	cups chopped rhubarb
2	cups Maine blueberries
2	tablespoons brown sugar
⅛	teaspoon cinnamon

Coat pork chops with flour and season with salt and pepper. In a skillet sprayed with non-stick cooking spray, cook pork chops over medium heat until browned on both sides.

Combine rhubarb, blueberries, sugar and cinnamon; pour over pork chops. Simmer until pork is tender and cooked through.

Spiced Pork Tenderloin with Bacardi Gold BBQ Sauce, Sweet Potatoes & Apple Citrus Slaw

Executive Chef Christopher D. Stallard, of the Little Star in Knoxville, Tennessee, won "best of show" and $10,000 in the Johnson & Wales University/Bacardi Recipe Classic.

Makes 4 Servings

Bacardi Gold barbecue sauce:
1½ tablespoons olive oil
1 cup diced onion
3 cloves garlic, minced
1 cup orange juice
1 cup tomato juice
½ cup Worcestershire sauce
¼ cup Dijon mustard
2 tablespoons soy sauce
¼ cup packed brown sugar
2 tablespoons balsamic vinegar
1 cup ketchup
½ cup Bacardi Gold Rum
½ teaspoon ground coriander
½ teaspoon ground ginger
¼ teaspoon pepper
¼ teaspoon cumin
Pinch of kosher salt

Sweet potato sauté:
6 cups cubed sweet potatoes
2 tablespoons olive oil
1½ cups thinly sliced Vidalia onion
1½ cups Bacardi Gold BBQ sauce
   (above recipe)
Salt and pepper, to taste

For the barbecue sauce: Heat oil in a large saucepan over medium heat. Add onion and garlic; cook until onion begins to turn translucent. Add remaining ingredients. Bring to a boil, lower heat and simmer for 30 minutes. Strain sauce and keep warm.

For the sweet potatoes: In a large saucepan, bring enough water to a boil to cover sweet potatoes. Add potatoes and cook for about 15-20 minutes, until tender. Remove potatoes from water and place in an ice water bath.

Heat oil in a skillet over medium heat. Add onion; cook until translucent. Drain potatoes and add to skillet along with 1½ cups barbecue sauce; stir to combine. Season with salt and pepper.

RECIPE CONTINUED

Spiced pork tenderloin:
2 teaspoons cinnamon
2 tablespoons ground ginger
¼ cup ground coriander
¼ cup packed brown sugar
¼ cup plus 2 tablespoons Bacardi Gold Rum
3½ pounds pork tenderloin, fat trimmed, silver skin removed
Salt and pepper, to taste
3 tablespoons olive oil

Apple citrus slaw:
Grated zest and juice of 2 oranges
Grated zest and juice of 1 lemon
Grated zest and juice of 1 lime
¾ cup mayonnaise
3 tablespoons Bacardi Gold Rum
¼ cup sugar
¾ cup chopped cilantro
3 cups shredded savoy cabbage
2 cups julienned apple
¾ cup chopped peeled carrot
Salt and pepper, to taste

For the pork: Preheat oven to 400°F. Combine cinnamon, ginger, coriander, brown sugar and rum. Rub pork with cinnamon mixture. Season with salt and pepper.

In a large skillet, heat oil over medium heat. Add pork and sear until browned on all sides. Transfer pork to a baking sheet and bake for 15-20 minutes, or until it reaches an internal temperature of 155°F.

For the slaw: In a small bowl, combine orange, lemon and lime juice and zest, mayonnaise, rum, sugar and cilantro. In a large bowl, toss together cabbage, apples and carrot. Add orange juice mixture and toss to combine. Season with salt and pepper.

To serve: Put some sweet potatoes in center of each plate. Slice pork into 24 slices. Put 3 slices of pork on top of sweet potatoes on each plate. Top pork with some citrus slaw. Drizzle barbecue sauce around plate and over pork.

ALMOND-CRUSTED PORK LOIN WITH PEACH CHUTNEY

Gerard Gander, a chef in southern California for almost 20 years, won the "entrée" category at the Eat California Fruit Make It Special With California Peaches, Plums and Nectarines Recipe Contest. Crunchy almonds and a California plum paste jazz up a pork loin served with fresh California peach chutney.

Makes 4 Servings

Almond crusted pork loin:
4-5 medium California plums
2 tablespoons water
¼ cup miso paste
½ cup mirin*
½ cup rice wine vinegar
2 tablespoons chopped canned chipotle peppers**

Pork loin:
2½ pounds pork loin
2 cups sliced blanched almonds

Peach chutney:
3 yellow California peaches
3 white California peaches
3 tablespoons olive oil
1 medium red bell pepper, chopped
2 medium green bell peppers, chopped
1 tablespoon minced seeded jalapeño
2 medium red onions, chopped
3 cups peach nectar
1 cup champagne vinegar
1 cup orange juice concentrate
1 cup brown sugar
Salt and pepper, to taste

For the plum paste: Cut a small **X** on bottom of each plum. Dip in boiling water for 30 seconds, then remove to a bowl of ice water for 1 minute. Peel and chop plums. In a saucepan over medium heat, heat 2 tablespoons of water and chopped plum; cook until softened, then cool slightly. Add miso paste, mirin, rice wine vinegar and chipotle peppers. Purée mixture in a food processor to form a paste.

For the pork: Preheat oven to 350°F. Roast pork until ⅔ done (with an internal temperature of 120°F). Cool for 20 minutes. Cut pork loin into 8 (4½-ounce) portions. Toast almonds slightly, then crush. Coat pork with plum paste, then roll in crushed almonds. Roast for about 10 minutes, until done. Serve with peach chutney.

For the chutney: Halve peaches and cut into ½-inch slices. Heat oil in a skillet over high heat. Add red and green bell pepper, jalapeño and onion; cook until onion is translucent. Add peach nectar, champagne vinegar, orange juice concentrate and brown sugar; bring to a boil and cook until liquid is reduced by half. Add peaches. Bring to a boil, lower heat and simmer for 10 minutes. Remove from heat. Season with salt and pepper.

*Note: Mirin is salted, sweet rice cooking wine found in the Asian section of larger groceries.

**Note: Chipotle chiles are smoked jalapeño peppers that can be found in the Mexican section of most groceries.

SAUSAGE-STUFFED, BACON-WRAPPED PORK TENDERLOIN WITH BACON & CHERRY RELISH

Jeni Dise of Phoenix, Arizona, won first prize in the "entrée" category at the Farmer John Meats' Everything's Better Wrapped in Bacon Recipe Contest.

Makes 10 Servings

Pork tenderloin:

1⅓	pounds Farmer John Pork Tenderloin (2 tenderloins), butterflied
¾	cup Farmer John Roll Hot Sausage
⅓	cup chopped red onion
¼	teaspoon pepper
12	slices Farmer John Bacon

Bacon and cherry relish:

6	slices Farmer John Bacon
1	cup bing cherries, pitted and chopped
1	tablespoon minced, seeded serrano chile pepper
1	tablespoon chopped cilantro

For the pork tenderloin: Preheat oven to 400°F. Pound each pork tenderloin between 2 pieces of plastic wrap to ¼- to ½-inch thick. Cook sausage in a skillet over medium heat until cooked through. Stir in onion and black pepper; cook for 3 minutes. Drain and set aside.

Lay each pork tenderloin on top of 6 slices of bacon. Spread half of sausage mixture over each tenderloin. Fold tenderloins in half, enclosing sausage mixture inside. Wrap tenderloins with bacon. Secure with toothpicks.

Put tenderloin on a baking sheet or in a roasting pan and roast until bacon is crisp and tenderloin is cooked through, about 30 minutes. Remove from oven and let stand for 5 minutes. Slice and serve with warm bacon and cherry relish.

For the relish: Cook bacon until crisp; remove from pan, drain on paper towels and crumble. Pour off all but 2-3 tablespoons of bacon drippings from pan. Add cherries and chile; cook for 3 minutes. Stir in cilantro and bacon; remove from heat.

PORK WITH MOLE SAUCE & PUMPKINSEED VINAIGRETTE

The Taste of Elegance is one of the major cooking events for professional chefs. Sponsored by the National Pork Board, this culinary competition is designed to inspire innovative and exciting ways to use pork. The "Premium Chef" title and $1,000 went to chef Todd M. McDunn of Café Limited in Columbus, Ohio.

Makes 4 to 6 Servings

Pork belly (or bacon):
¼   teaspoon ground cloves
1   teaspoon coriander seeds
1   teaspoon black peppercorns
1   cinnamon stick
½   cup kosher salt
1   clove garlic, minced
¼   cup sugar
2   bay leaves
7   sprigs thyme
7   sprigs oregano
2   pounds lean raw pork belly
     (unsmoked bacon)
Mirepoix*
8   cups chicken stock

Onion, apple & cherry sauté:
12-16 cippolini onions
1   tablespoon butter
1   large Gala apple, small dice
2   tablespoons dried cherries

Vinaigrette and pork tenderloin:
¼   cup olive oil
¼   cup pumpkin seed oil
¼   cup pumpkin seeds, toasted
¼   cup peanuts, toasted
2   tablespoons white wine vinegar
1   tablespoon sherry vinegar
2   tablespoons water
2   tablespoons grape seed oil
1   (12-ounce) pork tenderloin

For the pork belly: Preheat oven to 400°F. Toast cloves, coriander, peppercorns and cinnamon in oven for 5 minutes; crush in a food processor, then combine with salt, garlic, sugar, bay leaves, thyme and oregano. Score the fat of the pork belly with a knife and rub in spice mixture. Cover and refrigerate for 24-48 hours.

Preheat oven to 350°F. Rub spices off pork. Put mirepoix in a Dutch oven or oven-proof skillet with a lid. Top with pork belly. Add chicken stock. Bring to a boil on stove, then cover and transfer to oven. Roast for 3 hours. Uncover pan and roast for 30 minutes longer, basting every 10 minutes. Slice into 2x2-inch squares; set aside.

For onion, apple and cherry sauté: Cook onions in salted boiling water for 3 minutes; cool and peel. Heat butter in a skillet over medium heat. Add onions; cook for 5 minutes. Add apple and cherries; cook until apple is tender. Season with salt and pepper; set aside.

For the vinaigrette and pork tenderloin: Make vinaigrette by puréeing olive and pumpkin seed oil, pumpkin seeds, peanuts, white wine and sherry vinegar and water. Strain through a fine sieve. Season with salt and pepper.

Heat grape seed oil in a skillet over medium heat. Season pork tenderloin with salt and pepper. Add pork to skillet and cook, browning all sides, for 10-15 minutes, or until internal temperature is 150-155°F. Remove pork and let stand for 5 minutes, then cut into ½-inch slices.

Mole sauce:

1	ancho chile, seeded and chopped
1	canned chipotle chile, seeded and chopped*
3	tablespoons bacon fat (or lard)
1	large onion, diced
3	cloves garlic
1	jalapeño, seeded and chopped
1	small green apple, chopped
¼	cup chopped almonds, toasted
¼	cup chopped pumpkin seeds, toasted
¼	cup chopped peanuts, toasted
1	tablespoon sesame seeds
½	teaspoon cinnamon
2	whole cloves
¼	teaspoon nutmeg
5	dried apricots, diced
¼	cup dried cherries
¼	cup raisins
2	tablespoons dried cranberries
2	tablespoons dried blueberries
3	cups chicken stock or broth
1	teaspoon minced fresh oregano
3	sprigs of thyme
2½	ounces good quality dark chocolate, chopped
½	cup chopped Challah bread

Salt and pepper, to taste

For the mole: Put ancho and chipotle chiles in a skillet over medium heat; cook for 10 minutes. Add bacon fat, onion, garlic, jalapeño and apple; cook for 10 minutes. Add almonds, pumpkin seeds, peanuts, sesame seeds, cinnamon, cloves and nutmeg; cook for 7-10 minutes. Add dried fruits; cook for 10 minutes. Add chicken stock, oregano and thyme; cook for 15 minutes. Add chocolate and bread; cook for 20 minutes. If sauce is too thick, thin with more chicken stock. Purée sauce in a food processor or blender, then strain through a fine sieve. Season with salt and pepper. Keep warm.

To serve: Spoon some mole in center of each plate. Place alternating slices of pork tenderloin and pork belly on top of mole, 3 slices of each per serving. Drizzle some vinaigrette around edges of each plate. Top pork with some cippolini onion mixture.

*Note: A mirepoix is a mixture of onion, celery and carrot used as a base for braising (browning meat on stove, then roasting, covered). To make a mirepoix, melt 1 tablespoon of butter in a small skillet over medium heat. Add ½ cup chopped onion, ¼ cup chopped carrot and ¼ cup chopped celery; cook until soft.

**Note: Chipotle chiles are smoked jalapeño peppers canned in a spicy adobo sauce. They can be found in the Mexican food section of most larger groceries.

GRECIAN PORK-FILLED PUMPKIN FLATBREAD

Liz Deppe of Morton, Illinois, won first prize at the 2003 Morton Pumpkin Fest in Morton. Morton is the "Pumpkin Capital of the World," home of Libby's pumpkin packing plant, where over 85 percent of the world's canned pumpkin is produced.

Makes 4 to 6 Servings

Pumpkin flatbread:
2½ teaspoons yeast
2   tablespoons sugar
¼   cup lukewarm water
1   large egg
¾   cup Libby's canned pumpkin
1½ teaspoons salt
5½ cups all-purpose flour
2   tablespoons olive oil
1½ cups milk

Pork:
2½ pounds boneless pork loin
Juice of 1 lemon
1   teaspoon dried oregano
½   cup Pinot Grigio wine
3   tablespoons olive oil
¼   teaspoon salt
½   teaspoon dry mustard
2   cloves garlic, minced

Pumpkin sauce:
¼   cup Libby's canned pumpkin
3   tablespoons mustard
½   teaspoon garlic powder
½   teaspoon dried oregano
½   teaspoon Greek seasoning
3   tablespoons olive oil
½   teaspoon kosher salt
4 grinds of pepper
½   cup quartered kalamata olives
Sliced red onion, for garnish
Tzatziki sauce, for serving*

For the flatbread: Mix and knead all flatbread ingredients in a food processor for about 3 minutes. Let rise in processor until doubled in size. Process down and chill. Shape lemon-size portions of dough into ¼-inch thick flat round disks. Stack between sheets of parchment paper on a baking sheet. Cover and refrigerate overnight. Grill on a very lightly greased griddle, turning once. Cool slightly. Cover and set aside until serving.

For the pork: Freeze pork slightly, then slice very thinly. Combine lemon juice, oregano, wine, olive oil, salt, dry mustard and garlic in a ziplock plastic bag. Add pork and turn to coat. Seal bag and refrigerate overnight.

For the pumpkin sauce: Combine pumpkin, mustard, garlic powder, oregano, Greek seasoning, olive oil, salt and pepper in a microwaveable bowl.

To serve: Remove pork from marinade; discard marinade. Grill pork or cook in a lightly oiled skillet until browned and cooked through. Heat pumpkin sauce in microwave. Stir in kalamata olives. Spoon sauce over middle of warmed flatbread. Top with pork and red onion slices. Spoon tzatziki sauce over all and roll or fold up.

*Note: Tzatziki is a Greek cucumber sauce. To make tzatziki, combine ½ cup plain low-fat yogurt, 1 cup peeled, seeded and diced cucumber, ¼ teaspoon garlic powder, 1 teaspoon dried dill, 8 fresh dill sprigs and ½ teaspoon salt. Mix well, cover and chill until serving.

BEEF & VENISON

GRILLED STEAKS BALSAMICO

Lori Welander of Richmond, Virginia, won the $50,000 grand prize at the 25th National Beef Cook-off.
The 2003 competition focused on ways busy families can get dinner on the table, such as this simple steak.

Makes 4 Servings

⅔ cup balsamic vinegar
¼ cup fig preserves or chopped
   dried figs
4 (6- to 8-ounce) beef shoulder
   top blade (flat iron) steaks or
   boneless beef chuck eye
   steaks, cut 1-inch thick
Salt and pepper, to taste
1 (5.2-ounce) package herb and
   garlic soft spreadable cheese

Purée balsamic vinegar and fig preserves in a blender or food processor. Put fig mixture and steaks in food-safe plastic bag; turn to coat. Seal bag and refrigerate for at least 2 hours.

Preheat grill to medium. Remove steaks from bag; discard marinade. Grill steaks, covered, turning occasionally, for 10-14 minutes (for medium-rare to medium doneness). Remove steaks from grill and season with salt and pepper. Let steaks stand for 5 minutes.

While steaks rest, heat cheese in a small saucepan over medium-low heat, stirring frequently, until melted, about 2-4 minutes. Serve steaks with cheese sauce.

SOUTH PACIFIC STEAKS

Linda Morten of Katy, Texas, won first prize and $10,000 in the "grilled beef" category at the 2003 National Beef Cook-off. Non-traditional ingredients, such as this tropical combination of hoisin sauce and fresh pineapple, add a unique flavor flair to these steaks and kabobs.

Makes 4 Servings

1½ cups fresh pineapple chunks packed in juice
½   cup hoisin sauce
4   beef chuck eye steaks, cut 1-inch thick or 4 beef shoulder top blade (flat iron) steaks (6- to 8-ounces each)
1   large red bell pepper, cut into 1½-inch pieces
1   small red onion, cut into 8 wedges
⅓   cup apricot preserves
2   tablespoons fresh lemon juice
2   tablespoons chopped cilantro, for garnish

Drain pineapple; reserve ½ cup of juice. Combine hoisin sauce and reserved pineapple juice. Put steaks in a food-safe plastic bag. Add ¼ cup of hoisin mixture and turn to coat. Seal bag and refrigerate for 30 minutes.

Alternately thread pineapple, bell pepper and onion on 4 (12-inch) skewers. Put skewers in a glass dish; brush with ¼ cup of hoisin mixture. Cover and refrigerate for 30 minutes.

Preheat grill to medium. Remove steaks and kabobs from marinade; discard marinade. Grill steaks and kabobs for 10-14 minutes, covered, turning occasionally, until steaks are medium-rare to medium and kabobs are crisp-tender.

When steaks are almost done, in a small saucepan over medium heat, heat apricot preserves, lemon juice and remaining ½ cup of hoisin mixture, stirring, until hot. Pour sauce over steaks. Sprinkle with cilantro to serve.

GARLICKY SKIRT STEAK NACHOS WITH TOMATILLO SALSA

Chef Ryan Brown of Sol Kitchen in Delray Beach, Florida, won second prize in the "Appetizer" category at the 2003 Delray Beach Garlic Fest. In this head-to-head competition, each chef has identical ingredients and one hour to produce three gourmet dishes for the judges.

Makes 4 Servings

Tomatillo salsa:
8   tomatillos, husked, grilled and chopped*
1   red onion, finely chopped
1   large clove garlic, minced
Juice of 2 limes
1   jalapeño, seeded and minced
½   bunch cilantro, finely chopped
Pinch of salt

Skirt steak nachos:
2   (10- to 12-ounce) skirt steaks
1   large clove garlic, minced
Juice of 2 limes
½   bunch cilantro, finely chopped
1   teaspoon toasted cumin seeds, ground (or cumin powder)
2   tablespoons olive oil
1   (13-ounce) bag tortilla chips
2   cups grated smoked Monterey Jack cheese

Green onion sour cream:
Juice of 2 limes
1   cup sour cream
1   bunch green onions, thinly sliced

For the salsa: Combine all salsa ingredients. Cover and refrigerate until serving.

For the skirt steak nachos: Put steaks in a glass baking dish. Whisk together garlic, lime juice, cilantro, cumin and olive oil; pour over steaks. Cover and refrigerate steaks for 30 minutes to marinate.

Preheat grill. Grill steaks to desired temperature, then slice into thin strips. Preheat oven to 400°F. Put tortilla chips on a large, oven-proof platter. Scatter skirt steak over chips. Sprinkle with cheese. Bake for 2-3 minutes, or until cheese is melted. Top with tomatillo salsa and sour cream mixture to serve.

For the sour cream: Combine all ingredients.

*Note: Tomatillos are small, tart Mexican green tomatoes with a papery husk that is easily removed. They can be found in most larger groceries.

FORTY CLOVES OF GARLIC & BALSAMIC-BRAISED SHORT RIBS

Now in its fifth year, the Delray Beach Garlic Fest continues to offer Florida garlic fans the opportunity to celebrate the most widely used and loved food in the world – garlic! Chef Cathy Cox of the Old Calypso in Delray Beach took second prize in the "entrée" category at the 2003 festival.

Makes 6 to 8 Servings

5	pounds beef short ribs
1¼	teaspoons salt
1¼	tablespoons paprika
2½	teaspoons granulated garlic
2½	teaspoons granulated onion
1¼	teaspoons white pepper
1¼	teaspoons black pepper
1¼	teaspoons cumin
½	cup canola oil, divided
4	cups chopped onion
1¼	cups chopped carrot
1¼	cups chopped celery
40	cloves garlic
1	cup balsamic vinegar
1	cup all-purpose flour
4	cups beef stock or broth

Trim excess fat from short ribs. Combine salt, paprika, granulated garlic and onion, white and black pepper and cumin; rub into meat.

Heat a Dutch oven over high heat until pan is very hot. Put ribs in Dutch oven, fat-side-down. Drizzle with oil, as needed, to brown short ribs well on both sides.

Remove short ribs and set aside. Lower heat to medium and add remaining oil, onion, carrot, celery and garlic cloves; cook until onions are translucent.

Preheat oven to 350°F. Deglaze pan with balsamic vinegar, stirring to scrape browned bits free. Add flour and stir well. Slowly add beef stock, stirring until flour mixture is incorporated. Bring to a boil, then remove from heat and carefully return short ribs to pan.

Cover and roast for 3 hours, until short ribs are tender. Serve ribs with pan vegetables, pan juices and fresh pasta or roasted potatoes.

GAME NIGHT BARBEQUE BEEF PIZZA

Jamie L. Koch of Yukon, Oklahoma, won first prize in the "quick & easy beef" category at the 25th Oklahoma Beef Cook-off. Oklahoma is one of the nation's leading producers of beef, with 64,000 farms and ranches devoted to cattle raising.

Makes 4 Servings

1   (12-inch) pre-baked pizza crust
1   tablespoon mild olive oil
½   cup plus 2 tablespoons pizza sauce
12 ounces KC Masterpiece Shredded Barbecue Beef*
1   cup grated mozzarella cheese

Preheat oven to 450°F. Place oven rack in lowest position in oven. Put crust on a 15-inch pizza stone or a baking sheet. Brush crust with olive oil. Spread sauce over crust. Mash barbecue beef, then spread over crust. Sprinkle with cheese. Bake for 10-12 minutes, or until cheese is melted. Remove pizza from oven and cut into 8 slices.

Tip: Sharp or smoked cheddar cheese is also delicious on this pizza.

*Note: KC Masterpiece Shredded BBQ Beef is fully cooked barbecue beef, available in the meat section of most groceries.

GINGER BEEF & NOODLE BOWLS

The 25th annual National Beef Cook-off focused on ways busy families get dinner on the table. Kristine Snyder of Kihe, Hawaii, won the $10,000 prize in the "one-dish meals" category at the 2003 event with this Asian noodle bowl recipe, which takes only 30 minutes to prepare!

Makes 4 Servings

1   pound beef shoulder top blade (flat iron) steaks or 1 (¾-inch thick) beef top round steak
1   tablespoon dark sesame oil, divided
2   tablespoons minced peeled ginger
2   large cloves garlic, minced
Salt and pepper, to taste
2   (14-ounce) cans beef broth
¾   cup thinly sliced green onions
2   tablespoons mirin or rice wine vinegar*
6   cups cooked fresh Asian-style thin-cut noodles or unseasoned instant ramen
½   cup julienned carrot

Cut steaks crosswise into ¼-inch thick strips; cut strips in half. Heat 1½ teaspoons of sesame oil in a large skillet over medium-high heat. Add ginger and garlic; cook for 1 minute. Add half of beef and stir-fry for 2 minutes, or until outside surface of beef is no longer pink; remove from skillet. Repeat with remaining sesame oil and beef. Season with salt and pepper. Set aside and keep warm.

Add beef broth, green onions and mirin to skillet. Bring to a boil, lower heat and simmer for 8-10 minutes. Divide noodles and beef among 4 large soup bowls. Bring broth mixture to a boil over high heat; ladle broth over beef and noodles. Garnish with carrots to serve.

*Note: Mirin is salted, sweet rice cooking wine found in the Asian section of larger groceries.

Beef in a Blanket

These handheld kid pleasers from Joyce Grady of Bethany, Oklahoma, won the grand prize at the 25th Anniversary Oklahoma Beef Cook-off. These pies make great after-school snacks!

Makes 20 Small Pies

1   pound ground round beef
¼   cup finely chopped onion
¼   cup finely chopped tomato
¼   cup finely chopped bell pepper
    (optional, but tasty)
½   teaspoon cinnamon
⅓   cup grated Italian mozzarella
    and Parmesan cheese blend
2   (10-count) cans refrigerated
    buttermilk biscuits
Salt and pepper, to taste
Warm marinara sauce, for serving
    (optional)

Preheat oven to 450°F. Brown ground beef in a skillet over medium heat. Drain grease, if necessary. Add onion, tomato, bell pepper, cinnamon, salt and pepper; mix thoroughly and cook for about 1 minute. Remove from heat and stir in cheese until melted and combined.

Separate biscuits. On a floured surface, roll biscuit dough out flat. Put about 1 heaping tablespoon of beef mixture on each biscuit. Fold sides of biscuit dough over beef mixture; pinch together to form a closed, rectangular pie. Place pies on a baking sheet sprayed with non-stick cooking spray. Bake for 10 minutes, or until golden brown. Remove from baking sheet and cool for several minutes. Serve with warm marinara sauce, if desired.

Note: After baking, meat pies may be sealed in plastic freezer bags and frozen. To serve, heat in microwave for about 30 seconds.

FIRECRACKER BEEF BURGERS

The cattle industry is Oklahoma's leader in agriculture. Oklahoma beef is internationally recognized as some of the best available, and the Oklahoma Beef Cook-off is a showcase for it. Rosalie Seebeck of Bethany, Oklahoma, won first prize in the "grilled beef" category with these spicy burgers.

Makes 4 Servings

Roasted jalapeño salsa:
2   jalapeños, halved and seeded
2   large onions, sliced into ½-inch wide slices, divided
1   (7-ounce) jar roasted red bell peppers, drained and chopped
½   teaspoon Szechuan-style pepper blend seasoning
1   teaspoon sweet, hot mustard

Firecracker beef burgers:
1½   pounds ground chuck beef
½   teaspoon salt
½   teaspoon pepper
Szechuan-style pepper blend seasoning, to taste
4   slices Swiss cheese
4   crusty hamburger buns
Sweet-hot mustard, to taste

For the salsa: Preheat grill to medium. Spray a grill pan with non-stick cooking spray. Grill jalapeños and onions on grill pan for 3-5 minutes, until lightly browned and tender. Remove from heat.

Chop jalapeños and half of onions (reserve unchopped grilled onions for topping burgers). In a bowl, combine chopped jalapeños and onions, bell peppers, Szechuan seasoning and mustard.

For the burgers: Shape ground beef into 8 thin, 4-inch diameter patties. Spread 2 tablespoons of the roasted jalapeño salsa on each of 4 patties to within ¼-inch of edges. Top with remaining patties; pinch edges to seal. Sprinkle with salt, pepper and Szechuan pepper blend.

Grill burger patties over medium heat for 11-13 minutes, turning once, or until done to your taste.

Grill hamburger buns until lightly toasted. Put 1 piece of cheese on each hot patty. Spread buns with mustard and place patties and reserved grilled onions on buns. Serve with remaining roasted jalapeño salsa.

ROYAL CRAVE CASTLE BREAD

*Kenny Schrader of Edison, New Jersey, won the 2003 White Castle Crave Time Cook-off and the title of
"Chef de Crave." Schrader won over the hearts and taste buds of the judges for the best use of 10 White
Castle hamburgers. His prize was one "Crave Case" of White Castle hamburgers per week for a year.*

Makes 16 Servings

All-purpose flour
2   (16-ounce) packages pizza
     dough
10 White Castle hamburgers (no
     pickles)
½   teaspoon rosemary
½   teaspoon sage
½   teaspoon salt
3   large eggs, beaten
¼   teaspoon ground cloves
1   pound mozzarella cheese,
     grated
¼   teaspoon allspice
¾   cup grated Parmesan cheese
¼   teaspoon pepper
2   teaspoons dried basil
2   teaspoons dried oregano

Preheat oven to 375°F. On a lightly floured surface, roll
out dough into 2 (¼-inch thick) rectangles. Crumble
hamburgers into very small pieces and combine with the
remaining ingredients. Divide hamburger mixture among
dough rectangles.

Roll up dough jelly-roll style into 2 rolls, pinching seams
to seal. Put loaves on a lightly greased baking sheet,
seam-side-down, and bake for 40-45 minutes, until
crusty and browned. Cool on wire racks, then slice with
a sharp serrated knife.

Tip: This bread is great served with warm marinara sauce
(like a calzone). Or, top the hamburger mixture with
marinara sauce before sealing the dough.

GREEK ISLES BEEF WITH FETA & MINT

Susan Runkle of Walton, Kentucky, won the grand prize in Swanson Broth's Culinary Creations Recipe Contest. Runkle said, "I've always loved Greek food, and creating this dish gave me an opportunity to recapture the wonderful Mediterranean flavors that I enjoyed on a trip to Crete a few years ago."

Makes 6 Servings

2   tablespoons olive oil
1½   pounds boneless beef sirloin
     steak, cut into 1-inch cubes
1½   cups chopped onion
1   small eggplant, cut into ½-inch
     cubes
1   tablespoon minced garlic
1   teaspoon dried oregano
1   (14-ounce) can diced tomatoes
1   (14-ounce) can Swanson
     Beef Broth or Lower Sodium
     Beef Broth
¼   cup golden raisins
¾   teaspoon pepper
1   (19-ounce) can cannellini
     beans (white kidney beans),
     drained and rinsed
Hot cooked couscous
¾   cup crumbled feta cheese, for
     garnish
3   tablespoons minced mint, for
     garnish

Heat oil in a saucepan over medium heat. Add beef; cook until browned on all sides. Add onion; cook until lightly browned. Add eggplant, garlic and oregano; cook for 5 minutes. Add tomatoes, broth, raisins and pepper. Bring to a boil, lower heat, cover and simmer for 1 hour. Add beans; heat through. Serve with couscous. Sprinkle with feta and mint.

MEDITERRANEAN VEAL WITH GRILLED VEGETABLE COUSCOUS

Beeftips.com and the National Beef Council's 2003 WKTI Veal Grill-off drew a variety of entries.
Karim Elkouh of Milwaukee, Wisconsin, won first prize with this Mediterranean veal.
The secret to this recipe is the marinade.

Makes 6 Servings

Mediterranean veal:

12	pieces veal cutlet
2	tablespoons balsamic vinegar
¼	cup extra-virgin olive oil
Splash of white wine	
1	teaspoon sugar
Juice of 1 lemon	
Grated zest of ½ lemon	
1	jalapeño, seeded and minced
3	cloves garlic, minced
1	teaspoon pepper
1	tablespoon Italian seasoning
6	kalamata olives, chopped
4	ounces Wisconsin feta cheese, crumbled
2	tablespoons chopped mint
2	tablespoons chopped flat-leaf parsley

Grilled vegetable couscous:

2-3	tablespoons olive oil, divided
1	small zucchini
1	yellow squash
½	fennel bulb
1	red bell pepper, halved
1	sweet onion (such as Vidalia)
1	small carrot, diced
2	cloves garlic, minced
1	cup couscous
1¾	cups water
Salt and pepper, to taste	

For the veal: Pound out veal between 2 sheets of plastic wrap to ⅛-inch thick. Cut cutlets into 12 (1- to 2-inch wide) strips. In a wide dish, combine balsamic vinegar, olive oil, wine and sugar; stir until sugar is dissolved. Add lemon juice, lemon zest, jalapeño, garlic, pepper and Italian seasoning; mix well. Add veal; cover and refrigerate for 1-3 hours, or longer.

For the couscous: Brush zucchini, squash, fennel bulb, bell pepper and onion with 1-2 tablespoons of olive oil. Grill vegetables until tender; cool. Chop zucchini, bell pepper and yellow squash into small dice. Slice onion and fennel.

Heat remaining 1 tablespoon of olive oil in a saucepan over medium heat. Add carrot and garlic; cook for 3-4 minutes. Add couscous and cook, stirring, for 1 minute. Add water, salt and pepper. Bring to boil, lower heat, cover and simmer for 20 minutes, or until couscous is tender. Fluff with fork, then stir in grilled vegetables.

To finish: Preheat grill. Put veal on skewers. Grill for 1½-2 minutes per side. Serve over grilled vegetable couscous. Top with olives and crumbled feta cheese. Garnish with mint and parsley.

Grilled Veal Chops with California Figs & Brie Cheese

Jason Beecher of Redwood City, California, won the California Fig Advisory Board recipe contest. Figs have been lauded for their nutritional qualities from as early as 2900 B.C. In many cultures, including ancient and modern Greek, Egyptian and Roman, figs have a symbolic and spiritual significance beyond their great taste.

Makes 4 Servings

2	teaspoons olive oil, plus extra for rubbing on chops
2	tablespoons diced onion
½	cup sliced (¼-inch thick) dried California figs
1	tablespoon balsamic vinegar
½	teaspoon dried thyme
½	cup chicken broth
4	(¾-inch thick) veal chops

Salt and pepper, to taste

1	ounce Brie cheese, cut into small pieces

Heat 2 teaspoons of olive oil in a small saucepan over medium heat. Add onions; cook until softened (do not brown). Add figs, balsamic vinegar, thyme and chicken broth. Lower heat and simmer gently for 10-15 minutes, until liquid is reduced by almost half; keep warm.

Preheat grill to high. Rub veal chops with a little olive oil and season with salt and pepper. Grill chops to desired temperature, about 3-4 minutes per side for medium.

When chops are ready, whisk Brie cheese into fig mixture in saucepan until melted and combined. Season with salt and pepper. Spoon fig mixture over chops to serve.

MEDALLIONS OF VENISON WITH CARAMELIZED APPLES

Douglas Petroski of Queensbury, New York, won the prize for "best entrée" in the Adirondack Life *apple recipe contest with this perfect fall combination of venison and rich, sweet caramelized apples and onions.*

Makes 8 Servings

Caramelized apples:
1   tablespoon butter
1   tablespoon olive oil
½   white onion, diced
3   cloves garlic, thinly sliced
1½ cups diced apple

Venison:
1   cup all-purpose flour
1   teaspoon salt
1   tablespoon onion powder
½   teaspoon pepper
Pinch of cayenne pepper
1   teaspoon garlic powder
1   tablespoon paprika
8   (1-inch thick) venison
    tenderloin steaks
1   tablespoon butter
1   tablespoon olive oil
1   cup apple cider
Juice of ½ lemon
¼   cup minced cilantro
2   tablespoons soy sauce

For the caramelized apples: Heat butter and olive oil in a skillet over low heat. Add onion, garlic and apples; cook until onion is soft. Set aside and keep warm.

For the venison: On a plate, combine flour, salt, onion powder, salt, black pepper, cayenne, garlic powder and paprika. Pound out venison medallions between 2 sheets of plastic wrap to 1½ times their original size. Dredge medallions in flour mixture to coat. Heat butter and olive oil over medium heat in skillet used to cook apples. Add venison and cook, turning frequently, about 4-6 minutes, or until internal temperature is 115°F. Cover with foil and let stand for 5 minutes.

Transfer venison to warm plates. Deglaze skillet with cider and lemon juice, stirring to scrape browned bits free. Stir in caramelized apple mixture, cilantro and soy sauce. Cook until apple mixture is heated through. Top venison with apple mixture to serve.

BAKED GOODS

Raspberry Raisin Bran Muffins

Rosalind Anderson of Hopkins, Minnesota, won second prize in the Hopkins Raspberry Festival Bake-off.
Raspberries belong to a large group of fruits known as brambles. Raspberries have perennial roots and
crowns, but the canes live for only two summers. These muffins, however, are always exceptional.

Makes 36 Muffins

1	(16-ounce) box raisin bran cereal
5	cups all-purpose flour
2	cups sugar
5	teaspoons baking soda
4	eggs, slightly beaten
1	cup vegetable oil
4	cups buttermilk
1	cup raspberries, or more to taste

In a large bowl, combine cereal, flour, sugar and baking soda. In a medium bowl, combine eggs, oil and buttermilk; add to cereal mixture and stir just until combined. Cover and refrigerate batter for 30 minutes.

Preheat oven to 325°F. Gently fold raspberries into batter. Pour batter into paper-lined or greased muffin cups and bake for 25 minutes.

Note: Batter will keep covered and refrigerated for 2-3 weeks – just add raspberries before baking.

STRAWBERRY KOLACHES

Paige Smith of Leasanton, Texas, won "Berry Best in Show" at the 2003 Poteet Strawberry Festival in Poteet, Texas, the "Strawberry Capital of Texas." Kolaches, arguably Czechoslovakia's greatest contribution to world cuisine, are fruit- and cream cheese-filled sweet buns that are perfect with coffee or tea.

Makes 3 Dozen

Kolache dough:
- 1   cup sour cream
- ½   cup sugar
- 1½   teaspoons salt
- 1   stick margarine, softened
- 2   packages active dry yeast
- ½   cup warm water
- 2   eggs beaten
- 4   cups all-purpose flour

Strawberry topping:
- 1   (8-ounce) package cream cheese, softened
- 1   egg yolk
- ¼   cup sugar
- ½   teaspoon vanilla extract
- 1   pound fresh strawberries, sliced

For the dough: Heat sour cream over low heat until warm. Stir in sugar, salt and margarine; transfer to a bowl and cool. Sprinkle yeast over warm water; let stand until yeast is dissolved, then add to sour cream mixture. Add eggs and flour; mix well. Put dough in a greased bowl; cover and refrigerate overnight.

The next day, form dough into 36 balls. Put balls on a greased cookie sheet. Flatten to ½-inch thick and let rise for about 10 minutes. Make indentations in dough; put a little strawberry topping in each indentation. Let rise until doubled in size. Preheat oven to 350°F. Bake kolaches for 10-12 minutes, until golden brown.

For the topping: Combine cream cheese, egg yolk, sugar and vanilla until smooth. Stir in strawberries.

Citrus Sweet Rolls

More than 100 bakers from 54 counties across Oklahoma entered the 2003 Wheatheart Bread Baking Contest, held annually at the Oklahoma State Fair. Katherine Urban of Woods County, Oklahoma, took first prize in the "senior division sweet bread" category with these rolls.

Makes about 18 Rolls

Dough:
4-5 cups all-purpose flour, divided
½ cup sugar
2 packages active dry yeast
1 teaspoon salt
1 cup milk, warmed
1 stick butter, melted and divided
Grated zest of 2 large oranges
½ teaspoon almond extract
2 eggs, beaten

Filling:
½ cup sugar
Grated zest of 2 large oranges
½ stick butter, melted
1½ cups grated coconut, toasted*

Glaze:
1¾ cups powdered sugar
¼ cup orange juice

For the dough: In a large bowl, combine 3 cups of flour, sugar, yeast and salt. In a small bowl, combine milk, ½ stick of melted butter, orange zest, almond extract and eggs; add to flour mixture and mix well. Add just enough of remaining 1-2 cups of flour to make a dough that is easy to handle. Turn dough onto a lightly floured surface; knead until soft, smooth and elastic, about 10 minutes.

Shape dough into a ball and place in a greased bowl, turning once to coat the top surface. Cover with a damp cloth or a piece of plastic wrap and let rise in a warm place until doubled in size, about 1 hour.

Punch dough down and roll into a rectangle. Brush dough with remaining ½ stick of melted butter. Spread filling over dough. Roll up dough, beginning with the long side; pinch seams together. Cut rolls 1-inch wide and put them cut-side-down on a greased baking sheet. Cover and let rise until doubled in size, about 45 minutes. Preheat oven to 375°F. Bake for 20-25 minutes. Drizzle glaze over warm rolls.

For the filling: Combine sugar, orange zest and butter; stir in coconut.

For the glaze: Combine powdered sugar and orange juice.

*Note: To toast coconut, spread coconut in a thin layer on a baking sheet. Bake for 5-10 minutes in a preheated 350°F oven, stirring occasionally, until light brown.

CHERRY PECAN STICKY BUNS

A group of students at the Northwestern Michigan College of Culinary Arts won over judges with these sticky buns at the National Cherry Festival's Taste of Cherries Recipe Contest. The Food Network ranked the Cherry Festival as 2003's "Top Amazing Food Celebration."

Makes 24 Rolls

Sweet dough:

2	cups milk
1	stick butter, melted and divided
2	eggs, lightly beaten
1	tablespoon active dry yeast
½	cup white sugar
½	teaspoon vanilla extract
½	teaspoon nutmeg
1½	teaspoons salt
3	cups all-purpose flour, more if needed
1	tablespoon cinnamon
½	cup packed brown sugar
¾	cup chopped dried cherries
1	cup pecan pieces

Topping:

½	cup packed brown sugar
1½	teaspoons cinnamon
1½	sticks butter, softened
¼	cup plus 2 tablespoons corn syrup
½	cup honey, warmed slightly

For the dough: Heat milk until a skin forms on surface. Remove from heat and stir in half of melted butter; let mixture cool, then transfer to a bowl. Mix in eggs, yeast, white sugar, vanilla and nutmeg. Stir in salt. Gradually stir in enough flour to form a smooth, but sticky dough. Cover and let rise in a warm place until doubled in size.

Roll dough into a large rectangle. Brush with remaining melted butter. Mix cinnamon and brown sugar; sprinkle over dough. Sprinkle cherries over dough. Roll dough up jelly-roll style; seal edges tightly. Cut dough into 1½-inch circles.

Spread ½-⅔ of topping on a rimmed 12x18-inch baking sheet. Sprinkle pecans evenly over topping. Place rolls on top of pecans, about ½-inch apart. Put pan in a warm place and let rolls rise until almost doubled in size. Spread remaining topping over tops of rolls.

Preheat oven to 350°F. Bake rolls for 20-25 minutes, or until topping is a rich amber color. Remove from oven; immediately invert rolls onto a plate with a spatula.

For the topping: With a mixer on medium speed, cream together brown sugar, cinnamon and butter. Beat in corn syrup and honey until smooth.

SCOTTISH PEAR & LEMON TEA BREAD

Launi McKean Ruvolis of Shohola, Pennsylvania, won first prize in the "breads" category at the Pear Blossom Cook-off in Milford, Pennsylvania. Pear blossoms herald spring, typically blooming in early April. Their promise of warmer months is worthy of this delicious tea bread!

Makes 2 Loaves

Scottish pear bread:
1   cup shortening
2   cups plus 2 tablespoons sugar
2½ cups all-purpose flour
⅓   teaspoon salt
2   teaspoons baking powder
1   cup milk
4   eggs
1¼ cups chopped walnuts
Grated zest of 2 lemons
2   pears, finely chopped

White drizzle icing:
1   tablespoon butter, melted
½   cup powdered sugar
¼   teaspoon vanilla extract
Milk

For the bread: Preheat oven to 350°F. Grease and flour 2 (9x5-inch) loaf pans. Cream shortening and 2 cups of sugar with a mixer. Add flour, salt, baking powder and milk; beat with mixer until combined. Beat in eggs, 1 at a time. Stir in nuts and lemon zest. Bake for 55 minutes, or until a toothpick inserted in center comes out clean.

In a saucepan, simmer pears and 2 tablespoons of sugar for 5 minutes. Remove loaves from pans while still warm. Prick tops with a toothpick. Spoon pear mixture over loaves. Drizzle with frosting.

For the icing: Mix butter, powdered sugar and vanilla. Stir in enough milk to reach a drizzling consistency.

Coconut Bread with Coconut Butter

Jo Lynn Watson of Tulia, Texas, won the Texas Co-op Power monthly recipe contest in November 2003, with her delicious coconut bread recipe. This entry beat out hundreds of others because it is as easy to make as it is rewarding to eat!

Makes 1 Loaf

Coconut bread:

2	cups all-purpose flour
1¾	teaspoons baking powder
¼	teaspoon salt
1⅓	cups sugar
¼	teaspoon baking soda
⅔	cup vegetable oil
⅔	cup buttermilk
½	cup coconut
2	large eggs
1½	teaspoons coconut extract
½	cup chopped pecans

Coconut butter:

1	stick butter (not margarine), softened
¼	cup real cream of coconut

For the bread: Preheat oven to 325°F. Spray bottom of a 9x5-inch loaf pan with non-stick cooking spray. In a large bowl, combine flour, baking powder, salt, sugar and baking soda. Add oil, buttermilk, coconut, eggs, coconut extract and pecans; beat well with a mixer. Pour batter into pan. Bake for 1 hour, or until a toothpick inserted in center comes out clean. Serve with coconut butter.

For the coconut butter: Beat butter and cream of coconut with a mixer until fluffy.

Sweet Potato Surprise Bread

Kathryn Jackson of Benson, North Carolina, won first prize in the "desserts" category at the Ham & Yam Festival in Smithfield, North Carolina. This is a surprisingly simple recipe that combines the sweet tartness of cranberries and orange with mellow sweet potatoes – it is the ultimate autumn quick bread!

Makes 1 Loaf

Bread:
1	(14-ounce) box cranberry-orange quick bread mix
½	cup grated sweet potato
¾	cup water
3	tablespoons vegetable oil
1	egg, beaten
1-2	tablespoons chopped pecans (optional)

Filling:
2	(3-ounce) packages cream cheese, softened
⅓	cup sugar
1	egg
½	cup grated sweet potato

Icing:
2	teaspoons milk
½	cup powdered sugar

For the bread: Preheat oven to 350°F. In a large bowl, combine bread mix, sweet potatoes, water and vegetable oil just until moistened. Pour half of batter into a greased and floured 9x5-inch loaf pan. Spoon filling over batter. Spoon remaining batter over filling.

Bake for 65-75 minutes, or until a toothpick inserted in center comes out clean. Cool for 15 minutes, then remove from pan and cool completely. Drizzle icing over bread. Sprinkle with chopped pecans, if desired.

For the filling: Beat cream cheese, sugar and egg with a mixer until smooth. Stir in sweet potatoes.

For the icing: Mix milk and powdered sugar until smooth. Add more milk, if needed, to form a drizzling consistency.

MAPLE COFFEE CAKE

Keren Wheeler of Swanton, Vermont, took top honors at the 2003 Vermont Maple Festival in St. Albans, Vermont. This sweet, dense cake is delicious with morning coffee or afternoon tea.

Makes 1 Cake

2	sticks butter, softened
1¼	cups pure maple sugar, divided
¼	cup white sugar
3	large eggs
2	cups all-purpose flour
2	teaspoons baking powder
½	teaspoon salt
2½	teaspoons baking soda
2	cups sour cream
½	cup pure maple syrup

Preheat oven to 350°F. Butter and flour a large tube or Bundt pan. In a large bowl, beat butter, ¾ cup of maple sugar and white sugar until light and fluffy. Add eggs; beat well.

In a medium bowl, combine flour, baking powder, salt and baking soda. Add flour mixture and 1 cup of sour cream alternately to butter mixture. Pour half of batter into pan. Sprinkle remaining ½ cup of maple sugar over batter. Pour remaining batter on top of maple sugar.

Bake cake for 60-70 minutes, until browned on top and a toothpick inserted in center comes out clean. Let cake cool for 10 minutes, then turn out onto a plate and cool completely. When completely cool, combine remaining 1 cup of sour cream and maple syrup; drizzle over cake.

SWEET POTATO BUTTERMILK BISCUITS

When you combine two classics like warm, fluffy buttermilk biscuits with comforting sweet potatoes, you are sure to have a winner. These biscuits, created by Flora Grantham of Smithfield, North Carolina, won third prize in the "breads" category at the Ham & Yam Festival in Smithfield.

Makes 12 to 14 Biscuits

1½ cup self-rising flour, divided
½ teaspoon baking powder
½ teaspoon baking soda
½ teaspoon nutmeg
½ teaspoon cinnamon
⅛ teaspoon salt
1 stick butter or margarine, chilled
½ cup mashed cooked sweet potatoes
½ cup buttermilk

Preheat oven to 425°F. In a large bowl, combine 1 cup of flour, baking powder, baking soda, nutmeg, cinnamon and salt. Stir in mashed sweet potatoes. With a pastry blender or 2 knives, cut in butter until mixture resembles a coarse meal. Add buttermilk and stir until mixture comes together.

Add enough of remaining ½ cup of flour to form a dough that is easy to handle. On a floured surface, knead dough. Roll out dough ½-inch thick. Cut with a biscuit cutter dipped in flour. Put biscuits on an ungreased baking sheet. Bake for 12-15 minutes, until golden and puffed and bottoms are crisp.

APPLE, CHEDDAR & BACON SCONES

Helen Decker Hart of Hendersonville, North Carolina, won first prize in the "breads" category at the North Carolina Apple Fest in Hendersonville, North Carolina. Hart said, "This recipe came from a British friend of my husband. I started to improvise and came up with this delicious variation."

Makes 16 Scones

2¼ cups self-rising flour
3 tablespoons sugar
¾ stick butter, chilled
1 cup grated cheddar cheese
3 slices bacon, cooked and crumbled
2 cups finely diced peeled Gala apples (about 2 apples)
1 cup buttermilk

Preheat oven to 425°F. In a large bowl, combine flour and sugar. Cut in butter with a fork until mixture is crumbly. Fold in cheese, bacon and apple. Fold in buttermilk.

Turn dough out onto a floured work surface. Divide dough into 2 pieces. Pat each piece into an 8- or 9-inch circle. Cut each circle into 8 pieces. Place scones on a lightly greased cookie sheet; bake for 18-20 minutes. Enjoy for breakfast, lunch or dinner. Great for kids' lunches as well.

ZUCCHINI HERB CORNBREAD

*This wildly popular recipe by Jaime Beckham of Windsor, California, won first prize in the "breads"
category at the Windsor Zucchini Festival. This cornbread was so popular that the festival sold out
of its souvenir cookbooks and had to reprint them simply because everyone wanted this recipe!*

Makes 16 Servings

6	cups grated zucchini
2	cups cornmeal
1	cup all-purpose flour
3	eggs, beaten
1½	cups milk
2	teaspoons salt, divided
3	tablespoons sugar
1	tablespoon baking powder
2	tablespoons minced fresh basil (or 2 teaspoons dried basil)

In a colander, toss zucchini with 1 teaspoon salt. Weigh down zucchini with a plate and let drain for 30 minutes.

Preheat oven to 350°F. Sift together cornmeal, flour, sugar, baking powder and remaining 1 teaspoon of salt into a large bowl. In a small bowl, beat eggs, milk and basil; add to flour mixture and stir to combine.

Rinse zucchini and squeeze dry. Stir zucchini into flour mixture. Pour batter into a greased 9-inch springform pan or 8x8-inch baking pan. Bake for 40 minutes, or until golden brown. Cool for 10 minutes, slice and serve.

HERB CHEESE ROLLS

The International Dutch Oven Society is involved in the promotion, education and preservation of the art and skill of Dutch oven cooking. Each year, winning teams from local competitions gather for the World Championship Cook-off. In 2003, Randy Macari of Pleasant and Corey Phillips of Roy, Utah, won first prize in the "bread" category.

Makes 24 Rolls

1	cup milk
1	cup water
2	tablespoons butter
3	tablespoons honey
1	egg
1½	cups grated sharp cheddar cheese
1	tablespoon salt
4	teaspoons garlic powder
1	teaspoon dried basil
1	teaspoon dried oregano
1	teaspoon thyme
1	tablespoon dough enhancer*
5-6	cups all-purpose flour
4½	teaspoons yeast

Combine milk, water, butter and honey in an 8-inch Dutch oven. Heat at low temperature to 100°F. Transfer milk mixture to a bowl. Add egg, cheese, salt, garlic powder, oregano, thyme and dough enhancer. Add flour then top with yeast. Mix well, then knead for 2 minutes (dough should be slightly sticky). Cover and let rise until double in size, about 40 minutes.

Grease a 12-inch Dutch oven. Form dough into rolls and place in Dutch oven. Let rise until almost doubled in size, about 30 minutes.

Preheat 22-26 charcoal briquettes to 350°F.** Bake for 40 minutes, rotating Dutch oven every 10 minutes, until top is browned.

*Note: Dough enhancer is used to give breads a smooth texture and a longer shelf life.

**Note: According to the International Dutch Oven Society, to test the cooking temperature of a Dutch oven, place a teaspoonful of flour in a small pie pan and put the pan inside a hot Dutch oven. Cover and heat for 5 minutes. After 5 minutes, if the flour has not turned brown, the oven is less than 300°F. If the flour is light brown, the oven is about 350°F.

WHOLE GRAIN WHEAT BREAD

Elizabeth Metheny of Edmond, Oklahoma, won first prize in the "whole grain bread" category in the Wheatheart Bread Baking Contest held annually at the Oklahoma State Fair.

Makes 2 Loaves

3   tablespoons plus ¼ cup brown sugar, divided
1¼ cups warm water (115°F)
2   envelopes active dry yeast
6-7 cups whole-grain wheat flour
¾   cup powdered milk
2   teaspoons salt
¼   cup plus 2 tablespoons vegetable oil
2   tablespoons molasses
Melted butter

Dissolve 1 tablespoon of brown sugar in warm water. Add yeast. In a large bowl (or in a mixer with a dough hook), combine 5 cups of flour, powdered milk, salt and remaining brown sugar. Mix gently for 30 seconds. Stir yeast mixture to dissolve yeast; add to flour mixture and mix for 30 seconds. Add oil and molasses; mix for 30 seconds.

Add just enough of remaining 1-2 cups of flour, ½ cup at a time, to make a dough that is easy to handle. Mix for about 5 minutes. On a lightly floured surface, knead dough for 7-10 minutes, or until smooth and elastic. Put dough in a greased bowl, turning once to grease top. Cover and let rise in a warm place (such as an unlit oven) until dough is doubled in size, about 1 hour.

Punch down dough, divide in half and shape into 2 loaves. Put loaves in 2 buttered 9x5-inch loaf pans (or shape into round loaves and bake on a baking sheet). Cover loaves and let rise in a warm place until doubled in size, about 30 minutes.

Preheat oven to 325°F. Bake loaves for 26 minutes, or until done. Immediately remove loaves from pan and place on wire racks. Brush tops with melted butter.

BAKED GOODS

ROASTED GARLIC & ROSEMARY BRAID

More than 100 bakers from 54 counties across Oklahoma entered the annual Wheatheart Bread Baking Contest at the Oklahoma State Fair. Jessica Magar of McClain County, Oklahoma, was the junior division grand champion in the "other wheat bread" category with this sophisticated loaf.

Makes 3 Loaves

Bread:
5 whole garlic bulbs
1 tablespoon olive oil
4 teaspoons dried rosemary
6-7½ cups bread flour, divided
½ cup sugar
3 packages active dry yeast
1 tablespoon salt
1½ cups milk, warmed
1 cup water, warmed
1 stick butter, melted
1 egg, beaten

Wash:
1½ teaspoons garlic salt
½ stick butter, melted

Preheat oven to 425°F. Remove papery outer skin from garlic bulbs (do not separate cloves). Cut off tops of bulbs. Put bulbs cut-side-up in a baking dish. Brush with oil and sprinkle with rosemary. Cover with foil; bake for 30-35 minutes, or until cloves are soft. Cool for 10 minutes. Separate cloves, squeeze into a bowl and mash.

In a large bowl, combine 4 cups of flour, sugar, yeast and salt. In a small bowl, combine roasted garlic, milk, water, butter and egg; add to flour mixture and mix well. Add just enough of remaining 2-3½ cups of flour to make a dough that is easy to handle. On a lightly floured surface, knead dough until it is soft, smooth and elastic, about 10 minutes. Shape dough into a ball and place in a greased bowl, turning once to coat the top surface. Cover and let rise in a warm place until doubled in size, about 1 hour.

Punch down dough and divide into 3 portions. Divide each portion into 3 pieces; shape each piece into an 18-inch rope. Put 3 ropes on a greased baking sheet and braid; pinch ends to seal and tuck ends under. Repeat with remaining dough. Cover and let rise in warm place until doubled in size, about 30 minutes.

Preheat oven to 350°F. Combine wash ingredients. Bake loaves for 15 minutes. Remove loaves from oven, brush with wash and then bake for 10-15 minutes longer, or until loaves are golden brown and sound hollow when tapped on the bottom. Cool loaves on a wire rack.

"A balanced diet

is a cookie

in each hand"

Unknown

COOKIES & BROWNIES

One-Bowl Triple Chocolate Oatmeal Jumbles

When creating the ultimate oatmeal cookie, Beth Royals of Richmond, Virginia, knew she couldn't go wrong with the combination of chocolate and oatmeal. She was right! She won the $6,250 grand prize in Quaker Oats' Search For The Ultimate Oatmeal Cookie. These one-bowl oatmeal chippers have just five ingredients, so they can be an "everyday" treat.

Makes 24 Cookies

1	stick Blue Bonnet 65% vegetable oil spread
1	(18-ounce) package devil's food cake mix
2	cups Old-Fashioned Quaker Oats
3	large eggs
⅔	cup white chocolate chips
⅔	cup semisweet chocolate chips

Preheat oven to 350°F. Put vegetable oil spread in a large microwaveable bowl; cover loosely with wax paper. Microwave on high for 30 seconds, or until melted; cool slightly. Add remaining ingredients; mix well (dough will be very stiff).

Drop dough by level ¼-cupsful, 2-inches apart, onto an ungreased cookie sheet; flatten slightly. Bake for 13-17 minutes, just until set (do not overbake – centers should be soft). Cool on cookie sheets for 1 minute, then, using a wide spatula, transfer to wire racks and cool completely.

Note: Devil's food cake mix with or without pudding may be used. To substitute quick cooking oats, decrease oats to 1½ cups (cookies made with quick oats will not be quite as "fudgy" as those made with old-fashioned rolled oats).

Cookies & Brownies

CHOCOLATE-DRIZZLED RASPBERRY CHOCOLATE CHUNK COOKIES

Jill Mott of Northville, Michigan, won both the "chocolate chip" category and overall grand prize in the AAA Michigan's Best Cookies in Michigan Baking Contest with these delectable cookies.

Makes About 36 Cookies

2	cups all-purpose flour
1	cup whole-wheat flour
1	teaspoon baking soda
1	teaspoon kosher salt
2	sticks butter, softened
¾	cup sugar
¾	cup packed brown sugar
½	teaspoon vanilla extract
½	teaspoon raspberry flavoring
2	large eggs
½	cup raspberry preserves
1	cup coarsely chopped walnuts
2	cups chocolate chunk morsels
6	ounces white chocolate
1	cup chocolate chips

Preheat oven to 375°F. Sift together all-purpose and whole-wheat flour, baking soda and salt into a small bowl. In a large bowl, cream together butter, white and brown sugar, vanilla and raspberry flavoring. Add eggs, 1 at a time, beating well after each addition.

Gradually stir in flour mixture, a little at a time. Stir in raspberry preserves, walnuts and chocolate morsels. Drop dough by tablespoonful onto a cookie sheet. Bake for 9-11 minutes; cool cookies.

Melt white chocolate; drizzle over cooled cookies, then cool until white chocolate is set. Melt chocolate chips; drizzle over cookies and cool until set.

TRIPLE CHOCOLATE KISSES

Marjorie Grunewald of Weimar, Texas, won the Texas Co-op Power's February 2003 recipe contest with these chocolate-filled meringue cookies. Texas Co-op Power *magazine is a 60-year tradition in over two million homes. The publication prides itself on choosing recipes that appeal to its many readers – this one is sure to please you, too!*

Makes 42 Cookies

2	egg whites
¼	teaspoon cream of tartar
½	cup sugar
¼	teaspoon almond extract
1	ounce semisweet chocolate, grated
42	milk Hershey's kisses

Unsweetened cocoa powder

Preheat oven to 325°F. Beat egg whites with a mixer on high speed until foamy. Add cream of tartar; beat until soft peaks form, about 6 minutes. Gradually add sugar, beating until stiff peaks form, about 6 minutes. Beat in almond extract. Fold in grated semisweet chocolate.

Insert a medium open-star tip in a pastry bag (or a ziplock plastic bag with a corner cut off). Fill bag with meringue. On lightly greased baking sheets, pipe 42 (1-inch) solid circles (like coins). Lightly press a chocolate kiss into center of each circle.

Pipe meringue around each kiss in continuous circles from the base to the top until kiss is completely covered. Dust with cocoa powder. Bake for 15-18 minutes, or until edges are lightly browned. Immediately remove to wire racks to cool.

Espresso Chews

Kim Troy won third prize in the "sheer chocolate artistry" category at the annual Chocolate Lovers' Fling, a fundraiser for the Boulder County Safehouse in Boulder, Colorado. Troy, a formally trained chocolatier, owns Bliss Confections, in Boulder, a "delightfully small" company dedicated to making life a little sweeter.

Makes 60 Cookies

½   stick unsalted butter
1   pound premium bittersweet chocolate, finely chopped (such as Valrhona or Scharffen Berger)
1½ cups plus 3 tablespoons sugar
4   eggs
1   tablespoon vanilla extract
¼   cup plus 1 tablespoon all-purpose flour
1   teaspoon baking soda
¼   teaspoon salt
2   tablespoons instant espresso powder
1¾ cups chocolate chips
½   cup chopped walnuts, lightly toasted
Powdered sugar, for garnish (optional)

Melt butter and chocolate in a double boiler over gently simmering water, stirring occasionally (or microwave on medium power, stirring every 20 seconds, until melted). Stir to combine and cool slightly.

In a large bowl, beat sugar and eggs with a mixer until pale and thick. Beat in vanilla. Stir in cooled chocolate mixture. Sift together flour, baking soda, salt and espresso powder into a small bowl; add to egg mixture and mix well. Stir in chocolate chips and nuts. Let dough rest until it reaches a scoopable consistency, about 30 minutes.

Preheat oven to 300°F. Scoop dough into tablespoon-sized balls; place on a baking sheet lined with parchment paper or sprayed with non-stick cooking spray (leave room for cookies to spread). Bake for 18-20 minutes (cookies will have a meringue-like crust around a chewy center). Cool, then dust with powdered sugar, if desired.

IRRESISTIBLE COOKIES

Jan Phelan of Meridian, Idaho, won the hearts of the judges in the Irresistible Cookie Jar's Home Sweet Home Cookie Recipe Contest. The recipe makes a large batch of "irresistible" cookies!

Makes about 36 Cookies

2	sticks butter, softened
1	cup packed brown sugar
1	cup white sugar
2	large eggs
1	teaspoon vanilla extract
2	cups all-purpose flour
1	teaspoon baking powder
½	teaspoon salt
1	teaspoon baking soda
1½	cups golden raisins
1½	cups coarsely chopped pecans
1	cup old-fashioned rolled oats
1½	cups orange almond granola
1	cup chopped dates

Preheat oven to 350°F. In a large bowl, cream butter, brown sugar and white sugar. Beat in eggs and vanilla.

Sift together flour, baking powder, salt and baking soda into a medium bowl; stir into butter mixture, a little at a time. Stir in raisins, pecans, oats, granola and dates.

Drop dough by tablespoonsful onto a lightly greased cookie sheet. Bake for about 10 minutes.

LES GALETTES AU CAFE DE KONA

Lincoln Gomes won first prize in the "dessert" category at the 2003 Kona Coffee Festival. Kona coffee was first planted by missionary Samuel Ruggles in 1828. Today, many Kona farmers can claim to being fifth generation coffee farmers, and they continue the tradition and honor their heritage with every harvest.

Makes 16 Bars

2	sticks butter
1⅓	cups sugar
4	tablespoons powdered instant Kona coffee
2	large eggs
1	teaspoon vanilla extract
1½	cups all-purpose flour
1	cup chopped macadamia nuts

Preheat oven to 350°F. Grease a 8x8-inch baking pan. In a medium bowl, cream together butter, sugar and Kona coffee. Beat in eggs and vanilla. Beat in flour. Mix in macadamia nuts until well blended.

Spread dough into pan (or make cookies by dropping dough onto a greased cookie sheet with a small ice cream scoop or by rounded tablespoonsful). Bake for 10-15 minutes. Cool on wire racks, then cut into 2x2-inch bars.

GHIRADELLI CHOCOLATE-ENHANCED LINZERTORTES

More than 5,000 people from all over the Southeast attended the first annual North Carolina Chocolate Festival in February 2003. Kathleen Burns of Newport, North Carolina, took first prize in the "cookie" category with her chocolatey take on the traditional linzertorte.

Makes About 50 Cookies

1¼ cups powdered sugar, plus extra for garnish
3¼ sticks unsalted butter
Grated zest of 1 lemon
3   egg yolks
4½ cups sifted all-purpose flour
¾   cup hazelnuts, finely ground and sifted
½   teaspoon cinnamon
1   cup pistachios or hazelnuts, ground
6   ounces Ghiradelli semisweet chocolate
¾   cup Smucker's seedless raspberry jam

In a large bowl, beat together powdered sugar, butter, lemon zest and egg yolks. In a small bowl, combine flour, ground hazelnuts and cinnamon; add to butter mixture and mix well to form a firm dough. Cover and refrigerate for 1 hour.

Preheat oven to 350°F. On a floured surface, roll out dough ⅛-inch thick. Cut dough with a floured cookie cutter. Put cookies on an ungreased cookie sheet. With a thimble or narrow tube, cut a hole in the center of half the cookies. Sprinkle all cookies with ground pistachios.

Bake cookies for 8-10 minutes, or until light golden brown. Cool for a few minutes, then transfer to wire racks and cool completely. Sprinkle powdered sugar over cookies.

Melt chocolate and spread a thin coat over the cookies without the hole cut in them; cool until set. Spread jam over chocolate. Top the jam-coated cookies with the cookies with the holes cut in them. With a baby spoon, add ¼ teaspoon jam to each cookie hole. Store cookies in an airtight container.

CHOCOLATE CREAM BARS

Laura Chandlee of Dubuque, Iowa, won the $1,000 first prize and a trip for two to the Sonoma Valley Culinary School in the Nestlé and Better Homes & Gardens' *Share the Very Best Recipe Contest. Chandlee, a mother of two, loves this recipe because it is so quick to make.*

Makes 15 Bars

2   (18-ounce) packages Nestle Toll House Refrigerated Chocolate Chip Cookie Dough, divided
3   (8-ounce) packages cream cheese, softened
1   cup sugar
2   large eggs
1   teaspoon vanilla extract
1   (12-ounce) package Nestle Toll House Semi-Sweet Chocolate Morsels, melted*

Preheat oven to 350°F. Grease a 9x13-inch baking pan. Press 1 package of cookie dough into bottom of baking pan. Beat cream cheese with a mixer on high speed for 30 seconds. Beat in sugar, eggs and vanilla extract until smooth. Spread cream cheese mixture over cookie dough in pan.

Cut remaining package of refrigerated cookie dough into 15 equal slices; place cookie slices on top of cream cheese mixture. Bake for 55 minutes, or until golden brown. Cool completely in pan on a wire rack. Refrigerate for at least 2 hours.

Let stand at room temperature for 20 minutes before slicing. Drizzle each serving with melted chocolate morsels. Refrigerate any leftovers.

*Note: Melt just enough of the chocolate morsels to top each serving; store the rest.

DIED & GONE TO HEAVEN

Charity Wessel of El Dorado, Kansas, won first prize in the "desserts & holiday favorites" category in the 2003 Wichita Eagle Holiday Cookbook Contest in Wichita, Kansas. This dessert is sure to please anyone with a sweet tooth.

Makes 24 Squares

1½   sticks margarine, divided
24   chocolate sandwich cookies (such as Oreo's), crushed
½   gallon vanilla ice cream
1½   cups chocolate syrup
1   (16-ounce) can sweetened condensed milk
½   teaspoon vanilla extract
8   ounces whipped topping
½   cup chopped peanuts

Melt ½ stick of margarine and combine with crushed cookies; spread into bottom of a 9x13-inch baking pan. Freeze crust for 30 minutes. Soften ice cream by setting it out on a counter. When crust is frozen, spread ice cream over it. Freeze for 30 minutes.

In a saucepan, combine chocolate syrup, sweetened condensed milk and remaining 1 stick of margarine. Bring to a boil, lower heat and simmer for 5 minutes. Stir in vanilla; remove from heat.

Let chocolate syrup mixture cool for a few minutes, then spread over ice cream layer. Freeze for 30 minutes. Cover with whipped topping and peanuts. Cover with foil and freeze for 24 hours. Cut into 2x2-inch squares to serve.

TART & GOOEY CRANBERRY PECAN PIE BARS

Mary Donovan-Haber of Eau Claire, Wisconsin, won first prize in the "fresh cranberry" category at the 30th annual Warrens Cranberry Festival. Known as the "Cranberry Capital of Wisconsin," Warrens has the largest concentration of cranberry marshes in the state, yielding 285 million pounds of the berries each year.

Makes 32 Bars

2	cups all-purpose flour
½	cup white sugar
⅛	teaspoon salt
2½	sticks butter or margarine, divided
1	cup light corn syrup
1	cup packed brown sugar
4	eggs, slightly beaten
12	ounces fresh or frozen cranberries
2½	cups pecans, finely chopped
1	teaspoon vanilla extract

Preheat oven to 350°F. Grease a 9x13-inch baking pan. In a bowl, combine flour, white sugar and salt. Using a pastry blender, cut in 1½ sticks of butter until mixture resembles fine crumbs. Press mixture into bottom of pan. Bake for 15-18 minutes, or until lightly browned.

In a medium saucepan over medium heat, combine corn syrup, brown sugar and remaining 1 stick of butter. Bring to a boil, stirring constantly, then remove from heat.

Put eggs in a bowl. Gradually stir about ½ cup of brown sugar mixture into eggs, then add egg mixture to remaining brown sugar mixture in saucepan. Stir in cranberries, pecans and vanilla. Pour cranberry mixture over baked crust. Bake for 30-32 minutes, until cranberry mixture is set. Cool in pan on a wire rack. Cut into bars and serve.

OLIVIA'S OREGON FRUIT OATMEAL BARS

Olivia Trusty of Indianapolis, Indiana, and Grandma Marsha Gillespie of Danville, Indiana, won the grand prize in the Oregon Fruit Products' annual Grandparent/Grandchild Recipe Contest. Olivia won a $500 college savings bond and her grandmother won a housecleaning gift certificate (for that messy kitchen).

Makes About 24 Bars

1	(18-ounce) package yellow cake mix
1½	cups quick oats
1½	sticks butter, softened
2	(16-ounce) cans Oregon Strawberries
1	(8-ounce) package cream cheese, softened
⅓	cup sugar
1	egg

Preheat oven to 375°F. Grease a 9x13-inch baking dish. Combine cake mix, oats and butter until crumbly. Press half of oat mixture into bottom of baking dish.

Drain strawberries; reserve ¼ cup of syrup. Combine reserved strawberry syrup, cream cheese, sugar and egg; spread over oat mixture in baking dish. Arrange drained strawberries on top of cream cheese mixture.

Top strawberries with remaining oat mixture; press down gently. Bake for 25-35 minutes, until top starts to turn golden brown. Cool and cut into bars.

CHEWY SOUR CREAM CRAISIN BARS

These delicious bars, created by Shirley Johnson of Warrens, Wisconsin, won first prize in the "processed cranberry" category at the 30th annual Warrens Cranberry Festival. In its first year, the festival was strictly local and had 3,500 attendees. Today, it has grown to an international event with 100,000 visitors.

Makes 20 Bars

1¼	cups quick-cooking rolled oats
1¼	cups all-purpose flour
1	cup packed brown sugar, divided
½	teaspoon baking soda
1½	sticks butter
4	eggs, separated
1	cup white sugar
2	tablespoons cornstarch
1½	cups dried cranberries or Craisins
½	cup raisins
½	teaspoon vanilla extract
2	cups sour cream
½	teaspoon cream of tartar
⅛	teaspoon salt
⅓	cup pecans, chopped

Preheat oven to 350°F. In a medium bowl, combine oats, flour, ½ cup of brown sugar and baking soda. Cut in butter until crumbly; press into bottom of an ungreased 9x13-inch baking pan. Bake for 15 minutes.

In a saucepan over medium heat, combine egg yolks, white sugar, cornstarch, cranberries, raisins, vanilla and sour cream. Cook, stirring constantly, until mixture begins to boil. Boil mixture, stirring, for 1-2 minutes, until thick; pour over baked crust.

Beat eggs whites, cream of tartar and salt until soft peaks form. Add remaining ½ cup of brown sugar; beat until stiff peaks form. Spread egg white mixture over cranberry mixture. Sprinkle with pecans. Bake for 15-20 minutes, until golden brown. Cool, then slice into bars and refrigerate until serving.

DATE-FILLED BAR COOKIES

Pauline C. Speer of Indio, California, won first prize in the National Date Festival Recipe Contest in Indio, near Palm Springs. The festival began as a celebration of the Coachella Valley's date harvest. The event now offers a little something for everyone, including camel races and alligator wrestling.

Makes 18 Bars

Crust:
1½   sticks butter
1   cup packed brown sugar
1¾   cups all-purpose flour, sifted
½   teaspoon baking soda
1   teaspoon salt
1½   cup old-fashioned rolled oats

Date filling:
3   cups chopped dates
½   cup sugar
1½   cups water
¼   teaspoon salt
2   tablespoons lemon juice

Icing:
2   cups packed brown sugar
3   tablespoons evaporated milk
2   tablespoons dark corn syrup
2   tablespoons butter

For the crust: Preheat oven to 375°F. Combine crust ingredients; press half of mixture into bottom of a greased 9x13-inch baking pan. Spread with date filling. Cover with remaining crust mixture. Bake for 30-35 minutes, until lightly browned. Cool slightly, then drizzle with icing and cut into bars.

For the date filling: Combine date filling ingredients in a saucepan over medium heat; cook for 5-10 minutes, until thick. Remove from heat and cool completely.

For the icing: Combine icing ingredients in a saucepan over low heat; cook, stirring, until butter and sugar are melted and combined.

COOKIES & BROWNIES

MIXED-UP BROWNIE DELIGHT

Virginia Prince of Grand Blanc, Michigan, won AAA Michigan's Best Brownies in Michigan Baking Contest. The contest attracted 300 bakers, who produced some of the state's chewiest, gooiest, chocolate treats.

Makes 18 to 24 Brownies

2	sticks butter or margarine
4	ounces unsweetened chocolate
2	cups sugar
4	eggs
2	teaspoons vanilla extract
1	cup sifted all-purpose flour
⅓	teaspoon baking powder
½	teaspoon salt
12	ounces caramels
2	tablespoons smooth peanut butter
½	cup evaporated milk
½	cup chopped walnuts
½	cup white chocolate chips
½	cup milk chocolate chips

Preheat oven to 350°F. Melt butter and unsweetened chocolate squares together; stir to combine. Mix in sugar. Add eggs, 1 at a time. Stir in vanilla. Add flour, baking powder and salt; mix well. Pour half of batter into a greased 9x13-inch baking pan. Bake for 14 minutes.

Heat caramels, peanut butter and evaporated milk, stirring frequently, until melted and combined. Remove brownies from oven; pour caramel mixture over brownies. Sprinkle nuts and white and milk chocolate chips over caramel layer. Pour remaining batter over chocolate chips and bake for 15 minutes. Cool before slicing.

Coffee Brownies with Kahlua Frosting

Martha L. Beres of Warren, Michigan won third prize in the annual AAA of Michigan's Best Brownies In Michigan Baking Contest. "Year after year, the recipes keep getting better," said an event judge. "What sets a recipe apart is that little extra touch, maybe an unusual ingredient or extra culinary creativity." Clearly, these brownies are something special.

Makes 16 Brownies

Coffee brownies:

1½	sticks butter or margarine
3	ounces unsweetened chocolate
1½	cups sugar
3	large eggs
1½	teaspoons vanilla extract
⅛	teaspoon salt
¾	cup all-purpose flour
1	tablespoon instant espresso coffee powder

Kahlúa frosting:

1½	cups powdered sugar
1	teaspoon Kahlúa
2	ounces unsweetened chocolate, melted
1-2	tablespoons milk

For the brownies: Preheat oven to 325°F. In a bowl, melt butter and chocolate in microwave; stir until smooth and combined. Whisk in sugar, eggs, vanilla and salt until combined. Stir in flour until combined. Spread batter into a greased 8x8-inch baking pan. Bake for 30-35 minutes, or until set. Cool in pan. Frost when cool.

For the frosting: Combine powdered sugar, Kahlúa and melted chocolate. Add milk, a little at a time, to make a smooth, spreadable frosting.

PIES & TARTS

CRANBERRY PECAN UPSIDE DOWN APPLE PIE

Nancy Wilhelm of Mukwonago, Wisconsin, won second prize in the "fresh cranberry" category at the Warrens Cranberry Festival in Warrens, Wisconsin, the largest cranberry festival in the world. Cranberries are Native American wetland fruit that grows on trailing vines like strawberries.

Makes 6 to 8 Servings

Crust:
1¾ cups all-purpose flour, divided
3 tablespoons sugar
Pinch of salt
¾ stick unsalted butter, chilled and cut into small pieces
⅓ cup lard, chilled and cut into small pieces
3-4 tablespoons ice water

Filling:
1 cup packed brown sugar
1 cup chopped pecans
1 cup fresh or frozen cranberries
1 stick butter, melted
¼ cup white sugar
2 teaspoons cinnamon
3 tablespoons all-purpose flour
1 teaspoon nutmeg
6 cups Granny Smith or other crisp, tart apples, peeled and sliced
Vanilla custard or ice cream, for serving

For the crust: Put flour, sugar, salt, butter and lard in a food processor (or use a hand pastry blender); process until mixture resembles a coarse meal. With processor running, add enough of the ice water through the feed tube for the dough to gather into a ball. Wrap dough in plastic wrap and refrigerate for at least 1 hour.

For the filling: Preheat oven to 375°F. Combine brown sugar, pecans, cranberries and melted butter; spoon into a 9-inch soufflé or other baking dish with at least 2-inch tall sides.

Divide chilled pastry dough in half. On a floured surface, roll out one piece of dough into an 11-inch circle; place on top of cranberry mixture. Combine sugar, cinnamon, flour and nutmeg; add apples and toss to combine well. Spread apple filling on top of crust in pan.

Roll out remaining piece of dough into an 11-inch circle; place on top of apple filling. Trim and crimp dough edges. Cut 4 steam vents in top crust. Bake for 40-50 minutes. Cool for 5 minutes. Put a serving plate on top of pie and turn upside down. Remove baking dish. Put any topping remaining in dish on top of pie. Serve warm with vanilla custard or ice cream.

PIES & TARTS

PEACHES & CREAM SUPREME PIE

Michele Plumb of Grand Junction, Colorado, took second prize at the Palisade Peach Festival in Palisade, Colorado. The festival's "Peach Days" has been a popular event since the 1800s. Today, the area's world-famous peaches are sought after by people who drive hundreds or even thousands of miles to enjoy them.

Makes 1 Pie

1   cup Hungarian all-purpose flour
1   stick butter, softened
1   cup finely chopped pecans
1   (8-ounce) package Philadelphia cream cheese, softened
1   cup powdered sugar
1   (8-ounce) container Cool Whip, thawed and divided
4   large Palisade peaches, peeled and sliced
1   (3½-ounce) package Jell-O instant vanilla pudding mix
1⅓ cups cold milk
1   teaspoon almond extract
Sliced almonds, toasted, for garnish
Caramel ice cream topping

Preheat oven to 350°F. Combine flour, butter and pecans; press into bottom and up sides of a greased 10-inch pie pan. Bake for 25 minutes. Cool completely.

Beat cream cheese and sugar with a mixer until fluffy. Fold in 1 cup of Cool Whip; spread over cooled crust. Arrange peaches on top of Cool Whip.

Whisk together pudding mix, milk and almond extract; spread over peaches. Top with remaining Cool Whip. Sprinkle with toasted sliced almonds and drizzle with caramel topping to serve.

GRANDMA'S PEACH PIE

Bea Tusberg of Grand Junction, Colorado, won first prize in the "pies and tortes" category at the Palisade Peach Fest in Palisade, Colorado. The United States is the largest peach producer in the world, and peaches are grown commercially in almost every region of the country.

Makes 1 Pie

Crust:
3 cups Hungarian all-purpose flour
1¼ teaspoons salt
⅔ cup shortening
7-10 tablespoons cold clear soda (such as 7-Up or ginger ale)

Filling:
6 cups sliced peeled Palisade peaches
1 (4-ounce) package Jell-O cook and serve vanilla pudding mix
¼ cup sugar
¼ teaspoon vanilla extract
¼ cup tapioca
1 tablespoon lemon juice
1 teaspoon butter, cut into small pieces
Cinnamon, to taste
Sugar, to taste

For the crust: Preheat oven to 375°F. In a large bowl, combine flour and salt. Cut in shortening until crumbly. Add enough soda to flour mixture to form a ball. Divide dough in half. Roll dough out into 2 crusts. Place one crust in a 9-inch deep-dish pie pan.

For the filling: In a large saucepan over medium heat, combine peaches, pudding mix, sugar, vanilla, tapioca and lemon juice. Cook until mixture starts to bubble, then spoon into pastry-lined pie pan.

Top peach filling with remaining crust. Cut slits into crust. Dot with butter. Sprinkle with cinnamon and sugar. Bake for about 45 minutes, or until done.

CARAMEL APPLE PIE WITH TOFFEE STREUSEL TOPPING

Marles Riessland of Riverdale, Nebraska, took first prize in the American Pie Council's eighth annual National Pie Championship, held at the Great American Pie Festival. The competition draws amateur and professional bakers and pie companies from around the United States and Canada.

Makes 1 Pie

Crust:
3   cups all-purpose flour
1   teaspoon salt
1   teaspoon sugar
1   cup plus 1 tablespoon butter-
     flavored shortening, chilled
⅓   cup ice water
1   tablespoon vinegar
1   egg, beaten

Filling:
6   cups sliced peeled apples
     (Jonathan or Granny Smith)
1   tablespoon lemon juice
½   cup packed light brown sugar
½   cup white sugar
¼   cup all-purpose flour
1   teaspoon cinnamon
¼   teaspoon nutmeg
¼   teaspoon salt
1   teaspoon vanilla extract
¼   cup heavy cream
½   stick butter

Toffee streusel topping:
½   cup all-purpose flour
3   tablespoons sugar, plus extra
     for topping
1   tablespoon butter
2   chocolate covered toffee bars
     or 3 ounces chocolate-covered
     peanut or pecan brittle, crushed
Beaten egg white

For the crust: In a large bowl, combine flour, salt and sugar. Cut in shortening with a pastry blender or 2 knives until mixture resembles a coarse meal. In a small bowl, mix water, vinegar and egg. Add vinegar mixture to flour mixture, 1 tablespoon at a time, tossing with a fork to form a soft dough. Chill dough for 30 minutes.

Shape dough into 2 discs. Wrap in plastic wrap and refrigerate for at least 3 hours (overnight is best). On a pastry cloth or floured surface, roll out dough, flipping dough at least once and adding a little more flour to the pastry cloth. Roll out 1 disc of dough and fit in pie pan.

For the filling: Sprinkle apples with lemon juice. In a large bowl, combine light brown and white sugar, flour, cinnamon, nutmeg and salt. Add apples; toss to coat. Stir in vanilla and cream. Melt butter in heavy skillet over medium heat. Add apple mixture and cook for about 8 minutes, until apples have softened. Add apples to crust.

For the topping: Preheat oven to 450°F. Combine flour and sugar. Mix in butter with a fork until mixture forms coarse crumbs. Stir in crushed toffee bars; sprinkle over pie. Roll out second dough disc and place on top of pie; seal and flute edges and cut vents in top. Brush crust with beaten egg white and sprinkle with sugar. Bake for 15 minutes. Lower heat to 350°F. Bake for 45 minutes more.

APPLE RASPBERRY PIE WITH CINNAMON CHANTILLY CREAM

The makers of Crisco recently invited people from across America to submit their favorite festive recipes to the Crisco Celebrates the Flavor of the Holidays Recipe Contest. This pie, from Gloria Bradley of Naperville, Illinois, took home the $5,000 grand prize.

Makes 8 to 10 Servings

Crust:
⅔ cup Crisco Butter Flavor Shortening
1⅔ cups all-purpose flour
⅔ cup sugar
½ cup finely ground almonds
½ cup Smucker's Seedless Red Raspberry Jam

Filling:
½ cup sugar
1½ tablespoons cornstarch
1 tablespoon grated orange zest
¾ teaspoon cinnamon
3 large Granny Smith apples, peeled and thinly sliced
¾ cup fresh raspberries (or cranberries)
1 tablespoon Crisco Butter Flavor Shortening

Topping:
3 tablespoons Crisco Butter Flavor Shortening
½ cup all-purpose flour
⅓ cup sliced almonds
¼ cup packed light brown sugar
½ teaspoon cinnamon

Cinnamon chantilly cream:
2 tablespoons powdered sugar
½ cup heavy cream
⅛ teaspoon cinnamon

For the crust: Preheat oven to 400°F. In a large bowl, combine shortening, flour, sugar and ground almonds with fingers or a pastry blender until mixture resembles coarse crumbs. Using well-floured fingers, press dough into bottom and up sides of a 10-inch tart pan with a removable bottom. Spread jam over crust.

For the filling: Combine sugar, cornstarch, orange zest and cinnamon. Add apples and toss to coat. Gently stir in raspberries. Arrange apple mixture in crust. Dot with shortening. Bake for 30 minutes.

For the topping: Combine topping ingredients with a fork until crumbly. After pie has baked for 30 minutes, sprinkle with topping. Bake pie for 15 minutes more. Remove pie from oven and cool on a wire rack. Serve pie warm or at room temperature with chantilly cream.

For the chantilly cream: Beat powdered sugar, cream and cinnamon with a mixer until thickened.

TIN ROOF CHOCOLATE PIE

Carol Piermarini of Holland, Massachusetts, won the grand prize and a trip to Walt Disney World in the 2003 Nestlé and Better Homes & Gardens' *Share the Very Best Recipe Contest. Carol combined several other pie recipes to create this winning entry.*

Makes 10 to 12 Servings

Pie:
2   cups Nestle Toll House Semi-Sweet Chocolate Morsels, divided
1   tablespoon butter
1   pre-baked (9-inch) deep-dish pie crust
20 vanilla caramels
1⅓ cups heavy whipping cream, divided
1½ cups lightly salted peanuts, coarsely chopped
15 large marshmallows
½   cup milk
¼   teaspoon vanilla extract
Whipped cream, for serving

Caramel topping:
3   caramels
2   tablespoons whipping cream
1   tablespoon butter

Heat ⅓ cup of chocolate morsels and butter in a small saucepan over low heat, stirring frequently, until morsels are melted. Spread chocolate mixture on bottom and up sides of pie crust. Refrigerate for 15 minutes, or until set.

Heat caramels and ⅓ cup of whipping cream in a small saucepan over medium heat, stirring frequently, until caramels are melted and mixture is smooth. Stir in nuts and spoon over chocolate layer; cover and refrigerate.

Heat 1⅓ cups of chocolate morsels, marshmallows and milk in a saucepan over low heat, stirring, until chocolate and marshmallows are melted and mixture is smooth. Remove from heat. Stir in vanilla. Cool completely.

Beat remaining 1 cup of whipping cream until soft peaks form; fold into cooled marshmallow mixture and spoon over caramel layer (pie will be full). Refrigerate pie for 3 hours or overnight. Drizzle caramel topping over pie. Sprinkle pie with remaining ⅓ cup of chocolate morsels and top with whipped cream to serve.

For the topping: Heat caramels, whipping cream and butter in a small saucepan over low heat, stirring, until smooth; cool slightly.

Sweet Potato Praline Cloud Pie

Amateur and professional pie makers alike come to compete in the American Pie Council's National Pie Championship on National Pie Day, January 23rd. Beth Campbell of Belleville, Wisconsin, took first prize in the "sweet potato pie" category in the eighth edition of this annual contest.

Makes 6 to 8 Servings

Filling:

2	sweet potatoes, peeled, cooked and mashed
½	stick butter, softened
1	cup sugar
2	eggs
½	teaspoon cinnamon
¼	teaspoon salt
½	teaspoon nutmeg
¼	teaspoon ground cloves
¼	teaspoon mace
1	cup evaporated milk
1	unbaked pie crust (see recipes on pages 214, 216 and 217 – halve recipes for this single crust pie)

Meringue:

¼	teaspoon salt
¼	teaspoon vanilla extract
1	teaspoon lemon juice
3	egg whites
6	tablespoons sugar

Topping:

2	tablespoons firmly packed dark brown sugar
2	tablespoons dark corn syrup
1	tablespoon butter
¼	teaspoon vanilla extract
⅓	cup chopped pecans

For the filling: Preheat oven to 350°F. Combine filling ingredients (except crust) and pour into crust. Bake until firm, about 35-40 minutes.

For the meringue: Combine salt, vanilla, lemon juice and egg whites; beat until foamy. Add sugar, 1 tablespoon at a time; beat until sugar dissolves and egg whites are stiff.

For the topping: In a saucepan over medium heat, combine brown sugar, corn syrup, butter and vanilla. Cook, stirring, until butter is melted and combined; remove from heat.

To finish: Spoon dollops of meringue in a ring around outside edge of pie. Sprinkle pecans over center of pie. Drizzle all or part of topping over pecan mixture. Bake for 15 minutes, or until golden brown. Cool pie to room temperature before serving. Cover and refrigerate leftovers.

STRAWBERRY SANDWICH

Jeanell Webb of Ashburn, Georgia, won first prize in the "pie" category at the annual Fire Ant Festival Strawberry Cook-off in Ashburn. The cook-off is sponsored by Calhoun Produce, a family farm with "pick your own" strawberry fields that produce some of the biggest, sweetest strawberries in the world.

Makes 1 Pie

Crust:
1   (15-ounce) package refrigerated pie crust (2 crusts)

Strawberry layer:
1   cup water
1   tablespoon strawberry gelatin
1   cup sugar
3   tablespoons cornstarch
Pinch of salt
2   cups strawberries, crushed and drained

Chocolate layer:
3   cups sugar
¾   cup unsweetened cocoa powder
1½   sticks margarine
¾   cup evaporated milk

Cream cheese layer:
¼   cup powdered sugar
1   (8-ounce) package cream cheese, softened

Topping:
Fresh strawberries, sliced or whole
Whipped topping (optional)
1   teaspoon powdered sugar

For the pie: Let pie crusts stand at room temperature for 15-20 minutes. Preheat oven to 450°F. Unfold 1 crust and place on a cookie sheet lined with parchment paper. Prick crust all over with a fork. Bake for 9-11 minutes, or until light golden brown. Cool for 15 minutes. Repeat with second crust.

For the strawberry layer: Combine water, gelatin, sugar, salt and cornstarch in a saucepan. Bring to a boil, then remove from heat and chill. When mixture has chilled (about 45 minutes), mix in crushed strawberries.

For the chocolate layer: In a bowl, combine sugar, cocoa powder, margarine and evaporated milk. Microwave, stirring occasionally, until margarine is melted and mixture is smooth. Spread on each crust; cool until set.

For the cream cheese layer: Beat powdered sugar and cream cheese until smooth. Spread cream cheese mixture on top of chocolate layer on one crust.

To assemble: Put crust with chocolate and cream cheese on a serving plate. Spread half of strawberry mixture over cream cheese layer. Top strawberry mixture with second crust. Spread remaining strawberry mixture over second crust. Top with fresh strawberries. Pipe whipped topping around edge of crust, if desired. Sprinkle with powdered sugar to serve.

KEY "LIMON" TART WITH FRESH RASPBERRIES

In the Johnson & Wales/Bacardi recipe contest, this tart earned Diana Dumitru the $5,000 first prize in the "plated dessert" category. Dumitru is a 1993 graduate of the Providence, Rhode Island, campus of Johnson & Wales University and now owns Cakes Plus in Fairview Park, Ohio.

Makes 10 Individual Tarts

Tarts:
2 (14-ounce) cans sweetened condensed milk
8 egg yolks
Grated zest of 2 Key limes or 1 lime
6 tablespoons Key lime or lime juice (about 6 Key limes or 4 limes)
½ cup Bacardi Limon Rum
10 mini (3½-inch diameter) graham cracker tart shells

Raspberry syrup:
1 cup water
1 cup sugar
¼ cup Bacardi Limon Rum
2 pints fresh raspberries

Topping:
1 cup heavy cream
2 tablespoons powdered sugar
Grated zest of 4 Key limes or 2 limes
Grated zest of 4 lemons
10 sprigs fresh mint

For the tarts: Preheat oven to 300°F. Put condensed milk in a stainless steel bowl. Whisk in egg yolks until mixture is smooth. Stir in Key lime zest. Gradually whisk in Key lime juice and rum. Divide mixture among tart shells. Bake for about 20 minutes, or until filling is set. Remove tarts from oven and cool. Refrigerate tarts for about 20 minutes. To unmold tarts, put a piece of parchment or wax paper over tarts, invert tarts, remove aluminum tins and flip right side up. Put tarts on a tray and refrigerate until serving.

For the raspberry syrup: In a small saucepan, bring water and sugar to a boil. Remove from heat and stir in rum. Cool mixture, then stir in raspberries. Gently mash a couple raspberries to make syrup slightly pink. Cover and refrigerate until serving.

For the topping: Beat heavy cream with a mixer. When it begins to thicken slightly, add powdered sugar. Continue beating until cream forms stiff peaks.

To serve: Place 1 tart in middle of each plate. Top with 1 spoonful of whipped cream. Drizzle raspberry syrup and some raspberries on plate (do not drizzle syrup over tart). Sprinkle Key lime and lemon zest over plate and tart. Garnish with a sprig of fresh mint.

CARAMEL MACADAMIA MILK CHOCOLATE MOUSSE TART

Edwina Gadsby of Great Falls, Montana, submitted this winning dessert to IGA's Hometown Holidays Recipe Contest. Buttery caramels are a perfect complement to the rich macadamias, and the milk chocolate mousse adds a lightness that makes this tart irresistible.

Makes 8 to 10 Servings

Crust:
1   (9-ounce) package Nabisco "Famous" chocolate wafers
5⅓ tablespoons unsalted butter, melted

Caramel macadamia filling:
16 Kraft vanilla caramels
2   tablespoons heavy whipping cream
1   teaspoon vanilla extract
1   cup macadamia nuts, coarsely chopped

Milk chocolate mousse:
2   tablespoons water
1   teaspoon unflavored gelatin
1   cup chilled heavy whipping cream, divided
1   (6-ounce) package Nestle milk chocolate morsels
Kraft caramels, melted, for garnish
Whipped cream, for garnish
White chocolate curls, for garnish

For the crust: Put chocolate wafers in a food processor; pulse until finely ground. Stir in butter. Press crust into bottom and part way up sides of a 9-inch springform pan. Chill crust.

For the filling: Melt caramels in a saucepan over low heat. Stir in cream. Remove from heat and stir in vanilla and nuts. Spread caramel mixture over crust; chill.

For the mousse: Put water in a small saucepan; sprinkle with gelatin. Let stand for 10 minutes. Stir over low heat until gelatin dissolves; set aside.

In a small saucepan over medium heat, bring ¼ cup of whipping cream to a simmer. Remove from heat. Add milk chocolate morsels; stir until chocolate is melted and mixture is smooth. Whisk in gelatin mixture until combined. Transfer to a bowl, cover and chill for 10 minutes.

Beat remaining ¾ cup of cream until stiff peaks form; carefully fold into milk chocolate mixture. Spread mousse over caramel filling in crust. Cover and chill until set, about 2 hours.

To serve: Remove tart from pan. Cut into wedges. Garnish each serving with melted caramels, whipped cream and white chocolate curls.

RICOTTA TART

The Italian Culinary Institute is committed to finding the best of Italy and Italian cuisine in America. The Institute scours the nation for the best recipes and chefs and brings them to you. This award winner from the Italian Cooking & Living *magazine recipe competition was created by executive chef Enzo Pezone of Pepolino in New York, New York.*

Makes 1 Tart

Crust:
1½ sticks plus ½ tablespoon unsalted butter, softened
1 egg yolk
¼ cup plus 2 tablespoons sugar
2¼ cups 00-grade or pastry flour

Filling:
2¼ cups ricotta cheese
½ cup sugar
2 large eggs
1 teaspoon vanilla extract
1 cup heavy cream
Powdered sugar, for garnish

For the crust: Preheat oven to 350°F. Mix butter, egg yolk and sugar with a wooden spoon. Add flour, a little at a time, gently mixing with hands until incorporated. Roll out dough ⅛-inch thick. Line an 8-inch springform tart pan with dough; set aside.

For the filling: Put ricotta, sugar, eggs, vanilla and cream in a food processor; process until very smooth and creamy. Spread filling in crust. Bake for about 60 minutes, or until a toothpick inserted in center comes out clean (begin checking after 40 minutes). Sprinkle tart with powdered sugar to serve.

*Note: 00-grade flour is a fine, Italian flour used in cakes and pastas. It is available at some gourmet and Italian specialty stores.

POACHED PEAR TART WITH VANILLA BEAN CUSTARD

Mary Sommers of Santa Cruz, California, won the Vanilla Company's Cabrillo Culinary Arts Students'
Vanilla Cook-off. An avid chef, Sommers overcame many personal obstacles to achieve such acclaim. She
immerses herself into all of her recipes – this pear tart is conceived from the heart!

Makes 1 Tart

Poached pears:
1   vanilla bean
1½   cups red wine
1½   cups water
1   cup sugar
1   bay leaf
1   sprig thyme
3   peppercorns
½   lemon, sliced
3   pears, peeled and halved
     (Bosc and Anjou work well)

Vanilla bean custard:
2   cups milk
1   vanilla bean
½   cup sugar
2   egg yolks
1   egg
3   tablespoons cornstarch,
     divided
½   cup sugar
1   tart shell (made in a 10-inch
     tart pan with a removable
     bottom), baked and cooled

For the pears: Split vanilla bean and scrape seeds into a large saucepan. Add vanilla bean pod and remaining poached pear ingredients, except pears. Bring to a boil, lower heat, add pears and simmer until softened, about 15 minutes. Remove pears, strain and cool (reserve poaching liquid for glazing the tart). Slice pears into very thin vertical slices and drain on paper towels.

For the custard: Put milk in a saucepan. Cut vanilla bean and scrape seeds into milk. Add cut vanilla bean pod and sugar to milk. Bring milk just to a boil, then remove from heat. In a metal bowl, whisk together eggs and 2 tablespoons of cornstarch. Whisk in sugar. Pour a little of the milk mixture into the egg mixture and stir; then pour egg mixture into remaining hot milk in saucepan. Cook over low heat until it is very thick; chill. When custard has cooled, remove vanilla bean pod.

To serve: Boil reserved pear poaching liquid until reduced by half. Combine 1 tablespoon of water with remaining 1 tablespoon of cornstarch; stir into pear poaching liquid until clear and thick. Remove and chill.

Evenly spread chilled custard into tart shell. Arrange pear slices around edge of tart so stem ends all meet in center. Fan pear slices over tart. Carefully brush reduced pear poaching liquid over pears to glaze. Chill and serve.

MAPLED NUT COMPANY BUTTER TART

Marsha Phillips, co-owner of Vermont Mapled Nut Company, won the title of "Vermont's Best Maple Cook" at the Vermont Maple Festival in St. Albans, Vermont.

Makes 1 Tart

½ cup Vermont maple syrup
5⅓ tablespoons butter, melted
1   egg, beaten
2   tablespoons milk
1   teaspoon vanilla extract
1   cup coarsely chopped Mapled Nut Company Maple Sugar Coated Pecans or Walnuts, plus extra for topping (optional)
1   (9-inch) unbaked tart or pie crust

Preheat oven to 350°F. Combine maple syrup, butter, egg and milk. Stir in nuts; pour into crust. Top with more nuts, if desired. Bake for 25-30 minutes, until top is puffed and bubbly, and crust begins to brown. Cool for 20 minutes. Serve warm or at room temperature.

DESSERTS

PEANUT BUTTER CRUNCH CHEESECAKE

Ryan Nackers of Neenha, Wisconsin, wowed the judges with this delicious cheesecake at the 18th annual Great Wisconsin Cheese Festival cheesecake contest in Little Chute. Other events at the festival include a cheese curd eating contest, cheese tastings and a cheese carving demonstration.

Makes 12 to 14 Servings

Crust:
1⅓ cups crushed peanut butter cookies
5⅓ tablespoons melted butter

Filling:
3 (8-ounce) packages cream cheese
1 (14-ounce) can sweetened condensed milk
3 large eggs
½ cup sugar
1 tablespoon vanilla extract
3 tablespoons lime juice
1½ cups smooth peanut butter
3 tablespoons chocolate chips

Topping:
1 (24-ounce) squeeze bottle chocolate syrup
1 cup smooth peanut butter, melted
1 tablespoon chocolate chips, or more to taste

For the crust: Preheat oven to 325°F. Combine cookies and butter; press into bottom of a 9-inch springform pan. Bake for 5 minutes.

For the filling: Beat cream cheese and condensed milk until fluffy. Add eggs, sugar, vanilla and lime juice; mix until smooth. Transfer ⅓ of cream cheese mixture to a separate bowl; set aside. Spread half of remaining cream cheese mixture over crust.

In a double boiler, melt peanut butter with chocolate chips. Mix peanut butter mixture with the set aside ⅓ of cream cheese mixture; carefully spread over cream cheese layer in crust. Spread remaining cream cheese mixture over peanut butter/cream cheese layer (you will have 3 layers – 1 cream cheese/peanut butter layer sandwiched between 2 plain cream cheese layers).

Fill a pan larger than the springform pan with ¼-inch of water. Wrap springform pan tightly with foil and place in water-filled pan. Bake for about 55 minutes, or until cake reaches an internal temperature of 155°F. Cool completely, then remove pan.

For the topping: In a criss-cross pattern, drizzle chocolate syrup then melted peanut butter over top of cheesecake. Sprinkle with chocolate chips.

Red, White & Blue Cheesecake

Carla Brockman of Poteet, Texas, was the 2003 grand champion at the Poteet Strawberry Festival. The festival is recognized as the largest agricultural event in Texas. With crowds in excess of 100,000, the event pours five to six million dollars into the south Texas economy each year.

Makes 16 Servings

Crust:
5⅓ tablespoons butter, melted
1½ cups crushed shortbread cookies
⅓ cup ground almonds

Filling:
5 (8-ounce) packages cream cheese, softened
1 teaspoon vanilla extract
1½ cups sugar
3 eggs, beaten
2 egg whites
2 cups white chocolate chips, melted

Topping:
½ cup sour cream
1 cup sugar, divided
1 cup water
1 tablespoon cornstarch
1 cup sliced strawberries
1 cup blueberries
1 cup raspberries

For the crust: Preheat oven to 350°F. Combine melted butter, shortbread cookies and almonds. Press into the bottom and up the sides of a 10-inch springform pan. Bake for 6 minutes; cool.

For the filling: Beat cream cheese with a mixer until smooth. Beat egg whites until foamy. Add egg whites, vanilla, sugar, eggs and melted white chocolate to cream cheese; beat just until blended, then pour into crust. Bake for 55-60 minutes. Cool cheesecake, then remove from pan.

For the topping: Combine sour cream and ⅓ cup of sugar. In a small bowl, dissolve remaining ⅔ cup of sugar in water. Add cornstarch; stir to dissolve. Add strawberries, blueberries and raspberries; toss gently to coat and glaze.

To serve: Top cheesecake with sour cream mixture and glazed strawberries, blueberries and raspberries.

Turtle Brownie Cheesecake

At the 18th annual Great Wisconsin Cheese Festival in Little Chute, Michelle Benter of Green Bay, Wisconsin, won first prize in the cheesecake contest. Numerous cakes are entered each year, from traditional to elaborate. The best part for festival attendees is that all the cakes are sold by the slice after the contest.

Makes 16 Servings

Crust and brownie topping:
2   sticks butter
1½   cups sugar
¼   cup water
2   tablespoons vanilla extract
2   (12-ounce) packages semi-
        sweet chocolate chips, divided
4   large eggs
1½   cups all-purpose flour
1   teaspoon baking soda
1   teaspoon salt

Filling:
3   (8-ounce) packages cream
        cheese
1   cup sugar
1   teaspoon vanilla extract
2   large eggs
1   cup white chocolate chips,
        melted
1½   cups sour cream

Topping:
½   cup fudge ice cream topping
Brownies (from crust and brownie
        topping above)
½   cup caramel ice cream topping
½   cup chopped pecans

For the crust and brownie topping: Preheat oven to 325°F. Melt butter, sugar and water in a saucepan over medium heat. Bring just to a boil, then remove from heat. Add vanilla and 2 cups chocolate chips; stir until chocolate chips are melted. Add eggs, 1 at a time, mixing well after each addition. Stir in flour, baking soda and salt. Stir in remaining chocolate chips (they will not be completely melted).

Line bottom of a 10-inch springform pan with parchment paper. Grease a 9x9-inch baking pan. Pour half of batter into the 9x9-inch pan to make brownies for topping. Bake for 35-37 minutes. Remove from oven, cool, cover and set aside. Pour remaining batter into springform pan and bake for 25 minutes.

For the filling: Lower oven temperature to 300°F. Beat cream cheese and sugar until fluffy. Beat in vanilla. Beat in eggs, 1 at a time. Mix in white chocolate. Mix in sour cream. Spread filling over crust. Bake for 90 minutes. Cover and chill, preferably overnight.

For the topping: When ready to serve, melt fudge topping in microwave until spreadable; spread over cheesecake. Cut half of the 9x9-inch pan of brownies into bite-sized chunks; sprinkle over fudge (enjoy remaining brownies on their own). Drizzle caramel topping over cheesecake. Sprinkle with pecans to serve.

ALOHA PEACHES 'N CREAM CHEESECAKE CUPCAKES

Julie Coleman of Grand Junction, Colorado, won first prize in the "miscellaneous dessert" category at the 2003 Palisade Peach Fest in Palisade, Colorado. Peaches are actually a member of the rose family. They are the fourth most consumed fruit in the United States.

Makes 24 Cupcakes

Cheesecake:

3	(8-ounce) packages Philadelphia cream cheese, softened
5	eggs
1	cup sugar
1	teaspoon vanilla extract
¼	teaspoon almond extract

Sour cream filling:

1	cup sour cream
3	tablespoons sugar
1	teaspoon vanilla extract

Peach mango topping:

2	cups peeled, chopped fresh ripe Palisade peaches, divided
2½	tablespoons cornstarch
⅓	cup sugar
½	cup Naked Juice Mighty Mango*

For the cheesecake: Preheat oven to 300°F. In a large bowl, beat cream cheese with a mixer on low speed until smooth. Add eggs, sugar, vanilla and almond extract; beat on medium speed until smooth. Fill paper-lined muffin cups ⅔-full. Bake for 30 minutes.

For the filling: Just before cupcakes are done, combine filling ingredients. Remove cupcakes from oven. The cupcakes will sink in the middle – at that point, put a spoonful of filling in center of each cupcake. Return cupcakes to oven and bake for 5 minutes more. Remove cupcakes from oven and cool.

For the topping: In a medium saucepan over medium heat, combine 1 cup of chopped peaches, cornstarch, sugar and mango juice; cook, stirring, until mixture thickens. Cool for 10 minutes, then stir in remaining 1 cup of chopped peaches. Spoon 1½-2 tablespoons of topping over sour cream filling in each cupcake to serve. Refrigerate leftovers.

*Note: Naked Juice Mighty Mango is a thick, refrigerated juice, like Odwalla. If unavailable, substitute any thick mango juice or mango nectar.

BLUEBERRY LEMON WISP

Maine wild blueberries have been found to have considerable nutritional value. The berries are harvested in August and the harvest is celebrated with the Machias Wild Blueberry Festival each year. Kathleen Fritz of Edgartown, Massachusetts, took first prize in the "baking" category with this recipe.

Makes 10 to 12 Servings

Crust:
2 cups crushed gingersnaps
½ cup finely chopped pecans
5½ tablespoons butter, melted
1 teaspoon cinnamon
1 tablespoon brown sugar

Filling:
2 envelopes Knox unflavored gelatin
½ cup orange juice
1½ cups Maine blueberries
2 (8-ounce) packages low-fat cream cheese, softened
1 (8-ounce) container low-fat blueberry yogurt
1 (8-ounce) container low-fat lemon yogurt
½ cup sugar
½ teaspoon vanilla extract
1 teaspoon lemon juice

Topping:
1 cup whipping cream
4-5 tablespoons powdered sugar, to taste
2 tablespoons lemon juice
½ cup Maine blueberries
Strips of lemon zest

For the crust: Preheat oven to 350°F. Combine crust ingredients; mix with a fork until crumbly. Pat evenly into bottom of a 10-inch springform pan. Bake for 10 minutes, or until lightly browned. Remove from oven and cool.

For the filling: In a small saucepan over low heat, dissolve gelatin in orange juice, stirring until gelatin is dissolved.

In a medium bowl, beat cream cheese, blueberry and lemon yogurt, sugar, vanilla and lemon juice with a mixer on medium speed until combined. Gradually beat in gelatin mixture on low speed, then beat on medium speed for about 2 minutes. Gently fold in blueberries. Pour into cooled crust. Chill for several hours, until set.

For the topping: Whip whipping cream until stiff. Slowly blend in powdered sugar and lemon juice.

To serve: Gently run a knife around pan; remove outer ring of pan. Transfer wisp to a plate. With a pastry bag (or a ziplock plastic bag with a corner cut off), pipe whipped cream around base and top of wisp in a decorative fashion. Top with blueberries and lemon zest.

CHOCOLATE RASPBERRY TRUFFLE TORTE

Over 700,000 young women have competed in America's Junior Miss since its inception in 1958. Past participants include Diane Sawyer of ABC News, Deborah Norville of Inside Edition and Debra Messing of NBC's Will & Grace. Courtney Basich, West Virginia's Junior Miss 2003, joins this esteemed group with this winning dessert.

Makes 16 Servings

Torte:
2   (10-ounce) packages frozen raspberries, thawed
4   sticks unsalted butter
1   cup sugar
12 ounces semisweet chocolate chips
4   ounces bittersweet chocolate, finely chopped
½   cup Chambord liqueur
½   teaspoon raspberry extract
8   eggs, room temperature

Topping:
2   tablespoons unsalted butter
⅔   cup whipping cream
8   ounces bittersweet chocolate, finely chopped
Fresh raspberries, for garnish
Mint sprigs, for garnish

For the torte: Preheat oven to 325°F. Butter bottom and sides of a 10-inch round cake pan. Line with wax paper. Strain raspberries into a bowl; reserve juice.

In a double boiler over simmering water, combine butter, sugar, semisweet chocolate and bittersweet chocolate. Cook, stirring, until chocolate is melted and mixture is smooth; remove from heat. Stir in reserved raspberry juice, Chambord and raspberry extract. Whisk in eggs, 1 at a time. Stir in raspberries.

Spoon batter into pan. Put cake pan in a larger pan; add enough water to come halfway up sides of cake pan. Bake for 60-80 minutes, or until a toothpick inserted in center comes out clean. Cool on a wire rack for 3 hours. Cover with plastic wrap and refrigerate for 3 hours or overnight.

For the topping: In a double boiler over simmering water, combine butter, whipping cream and bittersweet chocolate. Cook, stirring, until chocolate and butter are melted and combined. Cover with plastic wrap and chill for 30-45 minutes, stirring occasionally, until thickened to the consistency of pudding.

To serve: Loosen sides of torte from pan with a knife. Invert torte onto a plate and remove wax paper. Spread topping over torte. Top with raspberries. Cover and chill until serving. Garnish each serving with a mint sprig.

GERMAN CHOCOLATE KAHLUA CAKE

"Home on the Range," the theme for the 2003 Wichita Eagle *Holiday Cookbook Contest, is an apt one for the Wichita cooks who feel quite comfortable on range, grill, wok and oven. Arlene M. Shaver of Hutchinson, Kansas, won third prize in the "desserts and holiday favorites" category for this cake.*

Makes 16 Servings

1   (18-ounce) box German chocolate cake mix
½   cup vegetable oil
1   (4½-ounce) package instant chocolate pudding mix
¾   cup strong brewed coffee
4   large eggs, room temperature
¾   cup plus 3 tablespoons Kahlúa
1   cup milk chocolate chips
3   tablespoons butter

Preheat oven to 350°F. In a large bowl, combine cake mix, oil, pudding mix, coffee, eggs and ¾ cup of Kahlúa; beat with a mixer on medium speed until smooth, about 4 minutes. Pour into a well-greased Bundt pan. Bake for 45-50 minutes. Cool cake on a wire rack.

When cake is cool to the touch, remove from pan and cool completely. Melt chocolate chips and butter. Stir remaining 3 tablespoons of Kahlúa into chocolate chip mixture; stir to combine and drizzle over cake.

FUDGE CAKE

Margret Armantrout of Salem, Oregon, took first prize at the Oregon State Fair's Gerry Frank Chocolate Layer Cake Contest. Mr. Frank, the event's namesake, is a renowned chocolate connoisseur and the event's lead judge. He takes just two bites from each cake – one of frosting, one of cake.

Makes 1 Layer Cake

Cake:
3   ounces unsweetened chocolate
1   stick butter
2¼ cups brown sugar
3   large eggs
1   teaspoon vanilla extract
1   teaspoon chocolate extract
2¼ cups cake flour
2   teaspoons baking soda
½   teaspoon salt
1   cup sour cream
¼   teaspoon instant coffee crystals
1   cup boiling water

Chocolate frosting:
1   teaspoon vanilla extract
1¼ cups whipping cream
½   cup sugar
4   large egg yolks
1   pound bittersweet chocolate, finely chopped
1½ sticks unsalted butter, softened
⅛   teaspoon salt
½   cup light corn syrup
¼   cup sour cream

For the cake: Preheat oven to 350°F. Grease and flour 2 (9-inch) cake pans. Melt chocolate in a small saucepan over low heat. In a large bowl, beat butter and sugar with a mixer until smooth. Add eggs, 1 at a time, beating well after each addition. After last egg is added, beat on high speed until light and fluffy. Beat in vanilla, chocolate extract and melted chocolate.

Sift together flour, baking soda and salt into a bowl. Add flour mixture and sour cream alternately to egg mixture, beating on low speed after each addition just until blended. Dissolve coffee in boiling water; pour into batter and stir just until well blended. Pour batter into pans. Bake for 35 minutes. Cool cakes in pans for 10 minutes, then remove cakes from pans. Cool completely, then frost tops and sides of cakes.

For the frosting: In a large saucepan over medium-low heat, combine vanilla, cream, sugar and egg yolks. Cook, stirring, until mixture thickens (do not boil). Transfer to a bowl. Mix in chocolate, butter, salt and corn syrup; stir until smooth. Mix in sour cream. Chill frosting until it reached a spreadable consistency, stirring occasionally.

BUCKET OF DIRT & WORMS

Five-year-old Breanna Lynn of Furtner, Virginia took the cake with her blue bucket filled with brownies and Gummi worms in the "children under 8" category at the Clarke County Fair Bake-off in Winchester, Virginia. "We thought it was so cute that someone would come up with an idea like this," the judges said of Lynn's creation.

Makes 1 Bucket

1   (15-ounce) package brownie
     mix
A child's pail/bucket and shovel,
     (new or very clean)
Gummi worms

Prepare brownies according to package directions; cool, then cut into squares and place in bucket. Place shovel in bucket. Arrange Gummi worms on top of, sticking out of and in the brownies, so they look like worms crawling in the dirt.

HAWAIIAN CHOCOLATE MACAROON CAKE

Bill and Sue Kurtley of Ahwahnee, California, won the "Chocolate Chef of the Mountains" title at the 2003 Wild, Wonderful Chocolate Festival near Yosemite, California. The chocolate-loving women who run the festival offer chocolate recipes and little known wisdom such as, "If you eat chocolate and no one sees you eat it, it has no calories."

Makes 12 to 16 Servings

Cake:
4	large eggs, separated
1¾	cups sugar, divided
½	cup shortening
½	cup sour cream
1	teaspoon vanilla extract
½	cup brewed coffee
¼	cup buttermilk
2	cups all-purpose flour
½	cup Ghiradelli unsweetened cocoa powder
1	teaspoon baking soda
1	teaspoon salt

Filling:
1	large egg white
3	tablespoons sugar
2	cups flaked coconut, finely chopped
1	teaspoon all-purpose flour

Frosting:
1	cup Ghiradelli semisweet chocolate
3	tablespoons butter, softened
2	cups powdered sugar
5	tablespoons milk

Topping:
1	cup chopped macadamia nuts

For the cake: In a large bowl, beat egg whites on medium speed until soft peaks form. Gradually beat in ½ cup of sugar on high speed, 1 tablespoon at a time, until sugar is dissolved and stiff, glossy peaks form; set aside.

In a large bowl, cream remaining 1¼ cups of sugar and shortening. Add egg yolks, sour cream and vanilla; beat until creamy. In a small bowl, mix coffee and buttermilk. In a medium bowl, mix flour, cocoa, baking soda and salt; add to shortening mixture alternately with coffee mixture. Beat until combined. Fold in beaten egg whites.

For the filling: In a small bowl, beat egg white with a mixer on medium speed until soft peaks form. Gradually beat in sugar on high speed, 1 tablespoon at a time, until sugar is dissolved and stiff, glossy peaks form. Fold in coconut and flour; set aside.

Preheat oven to 350°F. Pour half of batter into an ungreased 10-inch tube pan with a removable bottom. Spoon filling over batter. Pour remaining batter over filling. Bake cake for 55-60 minutes, until a toothpick inserted in center comes out clean. Immediately invert cake onto a wire rack and cool completely, about 1 hour. When cool, run a knife around side of pan and remove cake. Frost tops and sides of cake. Sprinkle with macadamia nuts to serve.

For the frosting: Beat frosting ingredients until smooth and creamy.

TWINKIE CAKE

More than 5,000 people from all over the Southeast attended the first annual Carolina Chocolate Festival in Morehead City, North Carolina. The festival's baking contest proved to be one of the most popular events. Diane Willis of Harkers Island, North Carolina, won third prize in the "cake" category with this creation.

Makes 1 Layer Cake

Cake:
1   (18-ounce) box Duncan Hines Devils Food cake mix
3   large eggs
½   cup canola oil
1⅓ cups water

Filling:
1   (12-ounce) carton Cool Whip
¼   cup sugar
1   teaspoon vanilla extract

Frosting:
2   cups powdered sugar
¼   cup Hershey's unsweetened cocoa powder
¼   cup Crisco shortening
½   stick margarine, softened
Milk, as needed

For the cake: Preheat oven to 325°F. Prepare cake mix according to package directions. Divide cake mix among 3 greased and floured 9-inch round cake pans. Bake for 25-30 minutes; remove from oven and cool.

For the filling: Combine filling ingredients; beat with a mixer on high speed for 5-7 minutes, or until fluffy. Spread filling between cake layers.

For the frosting: Cream powdered sugar, cocoa powder, Crisco and margarine. Beat in enough milk to yield a spreadable consistency. Frost top and sides of cake.

BANANA SPLIT CAKE

Kristen Schultze of Poteet, Texas, won "best in show" at the 2003 Poteet Strawberry Festival. The strawberry was introduced to Texans by a Poteet gardener in 1921, when he invited guests from San Antonio to sample his newfound delicacy.

Makes 1 Layer Cake

Cake:

1	stick butter, softened
½	cup shortening
1¼	cups sugar
3	large eggs
1	teaspoon vanilla extract
3	cups all-purpose flour
2½	teaspoons baking soda
1	teaspoon salt
2	cups buttermilk
3	drops red food coloring
4	tablespoons strawberry ice cream topping, divided
4	tablespoons pineapple ice cream topping, divided
3	drops yellow food coloring
2	tablespoons unsweetened cocoa powder
2	tablespoons hot water
3-4	ripe bananas, thinly sliced
2	cups thinly sliced strawberries
	Chocolate ice cream topping (optional)

Frosting:

2	cups whipping cream, beaten until stiff
1	(4-ounce) package banana cream instant pudding mix

For the cake: Preheat oven to 350°F. Grease and flour 3 (9-inch) round cake pans. In a large bowl, beat butter, shortening and sugar with a mixer on medium speed until light and fluffy, about 3 minutes. Beat in eggs, 1 at a time. Beat in vanilla. In a small bowl, mix flour, baking soda and salt. Beat buttermilk and flour mixture alternately into sugar mixture, then beat for 1 minute more, scraping bowl constantly.

Divide batter among 3 bowls. Stir red food coloring and 2 tablespoons of strawberry topping into batter in one bowl. Stir 2 tablespoons of pineapple topping and yellow food coloring into batter in second bowl. Mix cocoa and hot water; stir into batter in third bowl. Pour each batter into a separate pan. Bake for 20-25 minutes, or until a toothpick inserted in center comes out clean. Cool for 10 minutes; remove cakes to wire racks and cool completely.

Put strawberry cake layer on a serving plate; spread with remaining 2 tablespoons of strawberry topping. Top with a layer of banana and strawberry slices. Spread with ¾ cup of frosting. Top with chocolate cake layer; spread with remaining 2 tablespoons of pineapple topping. Top with layer of banana and strawberry slices. Spread with ¾ cup of frosting. Top with pineapple cake layer. Frost sides and top of cake. Drizzle with chocolate topping and garnish with remaining banana and strawberry slices or other fruit toppings. Cover and refrigerate until serving.

For the frosting: Mix whipped cream and pudding well.

32K CARAMEL CARROT CAKE

This cake won first prize in Recipezaar's spring 2003 Ready, Set, Cook Recipe Contest. Is this a carrot cake with a rich caramel flavor or a caramel cake with a carrot undertone? Either way, this decadent layer cake with a caramel frosting and a butterscotch and chocolate glaze is sure to delight your guests.

Makes 12 Servings

Caramel carrot cake:
- 2 cups all-purpose flour
- 2 tablespoons baking powder
- 1 teaspoon salt
- 1½ sticks butter
- 10 caramels
- 1 cup packed brown sugar
- 3 large eggs
- 2 cups finely grated carrot
- ½ cup finely chopped pecans

Caramel frosting:
- ½ stick butter
- 15 caramels
- 3 tablespoons packed brown sugar
- 3 cups powdered sugar
- 4 tablespoons milk, divided

Glaze:
- ¼ cup butterscotch chips
- ½ cup chocolate chips

For the cake: Preheat oven to 350°F. Grease 2 (8-inch) round cake pans. Sift together flour, baking powder and salt into a small bowl. Melt butter and caramels in microwave; stir to combine.

In a large bowl, beat brown sugar and caramel mixture until combined. Add eggs, 1 at a time, beating after each addition. Beat in flour mixture on low speed, then beat on high speed for 3-4 minutes, until batter is smooth and light in color. Stir in carrots and pecans.

Spread batter into cake pans. Bake for about 30 minutes, until cakes are browned and just pulling away from sides of pan. Cool cakes on wire racks. When cool, frost tops and sides cake. Drizzle glaze over top of cake, letting some of the glaze drip down the sides as decoration.

For the frosting: Melt butter, caramels and brown sugar in microwave (about 2 minutes); stir to combine. In a bowl, beat caramel mixture, powdered sugar and 3 tablespoons of milk with a mixer. Add remaining 1 tablespoon of milk, if needed to reach desired consistency.

For the glaze: Melt butterscotch and chocolate chips in microwave (about 1 minute); stir until smooth.

Praline Pumpkin Cake

Diana Wara of Washington, Illinois, won the grand prize at the Morton Pumpkin Fest. Before the first Pumpkin Fest in 1967, Morton, Illinois was best-known for its pottery. "Little did anyone realize," writes Morton historian Mike Badgerow, "that the pumpkin had come to town, and with it a new, lasting and unifying identity."

Makes 1 Layer Cake

Cake:
2   sticks butter, softened
2   cups packed dark brown sugar
2   tablespoons vanilla extract
¾   teaspoon cinnamon
¾   teaspoon salt
1   cup Libby's Solid Pumpkin
3   large eggs, separated
2½   cups cake flour
2   teaspoons baking powder
½   cup white chocolate chips, finely chopped
½   cup finely chopped pecans
Caramel candies, melted, for garnish (optional)

Pralines:
2   large egg whites
2   cups sugar
2   tablespoons cinnamon
2   cups whole unsalted pecans

Frosting:
1   (16-ounce) box powdered sugar
1   teaspoon butter flavoring
1   teaspoon salt
¾   cup caramel syrup (see recipe on page 18)
¾   cup shortening
Cold water

For the cake: Preheat oven to 350°F. Grease and flour 2 (9-inch) round cake pans. In a large bowl, beat butter, brown sugar, vanilla, cinnamon and salt until light and fluffy. Add pumpkin and egg yolks; mix for 30 seconds. Add cake flour, ½ cup at a time, and baking powder; mix just until flour is incorporated. Stir in pecans and white chocolate chips. In a small bowl, beat egg whites until stiff peaks form; fold into batter. Pour batter into pans. Bake for 35-40 minutes, until a toothpick inserted in center comes out clean. Let cakes cool in pans for 15 minutes. Remove cakes to wire racks and finish cooling. When cool, cut tops off cakes to make even layers.

For the pralines: Lower oven temperature to 300°F. In a small bowl, beat egg whites until foamy. In a separate bowl, combine sugar and cinnamon. Add 1 cup of pecans to egg whites. Gently stir with a fork to coat pecans with egg white. Carefully transfer pecans to sugar mixture and gently coat. Remove pecans and lay flat on a parchment paper-lined baking sheet. Repeat with remaining 1 cup of pecans. Bake for about 25 minutes, stirring occasionally, until nuts are deep brown and crisp. Remove from oven; stir nuts to loosen. Cool completely on baking sheet.

For the frosting: Combine frosting ingredients with just enough water to make a spreadable mixture. Put 1 cake layer on a platter; frost top. Add second cake layer. Frost top and sides of cake. Top with pralines. Drizzle melted caramels over top and down sides of cake to serve.

Pumpkin Whoopie Pies

Valerie Lindner of Morton, Illinois, won third prize in the "cookie" category at the 2003 Morton Pumpkin Fest for this creative treat. References to pumpkins date back hundreds of years. The word "pumpkin" is derived from the Greek word "pepon," which means "large melon."

Makes 3 Dozen Small Pies

Pumpkin cookies:
1   cup vegetable oil
2   cups packed brown sugar
1½ cups Libby's canned pumpkin
2   eggs
3   cups all-purpose flour
1   teaspoon salt
1   teaspoon baking powder
1   teaspoon baking soda
1   teaspoon vanilla extract
1½ tablespoons cinnamon
1½ teaspoons ground ginger
1½ teaspoons ground cloves
Powdered sugar, for garnish
     (optional)

Whoopie pie filling:
1   egg white
2   tablespoons milk
1   teaspoon vanilla extract
2   cups powdered sugar, divided
¾   cup shortening

For the cookies: Preheat oven to 350°F. Spray 2 baking sheets with non-stick cooking spray. In a medium bowl, combine oil and brown sugar. Mix in pumpkin and eggs; beat well. Add flour, salt, baking powder, baking soda, vanilla, cinnamon, ginger and cloves; mix well.

Drop dough by heaping teaspoonsful onto baking sheets. Bake for 10-12 minutes; cool. Sandwich filling between 2 cookies. Dust with powdered sugar, if desired. Store in an airtight container with wax paper between pies.

For the filling: Beat egg white. Add milk, vanilla and 1 cup of powdered sugar; beat well. Beat in shortening and remaining 1 cup of powdered sugar until light and fluffy.

IRISH COFFEE ICE CREAM MERINGUE TORTE

Miss Meringue held its first recipe contest in 2003 – the Miss Meringue Holiday Scoop-off. The goal of the contest was to find great ways to use Miss Meringue's naturally fat-free and low-fat meringue cookies with ice cream.

Makes 8 Servings

Crust:
8   (5-ounce) packages Miss Meringue Classiques cappuccino cookies
¾   stick unsalted butter, melted
3   tablespoons sugar
2   tablespoons coffee-flavored liqueur (such as Kahlúa)

Filling:
1   quart coffee ice cream, slightly softened
¼   cup Irish whiskey
1   teaspoon instant espresso powder
1   tablespoon powdered sugar
½   cup whipping cream
Chocolate shavings, for garnish

For the crust: Preheat oven to 350°F. In a plastic bag or food processor, crush cappuccino cookies to fine crumbs. Mix crumbs, butter, sugar and liqueur; press into bottom of a 9-inch springform pan. Bake for about 8 minutes, until firm. Transfer pan to a wire rack and cool crust completely.

For the filling: Mix ice cream, whiskey, espresso powder, powdered sugar and whipping cream; spread over crust. Smooth top, cover and freeze. Garnish with chocolate shavings to serve.

TOASTED ALMOND PANNA COTTA

Chef Sally Camacho of the Four Seasons Hotel in Beverly Hills, California, won the $5,000 grand prize at the Almond Board of California's Almond Inspirations Recipe Contest. The winners were chosen by a distinguished panel of Bay Area chefs and food writers.

Makes 6 Servings

Toasted almond panna cotta:
1½   cups heavy cream
1½   cups whole milk
¼   cup plus 2 tablespoons sugar
½   cup sliced almonds, toasted
¾   cup water
1   tablespoon unflavored gelatin

Caramelized apricots:
¼   cup plus 2 tablespoons packed brown sugar
3   tablespoons butter
Seeds from ½ vanilla bean
6   apricots, each cut into 6 slices
¼   cup plus 2 tablespoons Cointreau or other orange liqueur
6   tablespoons sliced almonds, toasted, for garnish

For the panna cotta: In a saucepan, bring cream, milk and sugar just to a simmer, then remove from heat. Add almonds; cover and let stand for 10 minutes.

In a bowl, sprinkle gelatin over water. When gelatin is "spongy," place bowl over simmering water until gelatin melts. Stir into cream mixture.

Purée cream mixture in a blender; strain through a very fine sieve. Divide mixture among 6 (4-ounce) ramekins; cover and chill for at least 4 hours, or until firm.

For the caramelized apricots: In a skillet over medium heat, cook sugar, butter and vanilla bean seeds for 3-4 minutes, stirring occasionally, until mixture thickens to a caramel consistency. Add apricots; cook for about 30 seconds. Remove skillet from heat and stir in Cointreau.

Return skillet to heat and carefully flame Cointreau with a long match. Simmer for 2-3 minutes, shaking pan gently, until apricots are tender.

To serve: Dip a ramekin into hot water; invert panna cotta onto a serving plate and remove mold. Arrange 6 apricot slices around each panna cotta and spoon 2 tablespoons of apricot pan sauce around plate (do not let apricots or sauce touch panna cotta, as it will melt). Sprinkle each panna cotta with 1 tablespoon of sliced almonds.

Kona Coffee Flan with MacNut Cookie Crust

Maria 'ZeZe' Gonzalves of Keauhou, on Hawaii's Big Island, won first prize in the "professional dessert" category at the 2003 Kona Coffee Festival, the only coffee festival in the United States. This elegant dessert boasts a wonderful combination of textures and flavors, and is sure to delight all who taste it.

Makes 10 Servings

Kona coffee flan:

½	gallon whole milk
2	sticks cinnamon
2¾	cups sugar, divided
2	eggs
4	egg yolks
⅓	cup brewed Kona coffee
1	tablespoon Kona coffee liqueur
1	cup water

Macnut cookie crust:

8	ounces Mexican chocolate (Ibarra brand), softened in microwave for 20-30 seconds
2	tablespoons Kona coffee
¼	cup all-purpose flour
1	cup chopped macadamia nuts
½	stick butter
1	tablespoon Kona coffee liqueur

Kona coffee honey sauce:

1	cup honey
½	cup brewed Kona coffee
2	tablespoons brown sugar
2	tablespoons Kona coffee liqueur

For the flan: Heat milk, cinnamon and ¾ cup of sugar in a saucepan over medium-low heat. Simmer until reduced by half; discard cinnamon sticks. Transfer milk mixture to a food processor along with eggs, egg yolks, coffee and coffee liqueur; process thoroughly, then strain into a bowl.

Preheat oven to 300°F. In a small, heavy saucepan over low heat, combine remaining 2 cups of sugar and water over low heat; cook until sugar dissolves. Raise heat and boil, without stirring, for about 5 minutes, until mixture is a deep golden brown. Put 2 tablespoons of sugar mixture into each of 10 lightly greased ramekins. Add ½ cup of milk mixture to each ramekin. Put ramekins in a baking pan. Add enough water to pan to come halfway up sides of ramekins. Bake for 20 minutes, until set, but still slightly soft in center.

For the crust: Preheat oven to 375°F. Combine all crust ingredients; press into a ⅛-inch thick in bottom of a baking pan or baking sheet. Bake for 15 minutes.

For the sauce: Combine honey, coffee and brown sugar in a saucepan over medium heat; boil until mixture resembles a light syrup. Stir in coffee liqueur and cook for 5 minutes, then cool.

To serve: Cut circles in cookie crust that are the same size as ramekin used to make flan. Gently remove flans from ramekins and place on top of cookie crust. Drizzle with coffee honey sauce.

BANANA CREME BRULEE

Rene Rice of Santa Cruz, California, won the Vanilla Company's Cabrillo Culinary Arts Students' Vanilla Cook-off. The Cabrillo Culinary Arts program offers a commercial baking program that provides students with on-the-job baking experience, during which they produce breads and pastries that are sold on campus.

Makes 4 Servings

2	ripe bananas
2¼	cups heavy cream
¼	cup plus 8 teaspoons sugar, divided
4	egg yolks
1	vanilla bean, split

Slice one banana into thirds. In a saucepan over medium heat, combine heavy cream, sliced banana, ¼ cup of sugar and split vanilla bean. Cook, stirring, until steam rises, about 4-5 minutes. Let stand for 10-15 minutes.

Preheat oven to 325°F. Bring a pot of water to a boil. Strain cream mixture through a fine-mesh sieve into a small bowl; reserve vanilla bean pod and discard sliced banana. In a medium bowl, beat egg yolks. Add cream mixture to egg yolks, a little at a time, stirring constantly, until smooth.

Divide cream mixture among 4 (6-ounce) ramekins. Put ramekins in a deep baking pan. Add enough boiling water to come halfway up sides of ramekins. Bake for 30-35 minutes, until set. Remove ramekins from pan; cool to room temperature. Refrigerate for at least 2 hours.

Slice remaining banana crosswise into ⅛-inch thick slices. Arrange 7-8 slices on each crème brûlée. Sprinkle 2 teaspoons of sugar evenly over each crème brûlée. Heat sugar with a kitchen torch or under the broiler until sugar melts and lightly browns. Serve immediately.

CANDIED ORANGE CANNOLI

Pastry chef Iacopo Falai, of Barbalùc in New York, New York, was a winner in Italian Cooking & Living *magazine's recipe competition. The pairing of ricotta and orange is simultaneously rich and delicate, and sure to please your friends and family!*

Makes 10 Servings

Cannoli shells:
1¾ cups all-purpose flour
1 tablespoon sugar
1 tablespoon unsalted butter, softened
1 teaspoon instant coffee powder
1 teaspoon unsweetened cocoa powder
4 egg whites, divided
Pinch of salt
3 tablespoons red wine
Peanut or vegetable oil, for frying

Filling:
1 pound ricotta cheese
⅓ cup powdered sugar
2 tablespoons diced candied orange peel
1 tablespoon coarsely grated semisweet chocolate
2 tablespoons chopped pistachio nuts

For the shells: Mix flour, sugar, butter, instant coffee, cocoa powder, 3 egg whites and salt. Slowly add wine and mix with a wooden spoon until a dough is formed (add more wine, if needed.) Cover bowl with a dish towel and let stand for 1 hour.

For the filling: Combine ricotta and powdered sugar. Fold in candied orange peel, grated chocolate and pistachios. Cover and refrigerate for at least 1 hour.

On a floured surface, roll out dough ⅛-inch thick. With a cookie cutter, cut dough into 3-inch circles. Wrap each dough circle around a cannoli tube (available at specialty baking shops) or other 1-inch diameter tube.

In a clean bowl, beat remaining egg white. Seal cannolis by brushing edges with egg white and pressing together.

Heat 2 inches of oil to 325°F in a deep skillet. Fry cannolis in oil, 2 at a time, for 3-4 minutes, turning once with tongs, until golden brown. Remove shells and drain on paper towels. Cool to room temperature.

Spoon filling into a pastry bag fitted with a large round tip (or a ziplock plastic bag with a corner cut off) and fill cannoli shells with ricotta filling. Serve immediately.

Pear Apple Napoleon

The Pear Blossom Festival in Milford, Pennsylvania, is the finale of a month-long celebration of spring that includes the Pear Blossom Cook-off, live music and arts and crafts. Yolanda Goldsack of Milford, won first prize in the "dessert" category in the cook-off.

Makes 8 Servings

Almond cake:
2   sticks butter, softened
½   cup sugar
3   eggs
1   (12-ounce) can Solo almond filling
2¼   cups all-purpose flour
2   tablespoons baking powder
½   teaspoon salt
¼   cup milk

Pear apple Napoleon:
1   (16-ounce) package frozen puff pastry, defrosted
2   pears, peeled and chopped
2   apples, peeled and chopped
1   cup sugar
1½   cups water
½   cup powdered sugar
Milk or water
2   ounces semisweet chocolate, melted
Ice cream or sweetened whipped cream, for serving (optional)

For the cake: Preheat oven to 350°F. Grease and flour a 9x13-inch baking pan. In a large bowl, beat butter and sugar with a mixer until light and fluffy. Beat in eggs, 1 at a time. Beat in almond filling.

In a medium bowl, combine flour, baking powder and salt; beat into butter mixture alternately with milk. Spread batter in pan. Bake for 50-55 minutes, or until a toothpick inserted in center comes out clean. Cut top off cake to make an even layer.

For the Napoleon: Raise oven temperature to 400°F. Put puff pastry on a parchment paper-lined baking sheet. Cover with another piece of parchment paper. Weigh down with a heavy roasting pan. Bake for 35-40 minutes, until golden brown; cool and set aside.

In a saucepan, bring pears, apples, sugar and water to a boil; lower heat and simmer for 15 minutes, until fruit is tender and mixture is thickened. Cool and then chill.

To assemble: Cut puff pastry into 3 lengthwise pieces. Cut cake into 2 lengthwise pieces. Put 1 puff pastry piece on a plate. Top with a layer of cake, then a layer of pear mixture. Repeat layers, ending with puff pastry.

Combine powered sugar and enough milk or water to make a thick icing; spread over top layer of puff pastry. Drizzle chocolate over icing in a pretty pattern. Serve with ice cream or whipped cream, if desired.

BANANAS FOSTER DESSERT PIZZA

Diane Nemitz of Ludington, Michigan, beat over 1,000 other contestants to win the grand prize for the "best dessert pizza" in Mama Mary's Pizza Creations Contest. Nemitz won a trip to Disney World and a hefty supply of Mama Mary's pizza crusts.

Makes 8 to 10 Servings

1	Mama Mary's 12-inch Gourmet Pizza Crust
1	(3-ounce) package cream cheese
1	cup shortbread cookie crumbs
½	stick butter, melted
½	cup heavy cream
½	cup dark brown sugar
½	teaspoon cinnamon
1	teaspoon rum flavoring
1	teaspoon vanilla extract
1	pint vanilla ice cream
3	bananas, sliced
1	tablespoon rum (optional)
1	tablespoon banana liqueur (optional)

Preheat oven to 400°F. Put pizza crust on a vented pizza pan, baking sheet or pizza stone (if using a pizza stone, follow manufacturer's baking directions).

Spread cream cheese to edge of crust. Mix cookie crumbs and melted butter; sprinkle over cream cheese. Bake pizza for 10 minutes. Remove from oven; cool completely.

In a small, heavy saucepan combine heavy cream, brown sugar and cinnamon. Bring to a boil and boil for 4-5 minutes. Remove from heat; cool to room temperature. Stir in rum flavoring and vanilla extract.

Put pizza crust on a serving plate. Spread ice cream over crust. Add bananas to brown sugar mixture; spread over ice cream. If desired, warm rum and banana liqueur in a small skillet; carefully ignite with a long match, then carefully pour flaming rum mixture over bananas. Slice and serve immediately.

NACHO AVERAGE SWEETS

Frank Prud'homme of North Fork, California, created an extraordinary culinary delight for his entry in the Wild, Wonderful Chocolate Festival, for which he won first prize overall and "best presentation," as well as the coveted "Chocolate Chef of the Mountains" title.

Makes 8 to 12 Servings

Fruit salsa:
1 papaya, diced small
1 mango, diced small
1 Anjou pear, diced small
3-4 small Indian blood peaches
     (Autumn peaches), diced small
2 Bosc pears, diced small
2 cups diced fresh strawberries
1 cup fresh raspberries, diced
     small
2 tablespoons chopped mint
Sugar, to taste
2 shots Cointreau, or to taste

Chocolate dip:
2 (1-pound) Hershey's Special
     Dark chocolate bars
1 cup fresh raspberries, puréed
     and strained to remove seeds
2 shots Cointreau, or to taste

Nachos:
1½ cups white sugar
1 cup brown sugar
3 tablespoons cinnamon
3 tablespoons Hershey's
     unsweetened cocoa powder
12 large flour tortillas, cut into
     quarters or eighths
1 stick butter, melted
1 (4-ounce) block white chocolate

For the fruit salsa: Combine fruit and mint; toss gently. Add sugar, to taste. Stir in 2 or more shots of Cointreau. Cover and chill until serving.

For the chocolate dip: In a large double boiler, melt chocolate. As chocolate melts, fold in puréed raspberries. Stir in 2 or more shots of Cointreau. Keep warm.

For the nachos: Preheat oven to 300°F or use a deep fryer. Brush tortillas with melted butter and place on a baking sheet. Bake or fry until golden brown (watch carefully). Remove from oven and let stand until cool enough to handle. Brush lightly again with melted butter.

Combine white and brown sugar, cinnamon and cocoa powder. Toss warm tortillas in sugar mixture to lightly coat. Dip only a portion of each tortilla in chocolate dip. Put chips on a cookie sheet; chill until chocolate is set.

Just before serving, place chilled chips on a platter or plates. Grate white chocolate over chips and top with fruit salsa. If desired, purée some of the salsa and drizzle over nachos for a lovely color contrast.

CHOCOLATE & STRAWBERRY FILLED MERINGUE SHELLS

Strawberries from California's Oxnard Plain are so highly prized that the fertile growing area is now dubbed "California's Strawberry Coast." Each May, the California Strawberry Festival salutes Ventura County's top crop with this award-winning festival. Barbara Beautz of Simi Valley, California, won first prize in the 2003 strawberry recipe contest.

Makes 6 Servings

Meringue shells:
2   egg whites
¼   teaspoon cream of tartar
¼   teaspoon vanilla extract
Dash of salt
½   cup sugar

Filling:
2   (8-ounce) packages cream
       cheese, softened
1   cup powdered sugar
¼   cup unsweetened cocoa powder
1   cup Cool Whip
1   pint fresh strawberries, sliced,
       plus whole strawberries, for
       garnish
2   tablespoons sugar

For the meringue shells: Preheat oven to 300°F. Beat egg whites until foamy. Add cream of tartar, vanilla and salt; beat until soft peaks form. Gradually add sugar, beating until stiff peaks form. Spoon meringue into 6 mounds on a parchment paper-lined cookie sheet. Shape mounds into cups. Bake for 35 minutes. Turn off oven; leave meringue shells in oven for 1 hour to dry (do not open oven door). Remove meringue shells and cool on a wire rack.

For the filling: Beat cream cheese, powdered sugar and cocoa until fluffy. Fold in Cool Whip. In a blender or food processor, purée sliced strawberries (strain seeds, if desired); transfer to a bowl and mix in sugar. Divide cream cheese mixture among meringue shells. Top with puréed strawberry mixture. Garnish meringue shells with whole strawberries.

Fiesta S'mores

Chef Craig Pincus of Someone's in the Kitchen in Encino, California, won the "dessert" category and the grand prize in Mission Tortilla's Think Outside the Tortilla Recipe Contest. This recipe is a modern twist on a campfire favorite, combining dark chocolate, coffee liqueur, marshmallows, fudge-covered graham crackers and puffed flour tortilla balls.

Makes 4 Servings

12	Mission flour tortillas (any size; older tortillas are better)
2	large eggs, beaten
	Vegetable oil, for frying
2	cups graham cracker crumbs
4	large egg yolks
⅔	cup sugar
2¼	cups milk, divided
¼	cup all-purpose flour
¼	cup cornstarch
1	small vanilla bean, split
3	ounces bittersweet chocolate, grated
2	tablespoons coffee liqueur (such as Kahlúa)
1	cup marshmallow fluff
1	package fudge-covered graham crackers, broken into bite-size pieces
	Chocolate syrup, for garnish

Cut tortillas into 20 (2½-inch) circles with a biscuit cutter (16 tortilla balls are needed, but it's best to make extra, as not all will puff successfully). Roll edges of tortillas in beaten egg. With a fork, crimp edges of tortillas to help seal them. Let stand for 5-10 minutes until slightly dried.

Preheat oven to 325°F. Heat oil in a deep skillet to 325°F. Dip tortillas in beaten egg, then coat with graham cracker crumbs. Fry tortillas, gently spooning some oil over the top of each as they fry. When tortillas start to puff, turn them. Cook until golden brown. Remove tortillas; drain on paper towels. Place in oven for 3-5 minutes to crisp.

Combine egg yolks, sugar and ¼ cup of milk. Add flour and cornstarch; whisk until smooth. In a saucepan, bring vanilla bean and remaining 2 cups of milk to a boil. Slowly whisk about ⅓ of hot milk into egg yolk mixture, then whisk egg yolk mixture into hot milk in saucepan. Cook over medium-high heat until mixture starts to boil and thicken. Lower heat to low; cook for 3 minutes. Stir in chocolate and coffee liqueur. Strain mixture through a fine sieve and store in a container with plastic wrap over surface of mixture (to prevent a skin from forming).

To serve: Poke a hole in the bottom of a tortilla ball. With a pastry bag with a small tip (or a ziplock plastic bag with a corner cut off), fill ball with chocolate mixture. Put about 2 teaspoons of marshmallow fluff on each plate; top with a filled tortilla ball. Garnish with marshmallow fluff, fudge-covered graham cracker pieces and chocolate syrup.

CRANBERRY PINEAPPLE SORBET

Sharon Herbers of Hutchinson, Kansas, won over the judges in the Hutchinson News' *Holiday Recipe Cookbook Contest with this refreshing sorbet. The fresh cranberries, pineapple and orange create a tangy treat that will impress your guests at holiday gatherings.*

Makes 10 Servings

1	pound fresh cranberries
2	cups coarsely chopped fresh pineapple
1	cup sugar
½	cup chopped seeded orange
1	tablespoon grated orange zest
1	tablespoon Grand Marnier

Curls of orange zest, for garnish

Put cranberries, pineapple, sugar, orange and orange zest in a food processor; pulse until coarsely chopped. Transfer to large metal bowl. Stir in Grand Marnier. Cover and freeze until mixture is frozen 2 inches in from sides, about 2 hours.

After 2 hours, scrape down frozen part of mixture and beat with a mixer. Return to freezer for 2 hours. Repeat this process 2 more times, freezing again after the final beating. Spoon sorbet into serving dishes. Garnish with curls of orange peel to serve.

APPLE RICE PUDDING

Jack Pinson of Egan, Louisiana, was the "intermediate" and "tri-color" winner in the "rice dessert" category at the 2003 International Rice Festival in Crowley, Louisiana. This annual festival is one of Louisiana's largest and oldest events – over 7 million people have attended since its debut in 1937.

Makes 8 Servings

2   eggs
½   cup white sugar
½   cup sour cream
1   cup milk
¼   teaspoon salt
1   cooking apple (such as Rome
     or Gala), peeled and chopped
2½   cups cooked rice
1   cup grated cheddar cheese
⅓   cup raisins
¼   cup packed brown sugar
1   tablespoon all-purpose flour
½   teaspoon cinnamon
1   tablespoon butter or margarine,
     melted

Preheat oven to 350°F. In a large bowl, combine eggs, white sugar, sour cream, milk and salt. Stir in apples, rice, cheese and raisins. Spoon mixture into a lightly greased 2-quart baking dish.

In a small bowl, combine brown sugar, flour, cinnamon and melted butter; sprinkle over rice mixture. Bake for 45 minutes.

WHITE CHOCOLATE CRANBERRY MACADAMIA NUT FUDGE

This fudge took second prize at the 20th annual Cranberry Festival in Chatsworth, New Jersey. The festival celebrates New Jersey's cranberry harvest, the third largest in the United States. Long before the first Europeans arrived, the Lenni-Lenape Indians made their home in the area and harvested the berries, which they called "pakim," meaning "noisy berry."

Makes about 120 Pieces

1½   cups sugar
½   cup whipping cream
1   stick unsalted butter
½   teaspoon salt
1   (7-ounce) jar marshmallow cream
12   ounces good quality white chocolate, chopped (use chocolate made with cocoa butter, not vegetable oil)
¾   cup chopped dried cranberries
½   cup chopped macadamia nuts

Heat sugar, whipping cream, butter and salt in a heavy saucepan over medium heat, stirring constantly, until boiling. Boil for 5 minutes, then remove from heat.

Stir in marshmallow cream and white chocolate; mix until well blended. Stir in cranberries and nuts; mix well.

Spread fudge into a lightly buttered 9x13-inch baking pan. Chill until firm. Cut into small squares. Store in an airtight container in a cool place for up to 1 week.

Black Walnut
Chocolate Fudge

Margaret Klee of Mason County, Kentucky, won the "chocolate fudge" category at the 16th annual Pride of Kentucky Chocolate Festival in the 1700s village of Washington, Kentucky. Rivers of dark chocolate flow during this award-winning festival. Homemade treats, games and contests make for a fun-filled event.

Makes about 64 Pieces

1   cup chopped black walnuts
2   cups sugar
½   cup unsweetened cocoa powder
1   (14-ounce) can evaporated milk
2   tablespoons butter
1   teaspoon vanilla extract

In a saucepan, combine walnuts, sugar and cocoa. Add milk; bring to a boil. Cook, stirring constantly, until a small amount of the cocoa mixture forms a soft ball when dropped in cold water. Remove from heat; do not stir. Add butter and vanilla; cool. Beat until creamy; pour into a buttered 8x8-inch baking pan. Cool, then slice.

JAMAICAN COCONUT CANDY

Joseph Moulton of Clewiston, Florida, won first prize in the Sugar Festival's 17th annual Sweet Taste of Sugar Country Recipe Contest with this candy that his grandmother made for him when he was young. The Sugar Festival signals the end of the sugar season in the Glades, and is open to all residents of the cane-growing areas around Clewiston.

Makes 20 to 30 Pieces

2	cups finely minced fresh coconut (from 1-2 coconuts)*
2½	cups water
¼	pound ginger, peeled and finely minced
2	pounds light brown sugar
All-purpose flour	

Open coconuts and drain coconut water (save coconut water for another use, if desired). Using a sharp knife, remove coconut meat from shell (the outer thin brown skin of the coconut is edible and need not be removed). Finely mince coconut until you have 2 cups.

In a saucepan, bring water to a boil; add coconut and boil for about 10 minutes. Add ginger and brown sugar; lower heat and simmer, stirring, until mixture is thickened and sugar has dissolved.

Dust aluminum foil lightly with flour. Drop mixture by tablespoonsful onto foil. Let candy stand until hardened. Wrap in wax paper and store in an airtight container for up to 1 month, or freeze in a freezer bag for up to 1 year.

*Note: Do not use presweetened flaked coconut, it will not work in this candy.

INDEX

Seafood & Sausage Gumbo, 67
Smoked Salmon Frittata Gremolata, 37
South Pacific Steaks, 169
White Chicken Chili with Cheddar Hush-
    puppy Crust, 65

BLUEBERRIES
Blueberry Lemon Wisp, 323
Blueberry Rhubarb Porkchops, 159

C CHEESE
Asiago:
    Italian Potato Torte, 93
Boursin:
    Lobster Poblano Roulade over Aztec
        Succotash, 10
Brie:
    Grilled Veal Chops with California Figs
        & Brie Cheese, 179
Cheddar:
    Apple, Cheddar & Bacon Scones, 191
    Baked Lentils & Cheddar, 98
    Cheesy Carrot & Potato Soup, 56
    "Dip-in" the Palouse, 23
    Egglicious Sandwich, 41
    Herb Cheese Rolls, 193
    The Adult Grilled Cheese Sandwich, 88
    White Chicken Chili with Cheddar
        Hushpuppy Crust, 65
    Zucchini & Chicken Quiche, 43
Cream Cheese:
    Aloha Peaches N' Cream Cheesecake
        Cupcakes, 231
    Artichoke Breakfast Burrito, 42
    Awesome Healthy Cheesecake Smoothie, 49
    Banana's Foster Dessert Pizza, 250
    Chocolate Cream Bars, 205
    Chocolate & Strawberry Filled-Meringue
        Shells, 252
    Olivia's Oregon Fruit Oatmeal Bars, 208
    Peaches & Cream Supreme Pie, 215
    Peanut Butter Crunch Cheesecake, 228
    Red, White & Blue Cheesecake, 229
    Smoked Salmon Cheesecake, 9
    Smoked Salmon Wonton Puffs with
        Ginger Soy Sauce, 13
    South of the Border Potato Soup, 55

Strawberry Sandwich, 221
Sweet Potato Surprise Bread, 188
Turtle Brownie Cheesecake, 230
Feta:
    Chowder of Scallops, Celeriac & Potato, 73
    Greek Isles Beef with Feta & Mint, 177
    Greek Garden Rice Salad, 101
    Greek Six-Layer Dip, 22
    Grilled Raspberry Chicken & Spinach
        Salad, 80
    Mediterranean Veal with Grilled Vegetable
        Couscous, 178
    South of the Border Pesto Sauce, 30
Goat Cheese:
    Apple & Arugula Salad with Almond
        Brittle, 77
    Championship Guacamole, 24
    Honey Figs with Goat Cheese & Pecans, 19
    Phillips Crab & Goat Cheese Torte, 14
Gorgonzola:
    Eggplant & Gorgonzola-Stuffed Portobello
        Mushrooms, 94
    Grilled Flatbread with Caramelized Walla
        Walla Onions, Gorgonzola & Pesto, 21
    Spinach, Gorgonzola & Lemon Rice, 102
Gouda:
    BBQ Pork Smokehouse Cuban-Style
        Sandwich, 85
Monterey Jack:
    Chicken, Corn & Tortilla Soup, 59
    Texas Cowboy Skillet, 9
Mozzarella:
    Beef in a Blanket, 174
    Game Night Barbeque Beef Pizza, 172
    Royal Crave Castle Bread, 176
Parmesan:
    American Egg Bake, 40
    Beef in a Blanket, 174
    Eggplant & Gorgonzola-Stuffed Portobello
        Mushrooms, 94
    Farrotto with Pecorino & Pears, 99
    Green Goddess Oyster& Artichoke Salad, 82
    Royal Crave Castle Bread, 176
    South of the Border Pesto Sauce, 30
    Vidalia Onion & Apple Casserole, 95
Provolone:
    Sun-Dried Tomato Quiche, 45

Peaches & Cream Supreme Pie, 215
Praline Pumpkin Cake, 241
Savory Chicken Salad, 78
Sweet Potato Praline Cloud Pie, 220
Sweet Potato Surprise Bread, 188
Tart & Gooey Cranberry Pecan Pie Bars, 207
Turtle Brownie Cheesecake, 230
Pine Nuts:
Grilled Flatbread with Caramelized Walla
Walla Onions, 21
Lobster Poblano Roulade over Aztec
Succotash, 10
Nut-Crisped Mahi-Mahi with Mango
Sauce & Coconut Curry Rice, 123
South of the Border Pesto Sauce, 30
Walnuts:
Black Walnut Chocolate, 256
Chocolate-Drizzled Raspberry Chocolate
Chunk Cookies, 199
Espresso Chews, 201
Mapled Nut Company Butter Tart, 226
Mixed-Up Brownie Delight, 211
Scottish Pear & Lemon Bread, 186
Smoked Salmon Cheesecake, 9
South of the Border Pesto Sauce, 30

O OATS/OATMEAL
Cherry Peanut Granola, 48
Chewy Sour Cream Craisin Bars, 209
Date-Filled Bar Cookies, 210
Irresistible Cookies, 202
Olivia's Oregon Fruit Oatmeal Bars, 208
One-Bowl Triple Chocolate Oatmeal
Jumbles, 198

OYSTERS
Green Goddess Oyster & Artichoke Salad, 82
Gulf-Style Cajun Gumbo, 66
Oyster Wraps with Asian Dipping Sauce, 12
Seafood Gumbo, 68
Seafood & Sausage Gumbo, 67
Seared Rockfish Fillet with Oyster & Corn
Stew, 117

P PASTA
Bacon N' Basil Ravioli, 107
Black Japonica Ravioli with Blue Cheese

Cream, 106
Crab Canneloni with Roasted Red Pepper
Sauce, 109
Pecan Risotto with Smoked Gouda &
Caramelized Onions, 110

PEACHES
Almond–Crusted Pork loin with Peach
Chutney, 162
Aloha Peaches N' Cream Cheesecake
Cupcakes, 231
Grandma's Peach Pie, 216
Peaches & Cream Supreme Pie, 215

PEARS
Chowder of Scallops, Celeriac & Potato with
Caramelized Pear & Roasted Chestnuts, 73
Farrotto with Pecorino & Pears, 99
Pear Apple Napoleon, 248
Pear-Glazed Cornish Hens with Apple &
Pear Stuffing, 152
Poached Pear Tart with Vanilla Bean
Custard, 225
Scottish Pear & Lemon Bread, 186

PESTO
Grilled Flatbread with Caramelized Walla
Walla Onions, Gorgonzola & Pesto, 21
South of the Border Pesto Sauce, 30

PINEAPPLE
Banana Split Cake, 239
Cranberry Pineapple Sorbet, 253
JIF Tropical Fantasy, 86
Summer Fruit Salad with Mint Honey Lime
Dressing, 83
Texas Proud Pineapple Salsa, 25

PORK
Bacon:
Apple, Cheddar & Bacon Scones, 191
Crab & Veggie Quiche, 46
Egglicious Sandwich, 41
Sensational Smoked Salmon B.L.T.
Sandwich, 90
Oyster Wraps with Asian Dipping Sauce, 12
Pigeon Cove Lobster Company Clam

Seafood & Sausage Gumbo, 67
Spinach, Gorgonzola & Lemon Rice, 102
Southeast Asia Spiced Grilled Rainbow
   Trout with Lime Ginger Sauce, 120

S SALMON & SMOKED SALMON
Grilled Candied Garlic Salmon on Baby
   Asian Greens & Crispy Rice Noodles, 116
Potato Pancake with Smoked Salmon &
   Caviar, 35
Sensational Smoked Salmon B.L.T.
   Sandwich, 90
Smoked Salmon Cheesecake, 9
Smoked Salmon Frittata Gremolata, 37
Smoked Salmon Wonton Puffs with Ginger
   Soy Sauce, 13

SCALLOPS
Chowder of Scallops, Celeriac & Potato with
   Caramelized Pear & Roasted Chestnuts, 73
Gulf-Style Cajun Gumbo, 66
Mediterranean Ceviche, 8

SHRIMP
Crunchy Coconut Shrimp with Mango
   Dip, 127
Grilled Jumbo Shrimp with Spicy Crawfish
   Potato Salad, 128
Grilled Lemon Herb Shrimp, 125
Gulf-Style Cajun Gumbo, 66
Mediterranean Ceviche, 8
Picante Shrimp Burritos with Fruit Salsa, 126
Seafood Gumbo, 68
Seafood & Sausage Gumbo, 67
Three Fish Trawler Chowder, 70

STRAWBERRIES
Awesome Healthy Cheesecake Smoothie, 49
Banana Split Cake, 239
Chocolate & Strawberry Filled Meringue
   Shells, 252
Grilled Raspberry Chicken & Spinach Salad, 80
Olivia's Oregon Fruit Oatmeal Bars, 208
Red, White & Blue Cheesecake, 229
Strawberry Kolaches, 183
Strawberry Sandwich, 221
Summer Fruit Salad with Mint Honey Lime
   Dressing, 83

T TOMATOES & TOMATILLOS
Artichoke Breakfast Burrito, 42
Blake-O's Red Hot Sauce, 29
Championship Guacamole, 24
Chillie Willie's Chili Salsa, 26
"Dip-In" the Palouse, 23
Garlicky Skirt Steak Nachos with Tomatillo
   Salsa, 170
Gearjammer's Chili Verde, 61
Greek Six-Layer Dip, 22
Lobster Poblano Roulade over Aztec
   Succotash, 10
Mediterranean Ceviche, 8
Napoli Chicken Pasta Salad, 79
South of the Border Pesto Sauce, 30
Three Bean Mexistrone with Cornmeal
   Dumplings, 57

TROUT
Grilled Rainbow Trout Adobe with Roasted
   Corn Salsa, 119
Harvest-Style Trout Cakes with Chipotle
   Remoulade, 122
Parmesan-Battered Rainbow Trout with
   Vegetable Risotto, 121
Smoked Trout Salad, 81
Southeast Asian Spiced Grilled Rainbow
   Trout with Lime Ginger Dipping Sauce, 120

TURKEY
Eastern Wild Turkey Roulade with Orange
   Sauce, 153
Egglicious Sandwich, 41
Quick Turkey Ragout with Pimento
   Cornbread Dumplings, 52
Tacchino Di Perla, 154

Z ZUCCHINI/SQUASH
Greek Six-Layer Dip, 22
Mediterranean Veal with Grilled Vegetable
   Couscous, 178
Parmesan-Battered Rainbow Trout with
   Vegetable Risotto, 121
Zucchini & Chicken Quiche, 43
Zucchini Herb Cornbread, 192

APPENDIX

ADIRONDACK LIFE MAGAZINE APPLE RECIPE CONTEST
Jay, NY
www.adirondacklife.com
518-946-2191

ALMOND INSPIRATION RECIPE CONTEST
Modesto, CA
www.almondboard.org
209-549-8262

AMERICA'S JUNIOR MISS RECIPE CONTEST
www.ajm.org
800-256-5435

BASIL HARVEST FESTIVAL – BEST O' PESTO
Sycamore Farms
Paso Robles, CA
www.sycamorefarms.com
800-576-5288
Festival is October 9, 2004

BEST BROWNIES IN MICHIGAN &
BEST COOKIES IN MICHIGAN BAKING CONTEST
AAA Michigan
www.autoclubgroup.com/michigan
The contest is held annually in the spring with
the winners announced in June.

BEST OF GARDENBURGER RECIPE CONTEST
Gardenburger
www.gardenburger.com
800-459-7079

BLACK HISTORY MONTH RECIPE CONTEST
Bruce Foods "Original" Louisiana Hot Sauce
www.brucefoods.com
800-299-9082

CABRILLO CULINARY ARTS STUDENTS' VANILLA
COOK-OFF
Santa Cruz, CA
www.vanilla.com
831-477-3524

CALIFORNIA DRY BEAN FESTIVAL
Tracy, CA
www.tracychamber.org
209-835-2131
Festival is the first full weekend in August.

CALIFORNIA OLIVE INDUSTRY RECIPE CONTEST
California Ripe Olives
Fresno, CA
www.calolive.org

CALIFORNIA STRAWBERRY FESTIVAL
Oxnard, CA
www.strawberry-fest.org
888-288-9242
May 15 & 16, 2004

CAROLINA CHOCOLATE FESTIVAL
Morehead City, NC
252-504-2203
Held annually the weekend before Valentine's Day.

CASTROVILLE ARTICHOKE FESTIVAL
Castroville, CA
www.artichoke-festival.org
831-633-2465
May 15 &16, 2004

CHATSWORTH CRANBERRY FESTIVAL, THE
Chatsworth, New Jersey
www.cranfest.org
609-726-9237
Festival is October 16 & 17, 2004

CHEFS SAY BEAN APPETIT!
Northharvest Bean Growers Association
Frazee, MN
www.northarvest.org
218-334-6351

CHOWDER COOKOFF
Portland, OR
www.aglink.org
503-241-1487
Held at the Oregon State Fair, August 26-
September 6, 2004

CLARKE COUNTY FAIR & BAKING CONTEST
Winchester, VA
www.ccfairva.com
540-667-3200
August 15-21, 2004

CLEWISTON SWEET TASTE OF SUGAR
Clewiston Chamber of Commerce
Clewiston, FL
877-693-4372
April 17, 2004

CRAVE TIME COOK- OFF
White Castle Burgers
www.whitecastle.com

CLEAR SPRINGS FOODS - CLEAR CUTS RECIPE
CHALLANGE
www.clearsprings.com
800-635-8211

CRUNCHY CREATIONS CONTEST
French's Fried Onion
www.frenchs.net

DELICIOUS LIVING RECIPE CONTEST
Boulder, CO
www.healthwell.com
303-949-5680

DEL RAY BEACH GARLIC FESTIVAL
Delray, FL 33444
www.dbgarlicfest.com
(561) 274-4663
November 7-9, 2004

DOLE FIVE- A-DAY KIDS' RECIPE CONTEST, THE
Dole Food Company
www.dole.com

EGGS MAKE THE MEAL
Iowa Egg Council
Urbandale, IA
www.iowaegg.org
ipahls@qwest.net

ESSEX CLAMFEST
Cape Ann Chamber of Commerce

Essex, MA
www.capeannvacations.com
978-283-1601
September 25, 2004

EVERYTHING'S BETTER WRAPPED IN BACON
Farmer John Meats
www.farmerjohn.com
323-583-4621

FAIRCHILD TROPICAL GARDEN'S INTERNATIONAL
MANGO FESTIVAL
Coral Gables, FL
www.fairchildgarden,org
305-667-1651
July 9-12, 2004

FOOD FOR THOUGHT FESTIVAL
R.E.A.P Food Group
Madison, WI
www.reapfoodgroup.org
608-244-2342
Held annually in mid-September.

FIG RECIPE CONTEST
California Fig Advisory Board
Fresno, CA 93712
www.californiafigs.com

FIREANT STRAWBERRY FESTIVAL
Ashburn, GA
www.fireantfestival.com
229-567-9696
March 26-28, 2004

FLORIDA'S NATURAL GROWERS CITRUS RECIPE
COOK-OFF
Lake Wales, FL
www.floridasnaturalgrowers.com

FRANKS RED HOT RECIPE CONTEST
Frank's Red Hot
www.franksredhot.com

FRIENDSHIP SOUR CREAM RECIPE CONTEST
Jericho, NY
www.friendshipdairies.com

GERRY FRANK CHOCOLATE CAKE CONTEST
Salem, OR
www.oregonstatefair,org
503-947-3247
Contest is held during the Oregon State Fair
August 26-September 6, 2004.

GILROY GARLIC FESTIVAL
Gilroy, CA
www.gilroygarlicfestival.com
Recipe entries are due by the first of May. The
festival is July 23-25, 2004.

GOLD KIST FARMS' WINNING TASTE RECIPE CONTEST
www.goldkist.com

GOOD EARTH PEANUT COMPANY RECIPE CONTEST
www.goodearthpeanuts.com

GOT LECHE? RECIPE CONTEST
Got Milk
www.gotmilk.com

GRANDPARENT GRANDCHILD RECIPE CONTEST
Oregon Fruit Products
Salem, OR
www.oregonfruit.com

GREAT PETALUMA CHILI COOK-OFF, SALSA AND
BEER TASTING
Petaluma, CA
www.greatchilicookoff.com
707-778-2100 ext. 18
May 2, 2004

GREAT SANDWICH RECIPE CONTEST
Finlandia Cheese
www.finlandiacheese.com
973-316-6699
November 3, 2004

GREAT WISCONSIN CHEESE FESTIVAL, THE –
CHEESECAKE CONTEST
Little Chute, WI
www.littlechutewi.org
920-788-7390
June 4-6, 2004

GRITS ANYTIME
Georgia National Fair
Perry, GA
www.georgianationalfair.com
478-987-3247
October 8-17, 2004

GUMBO FESTIVAL
Bridge City, LA
www.hgaparish.org
504-436-4712
October 8-10, 2004

HAM & YAM FESTIVAL
Smithfield, NC
919-934-0887
May 1-2, 2004

HERB-OX COMFORT FOOD CONTEST
HERB-OX Bouillon
www.hormel.com

HOLTVILLE CARROT FESTIVAL
Holtville, CA
www.holtvillechamber.ca.gov
760-356-2923
January 30-February 8, 2004

HOPKINS RASPBERRY FESTIVAL
Hopkins, MN
www.hopkinsraspberryfestival.com
952-931-0878
Cook-off is July 17-18, 2004

HUTCHINSON NEWS – HOLIDAY RECIPE CONTEST
Hutchinson, KS
www.hutchnews.com
800-766-3311

I CAN USE PECANS IN THAT?" RECIPE CONTEST
National Pecan Shellers Association
Atlanta, GA
www.ilovepecans.org
404-252-3663
Held each April for National Pecan Month.

IGA HOMETOWN HOLIDAYS RECIPE CONTEST
www.iga.com

INTERNATIONAL RICE FESTIVAL
Crowley, LA
www.RiceFestival.com
337-783-3067
Held annually on the third weekend in October.

IRRESISTIBLE COOKIE JAR RECIPE CONTEST
Hayden Lake, ID
www.irresistiblecookiejar.com
208-664-1261

ITALIAN COOKING & LIVING MAGAZINE RECIPE
CONTEST
New York, NY
www.italiancookingandliving.com
212-725-8764

JOHNSON & WALES HIGH SCHOOL RECIPE CONTEST
Johnson & Wales University
www.jwu.edu

JOHNSON & WALES UNIVERSITY/BACARDI RECIPE
CONTEST
www.jwu.edu/culinary/contest

JM SMUCKER COMPANY MOST CREATIVE PEANUT
BUTTER SANDWICH CONTEST
www.jif.com

JUST SMOKED SALMON RECIPE CONTEST
www.justsmokedsalmon.com

KODIAK CRAB FESTIVAL
Kodiak Island, AK
www.kodiak.org/crabfest.html
Festival is Memorial Day weekend.

KONA COFFEE CULTURAL FESTIVAL
Kailua Kona. HI
www.konacoffeefest.com
November 11-17, 2004

KUMQUAT FESTIVAL
Dade City Florida Chamber of Commerce
www.dadecitychamber.org
352-567-3769
Festival is held annually at the end of January.

LOOMIS EGGPLANT FESTIVAL
Loomis, CA
www.ppgn.com/lbcc_eggplant.html
916-652-7252
Festival is held in October.

LUNDBERG FAMILY FARMS RECIPE CONTEST
Richvale, CA
www.lundberg.com
530-882-4551

MACHIAS WILD BLUEBERRY FESTIVAL
Machias, ME
www.machiasblueberry.com
Festival is August 20-22, 2004.

MAINE LOBSTER FESTIVAL
Rockland, ME
www.mainelobsterfestival.com
800-LOB-CLAW
August 5-8, 2004

MAKE IT SPECIAL WITH CALIFORNIA PEACHES,
PLUMS OR NECTARINES RECIPE CONTEST
California Tree Fruit Agreement
www.eatcaliforniafruit.com

MAPLE LEAF FARMS DUCK RECIPE CONTEST
Milford, IN
www.mapleleaffarms.com

MAUI ONION FESTIVAL
Whaler Village
Kailua, HI
808-661-4567
August 7-8, 2004

MEALTIME.ORG RECIPE CONTEST
www.mealtime.org

MEDINA LAKE CAJUN FESTIVAL
Lakehills, TX
www.cajunfestival-medinalake.com
End of September each year

MISS MERINGUE RECIPE CONTEST
www.missmeringue.com
760-539-1326

MORTON PUMPKIN FESTIVAL
Morton, IL
www.pumpkincapital.com
888-765-6588
September 15-18, 2004.

MRS. CUBBISON'S THANKSGIVING STUFFING COOK-OFF
Los Angeles Trade Technical College Culinary School
www.mrscubbinsons.com

MUSHROOM FESTIVAL, THE
Kennett Square, PA
www.mushroomfest.com
888-440-9920
September 11-12, 2004

NAPA VALLEY MUSTARD FESTIVAL
Yountville, CA
www.mustardfestival.org
(707) 938-1133
Held each February-March.

NATIONAL BEEF COOK-OFF
www.beefcookoff.org

NATIONAL CHERRY FESTIVAL
Traverse City, MI
1-800-TRAVERS
www.cherryfestival.org
Held annually on July 4th weekend.

NATIONAL CHICKEN COOKING CONTEST
www.eatchicken,com
This is a biennial contest. Recipes are due in
October 2004 with the cook-off in spring 2005.

NATIONAL CORNBREAD FESTIVAL
South Pittsburg, TN
www.nationalcornbread.com
423-837-0022
April 24-25, 2004

NATIONAL DATE FESTIVAL, THE
Indio, CA
www.palmsprings.com
800-811-FAIR
Held annually in mid-February at the Riverside
County Fair.

NATIONAL PIE CHAMPIONSHIP
Great American Pie Festival
Celebration, FL
www.piecouncil.org
407-566-3448
April 15-18, 2004

NORTH CAROLINA APPLE FESTIVAL
Hendersonville, NC
www.ncapplefestival.org
828-697-4557
Held annually on Labor Day weekend.

NORWALK HARBOR *SPLASH!* CLAM CHOWDER
COOK-OFF
Norwalk, CT
www.norwalk.ws/splashfestival.com
203-838-9444
June 6, 2004

OKLAHOMA BEEF COUNCIL COOK-OFF
Oklahoma City, OK
www.oklabeef.com
(405) 235-4391

OLD FARMERS ALMANAC RECIPE CONTEST, THE
Dublin, NH
www.almanac.com
(603) 842-8922

OREGON FRYER COMMISSION RECIPE CONTEST
Oregon Chickens
www.oregonchickens.com
866-333-6488

ORIGINAL HOUSTON HOT SAUCE FESTIVAL, THE
Houston, TX
www.houstonhotsauce.com
281-558-3518
September 15-19, 2004

OYSTER FEST
Shelton, WA
www.oysterfest.org
800-576-2021
October 2-3, 2004.

PALISADE PEACH FESTIVAL
Palisade, CO
www.palisadepeachfest.com
info@palisadepeachfest.com
August 21-22, 2004

PEAR BLOSSOM FESTIVAL – PEAR COOK-OFF
Milford, PA
570-296-3400
Held annually in April.

PHILLIPS FOODS CRAB MEAT RECIPE CONTEST
www.phillipsfoods.com
888-234-CRAB
Annual with a late September submission deadline.

PIZZA CREATIONS RECIPE CONTEST
Mama Mary's
Spartanburg. SC
www.mamamarys.com

POTEET STRAWBERRY FESTIVAL
Poteet, TX
www.strawberryfestival.com
830-742-8144
Held annually on the first weekend in April.

PRIDE OF KENTUCKY CHOCOLATE FESTIVAL
Washington, KY
www.washingtonky.com/ChocFest2002.htm
609-759-7423
Held annually the weekend before Easter.

PULLMAN LENTIL FESTIVAL
Pullman, WA
www.lentilfest.com
509-334-3565
August 21-22, 2004

RECIPEZAAR "READY SET COOK" CONTEST
www.recipezaar.com
206-228-ZAAR

TURKEY FOR ALL SEASONS RECIPE CONTEST
National Turkey Federation
www.eatturkey.com
Semi-annual contest - check website for details.

RICE TO THE RESCUE
USA Rice Federation
www.usarice.com
Recipe contest are held throughout the year at various festivals across the country.

ROCKFISH CELEBRATION COOKING CONTEST
Maryland Watermans Association Maryland
Annapolis, MD
410-841-5820
Held annualy on the first Saturday in February.

SAN FRANCISCO CRAB FESTIVAL – CHALLENGE OF THE MASTERS
www.sfvisitor.org
415-391-2000
A month-long celebration held each February.

SEARCH FOR THE ULTIMATE OATMEAL COOKIE RECIPE CONTEST
Quaker Oatmeal
www.quakeroatmeal.com

SANTA BARBARA FRENCH FESTIVAL
Santa Barbara, CA
www.frenchfestival.com
805-564-PARIS
Festival is held on Bastille Day weekend – July 17 & 18, 2004

SCHWEPPES GREAT CHOWDER COOK-OFF
Newport, RI
www.newportfestivals.com
June 4-6, 2004

SHARE THE VERY BEST RECIPE CONTEST
The Nestle Toll House
www.verybestbaking.com

SHUCKMAN'S FISH COMPANY & SMOKERY RECIPE CONTEST
Louisville, KY
www.kysmokedfish.com
502-775-6478

SIMPLE VEGETARIAN RECIPE CONTEST
Yoyoga
www.yoyoga.com

SOUTH CAROLINA APPLE FESTIVAL
Westminster, SC
www.westminster.com/festival
864-647-7223
September 6-11, 2004

TABASCO'S HOTTEST CHEF RECIPE CONTEST
Williams Creative Group (PR)
Brentwood, TN
(318) 227-1515

TASTE OF ELEGANCE COOKING CONTEST
Pork Board
www.iowapork.org

TEXAS CO-OP POWER MONTHLY RECIPE CONTEST
Austin, TX
www.texas-ec.org
512-454-0311

THINK OUTSIDE THE TORTILLA RECIPE CONTEST
Mission Foods
www.missionfoodsfsc.com

VEG•ALL RECIPE CONTEST
Allan Canning
www.vegall.com

VERMONT MAPLE FESTIVAL
St. Albans, VT
www.vtmaplefestival.org
802-527-0289
April 23-25, 2004

WALLA WALLA SWEET ONION FESTIVAL
Walla Walla, WA
www.sweetonions.org
July 20, 2004.

WARRENS CRANBERRY FESTIVAL, THE
Warrens, WI
www.cranfest.com
608-378-4200
September 24-26, 2004

WICHITA EAGLE – HOLIDAY COOKBOOK CONTEST
Wichita, KS
www.kansas,com

WHAT A CROCK RECIPE CONTEST
www.mom-mom.com

WHEATHEART BREAD RECIPE CONTEST
Oklahoma Wheat Commission
Oklahoma City, OK
www.state.ok.us/~wheat/recipes.htm
September 16-26, 2004

WILD WONDERFUL WOMAN'S CHOCOLATE
FESTIVAL, THE
Oakhurst, CA
www.wildwonderfulwoman.org
October 9, 2004

WILDLIFE ACTION WILD GAME COOK-OFF
Whiteville, NC
www.wildlifeaction.com
910- 640-2648

WINDSOR ZUCCHINI FESTIVAL
Recipe Contest
www.afn.org/~windsor/contact.htm
Held annually in May.

WKTI VEAL GRILL-OFF
www.beeftips.com

WORLD BEEF EXPO FIREHOUSE BEEF CHILI COOK-OFF
Beef Tips
www.beeftips.com

WORLD CHAMPIONSHIP CHILI COOK-OFF
International Chili Society
www.chilicookoff.com
877-777-4427
October 2-3, 2004

VIVA VARIETY RECIPE CONTEST
National Honey Board
www.honey.com
303-776-2337

YAMBILEE CONTEST
Opelousas, LA
www.members.tripod.com/yambilee/yambilee.htm
800-210-5298
Held annully in the first week of October.